SARAJEVO:

AN ANTHOLOGY FOR BOSNIAN RELIEF

edited by
John Babbitt, Carolyn Feucht and Andie Stabler

designed and produced by
Tina Leverenzzi

Elgin Community College
Elgin, Illinois
1993

Copyright 1993 by Elgin Community College.
Publication rights to individual works revert to authors.
First printing, 1993.

Published by Elgin Community College with assistance from
The Illinois Arts Council, The Writers Center at Elgin
Community College, ECC English Department, ECC Office of
Student Life and ECC Student Senate, and private donations
to The Sarajevo Project.

ISBN 0-963851-60-8

Sarajevo: An Anthology for Bosnian Relief
Edited by John Babbitt, Carolyn Feucht and Andie Stabler
Designed and produced by Tina Leverenzzi.
Faculty advisor: Patrick Parks
Printed in U.S.A. by United Graphics, Inc., Mattoon, Illinois.

All proceeds from the sale of this publication will be used to assist in relief efforts for victims of the war in Bosnia.

Funded in part by the Illinois Arts Council.

For more information, write to The Sarajevo Project,
C/O The Writers Center, Elgin Community College,
Elgin, Il 60123-7193, or call 708/697-1000, ext. 7265.

The Sarajevo Project staff would like to thank the writers who contributed their work to this anthology and to the many generous benefactors who donated to our project. We would also like to thank the Illinois Arts Council, Bob Anders, and Jim Vandenbroucke along with Dr. Paul Heath, president of Elgin Community College, and the ECC Board of Trustees for their support.

We are especially grateful to Richard Jackson, whose visit to our campus and whose account of the war in Bosnia were the inspiration for this anthology.

Acknowledgments

"The Evening News" by Tony Ardizzone appeared in *The Evening News*, 1986, Tony Ardizzone.

"Lines to King's Cross Terminal" by Janet Burroway appeared in *Critical Quarterly*.

"The Last Bear" by Andrei Codrescu was first heard on National Public Radio's *All Things Considered* in November, 1992.

"almost always" by Alvin Greenberg appeared in *Colorado Review*.

"Adagio" by Richard Jackson first appeared in *The AWP Chronicle*.

"True or False" by Richard Jackson appeared in *Alive All Day*, 1992, Cleveland State Press.

"The Border" by David Jauss was first published in *Shenandoah*.

"Interrogations," by Paul Lake was first published in *Pequod*.

"An Arch of Birches" by Joseph Maiolo was first published in *Shenandoah*.

"Map of Rivers" by Kevin McIlvoy is an excerpt from *Little Peg*, 1990,. Atheneum.

"Unsent Letter 2" by Carol Muske was published in *Red Trousseau*, 1993, Viking Press.

"A Measure of the Sin" by Kristy Nielsen will appear in *Spoon River Quarterly* in November, 1993. "The Hummingbird Between My Legs" will appear in *Amelia* in October, 1993.

"The Miracle" by Harry Mark Petrakis appeared in *Collected Stories*, 1986, Lake View Press.

"Revolutions" by James Plath was first published in *The Rectangle*.

"Divine Attention" by Paulette Roeske appeared in *Whetstone* magazine and *The Body Can Ascend No Higher*, 1992, Illinois Writers' Inc.

"An Essay on Liberation" by David St. John appeared in *No Heaven*, 1985, David St. John.

"Night Shift, after Drinking Dinner, Container Corporation of America, 1972" by Kevin Stein was first published in *The North American Review*.

"Voyage" by Lucien Stryk appeared in *American Poetry Review*.

Table of Contents

Adagio
Richard Jackson 1
True or False
Richard Jackson 11
Dead Space
Jonis Agee 17
The Evening News
Tony Ardizzone 25
Curse
Thomas Fox Averill 47
We Tried to Stop the War
Marvin Bell 71
Poetry & Politics – A Poet's Impressions
Christopher Buckley 73
Lines to King's Cross Terminal
Janet Burroway 91
The Last Bear
Andrei Codrescu 93
The Neighbors
Philip Dacey 95
On the Murder of Two Orphan Children by Sniper Fire
Robert Dana 97
Marie Antoinette Ocean
Connie Deanovich 99

She
  Helen Degen-Cohen 101
The Lessons of History
  Emilio DeGrazia 107
Crows
  Stephen Dixon 109
**What the Woman in the
Origami Village Remembers**
  Jim Elledge 119
A Story for Young Moderns
  S. P. Elledge 129
Dear Dagmar, Wie Sagst Du Denn Heimat?
  Lucia Cordell Getsi 135
almost always
  Alvin Greenberg 139
Heart Tones
  Dan Guillory 141
The Border
  David Jauss 143
True Crime
  W. P. Kinsella 145
Mother
  Ted Kooser 165
Interrogations
  Paul Lake 167
Mabel: A Life in Four Scenes
  Jean C. Lee 171
An Arch of Birches
  Joseph Maiolo 177
**Achilles Speaks of His Deception
in the Court of Lykomedes**
  Michael Martone 201

Map of Rivers
  Kevin McIlvoy 205
The Walls of Dubrovnik
  Christopher Merrill 227
Herself in White
  John Milton 233
Unsent Letter 2
  Carol Muske 249
Romeo and Julio
  Jay Neugeboren 251
A Measure of the Sin
  Kristy Nielsen 257
On Encountering Passionate Lovers of Poe in the Former Soviet Union
  Karen Lee Osborne 265
The Miracle
  Harry Mark Petrakis 267
Revolutions
  James Plath 277
Divine Attention
  Paulette Roeske 279
Epitaph for Contemporaries
  Maura Stanton 285
Night Shift, After Drinking Dinner, Container Corporation of America, 1972
  Kevin Stein 289
An Essay on Liberation
  David St. John 293
Oh Rage and Fury
  Jonathan Strong 295
Voyage
  Lucien Stryk 301

Compost
    Martha M. Vertreace 305
amalek
    S. L. Wisenberg 307
The Same Old Hatreds
Only More Deadly Now
    Maia Wojciechowska 311
The Earnest Man
    Paul Zimmer 317
Recurring Dreams: The Neglected
    Al Zolynas 319
Contributors 322

Adagio

by Richard Jackson

Vedran Smailovic. He may come to stand for the voice of the solitary artist against the sound of tank treads, the whoosh of mortar fire, the spine rippling crunch of 155 howitzer rounds. It is Sarajevo. Summer, 1992. Vedran used to play violin for the Sarajevo Opera. But now he is playing outside a bakery, in a small square. The town is situated in a mountain valley and can be sultry hot for several weeks in the summer. The promise of cooler, one would almost venture, innocent, times is given by the snow peaks of the mountains you can see by looking down to the end of almost any street. Today, Vedran Smailovic is playing Albioni's *Adiago* in front of this bakery. He is playing for the 22 people killed while waiting in a bread line at the bakery in May. You might remember the two or three days of outrage at this act in the West after the TV photos and the wails of the wounded, after the grotesque camera focus on the man who has just had his legs blown off trying to make his way to the camera. Vedran has vowed to play for 22 days in memory of the 22 slaughtered innocents. He is an easy target, one would think, for the dozens of snipers, if they get into position for a shot. "That is not the point," he says, "not the point at all."

Winter in Bosnia, several months later, is frightfully cold, and filled with images just as surreal. I have been talking to Boris Novak, head of the Slovene PEN Peace Committee in Ljubljana, on the phone this mild

Chattanooga January. I had just received another letter from him. He has more stories, but he almost seems afraid to speak. There is no firewood in Sarajevo, he reports. Most of the trees have already been cut to heat houses and apartments, none of which have window panes, electricity, or running water. You try to burn wood for heat by making a small fire in a pot or tub or wheel barrow brought in from outside, or the hood of a car, or a piece of sheet metal. You have to be inventive. But you can't very well burn most of the wood from the buildings because so much of it is soaked in resins and oils from decades, sometimes centuries of use and treatment— the fumes would be toxic. So you go to the cemetery which is filled with wooden crosses to mark the Christian graves and wooden panels or stakes to mark the Muslim graves. When you leave, there is no record of who is buried, but there seems a kind of quiet understanding and permission that the dead give from the grave— it's alright, just survive.

Just survive. The winter snows are already falling on Bosnia in full force. There's a little girl carrying her sled to a hill. Everything is quiet, and so, she thinks, it must be safe. There hasn't been any shelling in this part of the country for weeks. The new snow doesn't even have a track in it. Hardly any snow has fallen from the branches to ruffle the surface. There is only the quiet of the pale moon barely visible in the morning sky. The hill is not that steep, and she can't get much speed anyways on the way down, so she probably sits on the sled rather than lying down across it. She has no way of knowing that she is the sights of a sniper, and, as the saying goes, she never hears the shot from behind that blows her chest out in front of her across the snow.

There is no adagio, no grand requiem to play for this

girl— there are just too many stories like this, too many realities. I tell Boris I don't know how he can deal with these things daily. And he isn't even in the war zone. Slovenia is at peace. But like so many Slovene writers, he works as a volunteer at a refugee center. He's been taking care of 50 refugee writers, and through the Slovene Writers' Union he has been helping to get another 70 writers and their families out of Sarajevo. "I have never been so exhausted in my whole life," he had written. The red tape, the endless negotiations, the petty requirements, probably even the bribes to local border guards within Bosnia, must be draining. He sent along a poem, "Why Do You Cry Mother," by Dugic Jasmina who is only ten years old:

> while I am standing sadly by you
> kissing me like never before
> holding daddy's golden ring in your hand.
> I ask her if anything happened
> to our daddy and
> she caresses me
> as if she didn't hear me
> and I ask her again
> and she hugs me even more
> and says no my baby
> nothing happened to our daddy.

For a little while on the phone we talk about the children who are the long term tragedy of the war. One of the biggest worries is that the orphans of this war will grow up hating the other side— Serb, Muslim, Croat— and an endless cycle of reprisals will continue. Instead of playing a mock battle against alien creatures, or Nazis, the children— boys and girls alike— wage mock battles against Serbs, Croats, Muslims, whoever happens to be on the other side. In a few years they will be holding real guns. It is not going to stop.

On the other end of the phone, Boris is lamenting the ridiculous peace proposal presented by the American negotiator, Cyrus Vance and the British negotiator, Lord Owen, a gerrymandered map that caves in to the Serbian policy of ethnic cleansing by rewarding the Serbian Chetniks with most of their winnings. It is just another case of naive western negotiators trying to decide the fate of what they think is a minor or barbaric country in a way that won't interfere with the everyday workings of their own worlds. The boundaries are so complex, so unnatural, and emphasize ethnic differences so much, that the proposal seems certain to insure even more savage fighting as soon as— perhaps a few months after it is adopted, if it is— the parties solidify their strongholds. What will probably happen is a renewal of Serbian aggression and terrorism— even the Bosnian Serb legislature, made up of Serbs who want to break away from Bosnia and join Serbia, admits that any such peace proposal is just a holding action to temper world condemnation of their atrocities.

How does one negotiate with the Serbian Chetnik fighters (irregular troops, under at best a loose command structure) who claim a man wanted for bank robbery in western Europe as one of their commanders? "Arkan," Boris says. "They are dealing with the Arkans of the war." He's referring to the savage Serbian militia leader elected in December of 1992 to the Serbian Parliament: his real name is Zeljko Raznjatovic, and his troops have been responsible for many of the tens of thousands of systematic rapes, for many of the countless mass executions, tortures, the desecrations of bodies in several parts of Bosnia. The country, as well as Croatia, is studded with mass graves, with ashes from burnt bodies, the bodies that clog a few streams for a while like fallen boulders. There are a lot of children among the bodies. Outside one town lie the half buried remains of the tattered and torn bodies of Muslims crucified by Christian Serbs as a sort of sick joke — but what is the point? Indeed, Vance and Owen do negotiate with terrorists, like the Bosnian Serb leader, Radovan Karadzic, who has lied to his own people when he says that the Muslims in Bosnia want to establish an Islamic state and steal land. Never mind that the Bosnian Muslims were the most secular in the world, or that their president boasted just last year that Bosnia was like a Jackson Pollack painting in its harmonious ethnic diversity. What happened? You can almost hear Smailovic's adagio complain. It was politicians, especially Slobodan Milosevic of Serbia— these terrorists, these power hungry, these criminals who control the Serb press, radio and TV, the whole propaganda machine of the communists—that have misled the average person who has no other source of information. Most Serbs think they are fighting a war of national survival, when in fact they are fighting, as aggressors, a war for political power for their leaders.

Meanwhile the winter parades on. The town of Zepa, east of Sarajevo towards Serbia, is a town like so many we never hear from, but whose sufferings are in many ways worse than in Sarajevo itself. There are no concertos, no adagios, no music whatsoever to soothe the hours. No food has been available for a few months except a few scraps that can be scavenged. There are no more weeds or easily available bark to boil up in a makeshift soup. There are no more edible roots. Even the small animals have already been eaten, or have wisely fled to the hills. Someone has remembered you can eat shoe leather, but then there are no extra shoes, for most of the stores have been victims of mortar fire.

One night this winter it is especially cold. It hurts your nose to breathe, to even touch it. What happens here happens all over Bosnia: on this star-filled night, 51 children in the town of Zepa freeze to death.

Last September we had talked about the role of the writer— to reclaim and redefine the language that has been perverted by the twisted logic, slogans, and syntax of the generals and politicians, and to change the language of hate into a language of love. We had been sending off letters to heads of state, but it seems there are too many deaf ears, too many cowards. A story about Bosnia hardly ever gets more time on TV or space on a page other than a few papers like *The New York Times* than an ad for perfume or jeans. Maybe we had better begin with the children. This will be an endless task of building and rebuilding; it is Edvard Kocbek, the great Slovene poet who died over a decade ago, who has described this so well in a metaphor that speaks not of arrogance, not of accusations, but of building, of the future, and the desire for love. The poem is called, "This Evening, This Toy" and begins with the notion that the evening itself, that it, the approaching darkness, compels him to take it apart because its "sad song" is composed of "what is — in what is not,/and what is not" which is always "present in what is." Faced with such pervasive "emptiness" and loss he would try to dismantle and sort without losing anything, an impossible task.

> And there I am dismantling and sorting
> everything I lay my hands on.
> All by itself a new order arise
> I become a builder, a mason, a roofer,
> next I change into a painter and a rug weaver,
> finally I am a gardener. By then night has fallen
> and there are ever more things behaving ever more

mysteriously, till all that is left in my hand is something gentle and light, a bride's veil without the bride.

Perhaps the metaphoric bride will never arrive, but that is no reason to stop; everything in this part of the world moves slowly, everything is past or future, repetition or change, despair or hope. There can only be one choice. As writers, as human beings, it is our choice. We must look to a future we can hardly imagine, but which we must have the difficult faith to create.

I am interrupted in writing this by a letter from Ljubljana asking me to join a "Wake Up World" committee that will attempt to stage pacifist events to draw the worlds' attention to the plight not only in Bosnia but throughout former Yugoslavia. Besides the cost in people there is a cost in cultural heritage, identity, and art. Dozens of churches with valuable frescoes have been obliterated, writers have been killed. Architectural treasures, some of them whole cities, leveled. I remember the architecture around the home of Giuseppe Tartini in Piran, a walled, coastal town an hour's drive from here. He was born there in 1692, in the midst of another struggle between east and west. The Turks had taken Belgrade once again a few years earlier, and political alliances were dealing countries and ethnic groups across the table of the Balkans like cards in the back room of some inn. Maybe the kind of complex, interwoven wildness in Tartini's "Devil's Trill Sonata" might suit these times, too, which seem to echo the centuries old struggles of Serb and Muslim, Serb and Croat. It does not have the plaintive air of Albinoni's piece, but it contains some of the insanity of the times. It is a music on the verge of dissolution into fragmented detail, saved continuously by a strong

melodic background. One might have said, too, it was a
model for the tenuous state of affairs that held in
former Yugoslavia until the past several years. I stood,
in September of 1991, on the hill above Tartini's Piran,
at the beautiful baroque Parish Church of St. George,
and watched a small sailboat make its way down the
middle of the bay against the setting sun. Slovenia was
at peace, but across the bay no more than 5 kilometers,
smoke rose from just beyond the Croatian shore, and
there was the distinct rumble of artillery. It seemed
odd, this pleasure boat so close to the war. The boat, I
would later learn, was probably smuggling guns from
Italy or an offshore freighter, skirting the boundary line
to jump to the other side should a Slovene of Yugoslav
gunboat attempt to intercept it. Any peace will require
a difficult and long process of looking towards a
future— not just to the other coats, but to the sun on
the horizon that has the capability of enlarging
everything with its light and warmth.

   Difficult. Progress is going to have to follow the slow
movement of Smailovic's adagio. In another walled
coastal town last year, in Dubrovnik, the poet, Milisic,
was sitting as his desk in his apartment. Maybe he
was working on a new poem, maybe revising an old
one. I like to imagine him looking out at the beautiful
Adriatic, at the ominous gunboats just outside the
harbor, or maybe up the stone mountain that overlooks
the town and which holds the Serbian positions. In an
instant the whole room, most of the building, is
crunched by an artillery round. The flames are too hot
to approach, and if the firemen aren't careful, they too
will be victims. It is going to be very difficult. Boris
has a new poem that speaks to this difficulty. It's
called "South East of Memory"—

Cruel is the crystal of memory,
cruel when the living call
the dead forcing them
to voice their void—
a sacred, holiday silence
echoing in the winter wind.
Narrow is the skylight ever after:
leave the dead in the dusk!

Words are utterly painful
for the dead:
they prefer to watch buds
south-east of memory.
Hearing a stranger approach
they close their dreamy secrets.
Peaceful is the valley on the other side:
leave the dead in the dusk!

Call the living fields instead!
Let your children call you!
Call the morning, call tomorrow!
Who can understand the whiteness
flowing through the blood of crime?
Who are you to judge field poppies
wiping all the spilt blood?
Leave the dead in the dusk!

The air is too deep.
You will never catch
a shape in the shade.
Leave the dead in the dusk!

This is indeed a difficult and painful poem. It does not call for a loss of memory. It does not call for a return to innocence. The insistent refrain of the ballad form forces the dead to keep returning despite our psychological need to try to focus on the future.

Focusing on the past, the deep sadness, dishonors the dead, and perhaps leads to acts of revenge and reprisal, that is, to an even bleaker future. Boris' poem is a call for life, a call for love.

    I can't help thinking, as we hang up, of the image I heard last September at a writer's conference in Vilenica, Slovenia, just outside Trieste. It keeps returning like Boris' refrain, less for its horror than its haunting ambiguity. There are these Chetnik Serbian soldiers on a hill a few hundred yards from the center of Sarajevo. It seems like you could brush aside a branch and touch the city. In an open field, a few soldiers are throwing knives at a target. But it is not a target. It is a Muslim strapped tight against an old table leaning against a tree. It is not yet clear whether the object is to hit him or to narrowly miss him. It is not yet clear whether he is dead. It is not yet clear whether any of us in the west would have come to his aid. It is not clear yet, as we each hang up and the space widens between Chattanooga and Ljubljana once again, what we will do in the future.

True or False

by Richard Jackson

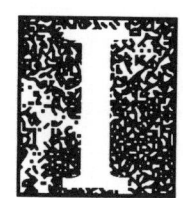

I have abandoned my life as a trapeze artist.
I will no longer hang my net from star to star.
Sept. 6, 1991, and I am push-starting Boris'
 Renault 4
down a hill into another era, swinging from
 the open
door to the roof bar as if I were one of the flying
Romanovs. It is 500 million years after
the increase in our oxygen led to skeletal animals.
A few hills behind us the Serbs are lobbing bombs
at a few Croatian churches. We are tracking a fugitive
future the way those aborigines in Australia follow
the dream paths that scientists think are the lines
of magnetic fields. They pause on a ridge, the last
drops of light soaking into the ground, listening
for the footsteps of old words kicking up a few stones
in front of them. Now the night begins its gossip
about the day. The important thing is to let
the momentum of your swing carry you smoothly,
without straining to reach, or you will break
the aerodynamic flow and miss the bar altogether.
Do you think we will make it all the way to Lipica?
Each time I enter a new dream of you, I find someone
has tampered with it. The world is only as true
as what you see through a commander's binoculars.
Therefore, I have abandoned my desire to fit
all my angels on the head of a pin. Over 96%
of visible matter is hydrogen or helium. Tank traps

litter the side of our road like a huge game of jacks
some giant
has abandoned. The body of the giant, Cormoran,
lies at Dinusul, England, which just happens to sit
on a bardic dream path as ancient as those of
the aborigines,
and includes Stonehenge and Glastonbury Abbey
where in 1539 Henry VIII hung, drew and quartered
the last abbot, Richard Whiting, while preparing to marry
his fourth wife. In that year Spain annexed Cuba.
Also, the first Christmas tree was introduced at Strasberg.
Why have I always been fascinated with dates?
This little Renault 4 can do over 80 in fourth gear.
Maybe I should abandon my desire to peek through
the keyholes of history. I have already abandoned
my desire to do a triple twist somersault
back through my own formative years. Maybe
I should just quietly lie inside you while our old selves
slip in and out of the back rooms of the soul.
Or maybe Descartes was right-we each become
two people, avoiding clandestine meetings
with ourselves. There are some people who try to arrange
their lives so they don't even have to be present.
Maybe that's why Rumor has wandered out of Vergil,
out of the fires and rubble of Carthage, only to huddle
under a streetlight in its oversized coat, studying the maps,
trying to find its way past the shanties of our hearts,
trying to find a life in the files of some general.
In a few minutes, we will pass this wreck and traffic
will flow smoother. Why do they always pull a coat
over the face of the old man who has been struck?
In Brazil, the boy who was born without a face
gradually had the few parts that were there arranged,
the rest being invented by the doctors until by now
everything has been done but incomplete. Only
the shallow, as Oscar Wilde said, will ever
know themselves.

Maybe I should abandon everything except a few harmless
details. We can just rest awhile in one of these
loopholes of the wind. I can stroke the soft petal of
  your belly.
No car. No war. No lies. The kind of life enjoyed
by broccoli in cheese sauce. Did you know that
horseback riding began in the Ukraine 6,000 years ago?
That there are 2 million atoms of nickel for every
four of silver in our galaxy? That Bernie Doyle and I
cut half a day in the 3rd grade coat room before
the nuns found us? If I pile up enough of these facts
we can all just forget about the truth. I remember
swinging from prank to prank along the ladder
on our schoolyard jungle gym. The curious thing
about the Renault 4 is that the gear shift is built
into the dashboard. Only 17% of Americans believe
Elvis is still alive. Believe me when I say that trapeze
artists are very big in this part of the world. In 1950
Edgar Rice Burroughs died while reading the comic pages.
That was about the time a whole flock of regrets started
descending over Croatia. In the third century the emperor
of China was buried with 6,000 individualized clay soldiers.
In 1980 Libya ordered England off its maps creating
a new arm of the North Sea. It would have taken more
than my incredible repertoire of aerial acrobatics
to avoid the train loads of errors shipped to us over time.
Like the TV detective of my childhood I just want the facts.
In 1955 the nuns marched us across the street from
St. Patrick's school to attend the wake of a classmate.
I had not yet abandoned my love for Maureen Brennan.
I bought my first telescope and saw my first binary star.
I leaned over, as I was told, to kiss the side of his face
not covered by bandages to hide the cancer.
On Mount St. Helens, patches of flowers are growing
of ash in the shape of decayed animals that died there.
If we ever wrecked this tin car we'd be dead.

For thirty years I couldn't attend another funeral.
On Sept 6, 1991 in Croatia seven men are laid out
by the side of the road like burnt wicks, throats cut,
testicles jammed into their mouths. For 30 years
I believed my friend, Bernie Doyle, had moved away,
but it was him, wasn't it, in that casket in 1955.
Every day, it seems, another dream is chained
to the cell wall. Even the flowers have put on
their gray trench coats. 12 billion light years from here
a gas cloud 100 times the size of the Milky Way is
getting ready to form a second generation of stars
from the elements of millions of supernovas,
which means that all life begins in a kind of fog
and no matter how many times we start over
we will never see clearly enough. Therefore,
I am abandoning my life as a fish, my reptilian brain,
even my allegiance to the lower animals. What we are is
62,000 miles of capillaries if we care to line them up.
It seems like every galaxy is tumbling through space
as if it, too, had missed in its grab for the bar.
According to the laws of entropy the more I write
the less true it all becomes. In fact, only the autobiographical
parts of this poem are true. Maybe we are just the abandoned
drafts of something better. Why had it taken me thirty years
to abandon my dream for Bernie? When we get to Lipica
I am going to clean the windshield. I will abandon
my communication with life on other planets. I abandon
the net, the chalk of a sure grip on these details,
the wristband that braced me against desire. Maybe our dearest
truths are shoes we abandon in some old dumpster. In 1910
thousands of people bought gas masks to protect
themselves from the cyanide in the tail of Halley's Comet.
In 1578 the Bishop of Magdeburg revealed that a comet is
the thick smoke of our sins. If this were true
the night sky ought to be a good deal brighter. If this car
doesn't make it all the way to Lipica we will have

to abandon it next to one of those burnt-out trucks
that stopped the tanks. I can still see the red freckles
covering Bernie's face. We had to write something
forgettable 1,000 times for skipping class. We will have
to wait for the night to slip back into its burrows.
Maybe we should forget about Lipica and head for Piran
and its topless beach. It is the home of composer
Giovanni Tartini (1692-1770) who wrote *The Devil's Trill
Sonata* which might as well be our theme song. Besides,
it seems our Renault 4 has taken a wrong turn somewhere
and we must abandon everything. Boris himself will invent us
from the smell of abandoned fruit stands. We will spend
the rest of the day inventing a kind of love that no longer
exists in the world, a kind of love no army can pillage
at the outposts, no rumor could bring to its knees like a traitor,
no heart will leave abandoned at the crossroads. Here
Truth is lounging beneath a great oak, waiting to bum
another ride. Somewhere, a nameless
star is collapsing, but its light won't stop arriving,
it won't ever stop arriving for millions of years.

Dead Space

by Jonis Agee

There is a funeral you imagine - the one where they roll your sister efficiently toward the hole. None of this effort of straining men. They have done everything they can, or know how to do already. Father's in a wheelchair. He can't lift a hand again. Ex-husband has taken his cynical smile to the cruel motel and waits. Maybe he has another bride. Who knows, maybe he's in the part of the cemetery dissolving into the overgrown hollow and abandoned cars beyond.

You know this because this is the funeral of November. So let's put him on the other side of the hollow, his careful pant legs stickered and ragged with weeds. He's been caught and rumpled in the bush. He's been stumbled and fallen in the dry creek. Morgan Creek. All the creeks have been drier since the great drought. This one is no exception. He caught a Gucci in between two rocks and went down on the mossy stones. His knees are wet - darkly wet. There's hope of blood, maybe mud. One of them would be worse. You want them to be muddy so he doesn't get the valor of wounds in the shower inspection. No, you just want him stranded in a knee high thicket of ragweed and blackberry and burrs. You want him in the possession of something with enough power to ignore and nag him, An irritation like a splinter on his attention.

Okay, this is the funeral. The air is slight and cold with wet, though it is not raining. Brothers who would be strong enough for coffin lifting have put themselves elsewhere. They're worried about what they'll have to steal to get home again. There's almost nothing in the cemetery of value–though in a wild moment they imagine backing a van to the slabs at night and stealing the very old Civil War ones. The weather has made them light enough to carry, and the faded spires with elaborate dull print might appeal to someone seeking a really unique object. They try to think if they know anyone like that. They glance at the bald head of her ex-husband, it's finally lost its shine. He looks poor today, he can't even afford to stand with the family.

When the coffin comes rolling onto the gurney, you're struck by the way the legs flop down and stand up under her. There, you want to say, that's what she needed - four long steel rods and wheels. You notice the brothers peeking in cars as the procession works its way along the roads.

At each family plot you must ask, "Will you have her?"

"We're crowded," they complain. "We don't remember her, where's her family?"

It takes an hour and a half of struggling the coffin over rocks and ruts to come to the lowest part of the cemetery. The oldest part sits on a small rise at the center, inaccessible by roads so you must walk on the heads and shoulders of the dead to speak to them. The coffin rocks perilously at the Spurlocks but their silence keeps her away. The newer members spread away from the old heart, gradually working their way to the road, the hollow, the little houses and the poor.

Mother walks behind, the chief mourner, though she wants to gallop ahead, lead the wagons. She's known where you're headed all along. There was never any question, but she's been told to stay behind, so she does. This is one time your sister gets to lead the way, and she's not giving up the authority of death. Not even to the powerful figure of her mother in black - a dark hum, a sound held and gutturalized. You have dressed her in galoshes - the old fashioned heavy black rubber kind with metal gripper fasteners that flop and clank with each step. She keeps wanting to kill the corpse again so the hair and fingernails don't grow. Someone has to be sure.

The father, miles behind, is going to ashes, so his wife doesn't have a chance at him. He wants a sure end to things - no growing out of control after the breath flattens and the tongue stills and softens. The first thing is rot, he once believed, until his wife told him of the cells whose job it was to keep living, growing, the dead rising again. Either you sat up with the body, waiting for the clack of teeth, the snort of breath, or you embalmed, killing again, or you burned killing again, every cell crackling and popping in the chocking dirt.

Grandmother Hettie's stone lies flat with her friend at her feet. They've got two trees to themselves. Keep the men at a distance. When you reach her, she won't recognize anyone - not even her son. She doesn't approve of this ragged lot. That's why she took her place here with someone who isn't even family.

Father pretends he doesn't notice, his knuckles yellow-white on the chair arms.

In the middle of the group your sister's daughter staggers under the load of jewelry, clothes, furniture, paintings and silver she carries. This is what envy brings her. She is a series of half-successful gestures. She was born old and has been catching up all her life. If there is grief pocketed in her, you can't see it beneath the accumulation of her mother's wealth. She thinks of putting something down, but can't make decisions like that. Not since her mother, you know -

Behind her daughter come the sisters. Dressed in bright blues and greens, bejeweled like queens or circus stars. You are afraid to touch anything. You're thinking of the bathroom at the motel, pure water with no aftertaste, no stink to soap your hands again and again. You'll never wear those clothes again. You'll discard the shoes edged with red clay, a tiny pebble caught between sole and stitching. The business is all physical - it makes you want to brush your teeth like an embarrassing smell has caught on the back of your tongue, along the rim of your gums. You can't admit you've never been in a graveyard. You don't have a fallback like the bandit brothers. Looking pretty is your only option. Each of you wears a rainbow of face makeup, greens and blues and pinks and yellows. It makes your faces look surprised, hopeful, an expression you have learned so that you won't be mistaken, hurt. The three of you, like harpies tamed to the hand, husbands trudging behind on little leashes, tinkling chains in the grey dull light. Their faces are scrubbed clean of features.

Finally, when the weight of refusals from the occupied stones shoves your little procession to the fringe, the edge where newly dead stretch rawly in the yellow grass, your eye notes how embarrassing it is, without trees, within clear view of the blacktop traffic and tumbledown shacks whose porches hold the overflow couches, appliances, boxes, an open air closet, something defiantly intimate that makes you turn your eyes away when you want to stare.

That's where the ground stops talking and the men stop the gurney. You'd like to say a hole appeared, that no one was asked to lend a hand. When it happens though, you only have to scoop a bit, your high heels sinking so you're rocked back, tilting away from the shovels of dirt.

It doesn't take long. The rain has helped. The rocks grind like molars on the metal blade, but it's not unpleasant. It feels good to be doing something, and soon even the brothers put their backs into it - though later they'll steal the shovel. Ex-husband is panting like a dog on the other side of the culvert. He drops to all fours, the Harris tweed filling quickly until he's bushy, with the bald spot like a bolus of tree fungus. "Don't worry," you say, "he can't get across."

Even mother gets into the act, happy she's worn galoshes after all since she won't throw anything away. She gives the shovel a hefty dig and pulls great amounts of dirt out, heaving them easily over her shoulder. Some of the dirt crumbles over her as it flies through the air. Good thing she wore black, you think.

Father won't get out of his chair. He shouts directions and caustic remarks everyone ignores. After all, what does he know, he's afraid of fingernails, hair, and his own cells.

By the time the chain gang husbands are done, the hole is as big as a house foundation and the men easily drive the gurney in, press a button and leave the coffin squatting bewildered in the middle of the scrapedred earth.

Now this is something, you think, as you look around. At this funeral, there is no minister, no stranger to the wills and wiles of the family. The coffin transport workers have faded from sight.

In a minute, you hear the backfire of the old hearse, which doubles as ambulance and scout expedition bus for the tiny town.

The brothers haven't stolen the shovel yet, but no one makes a move. You can wait a long time between efforts. The ex-husband's soft whimpers and growls get blown to pieces by the swooping caws of blackbirds who arrive like visiting gods and walk among the headstones behind you. Every motion elongated, slowed, deliberate until they resemble the grace of elephants, giraffes, draft horses—something bigger than possible.

It takes a while for you to recognize the clinking and clanking and turn your head to the figure of her daughter, a tumbledown tower of stuff shuffling to the hole. Descending the dirt ramp in the gurney tracks, the weight sinking her deeper and deeper. Each time she yanks a leg out, it leaves a pock surrounded by a puddle of colors and forms. She resembles a dinosaur making its gradual progress into the tar pit. By the time she reaches her mother's coffin, she is waist deep in muck and only her final shove of goods from her shoulders, back, and head keeps her from sinking out of sight. Miraculously, when the noise of metal and glass and cloth hits the bright anodized aluminum canister of the coffin, it doesn't sink.

Her daughter stands bare except for a simple black dress like her grandmother. Levering herself on the coffin, she pulls her legs out and stands naturally, but doesn't bother pushing at the mud caking her from the waist down. Instead, she is the one who begins to fill the hole. Using her hands, she digs ferociously at the sides, pulling the dirt down around her, then climbing out again, over and over.

You watch this. Then you look at mother who stands on the rim. One of her sisters hands her the shovel, but she has lost her strength now. The bandit brothers take the shovel and work hard—really hard, for the first time in years. They have things to do now. They need to finish before dark. Next the chain gang husbands, let of their leashes, get their backs into it, but the hole is taking much longer to fill than dig. By the time the sisters have to dirty their hands, you need to borrow dirt from surrounding graves. There just isn't enough to go around. Even father gets out of his wheelchair. He's so annoyed he can walk again, but he finds out what his advising voice didn't know: the coffin keeps rising foot by dirt filling foot until the hole is gone and the place marked by the giant bright cigar is anodized red. Your sister's grave.

After you're gone, her ex-husband comes sniffing by, lifts a leg to pee and gets an electric shock when the yellow stream hits the burnished red. He runs away howling.

In the motel room, you bathe her daughter, wash her hair, clean her fingernails and give her a plain practical life without tragedy and drama. Father gets lost in the corridors and whimpers until he hears the galoshes slurping. The husbands are in the bar getting drunk, trying to get some expressions back in their faces.

Out at the cemetery, the brothers have possession of the shovel and are passing it back and forth, estimating its weight and the price it will bring.

And your sister finally has what she wants.

The Evening News

by Tony Ardizzone

Their fears appear nightly, as routinely as the newscaster's face. Framed by the plastic black rectangle of the portable color television set Maria's parents had given them, the newscaster's head and shoulders normally fill two-thirds of the screen, and the man's face is always calm, pale salmon. Behind him is a soothing gray-blue backdrop. The other third of the picture is left to maps of Poland, El Salvador, the Falkland Islands. Paul wonders who chooses the colors for the maps. El Salvador is usually brown; Poland, nearly always red. Argentina is green and jagged. Paul likes to tinker with the knob labeled TONE to make the countries any color he wants them to be. Sometimes when Maria isn't in the room he turns down the BRIGHT knob and makes everything turn black. Paul's parents didn't have a color television when he was growing up. Whenever he watches baseball he likes the colors to be true, but not so gaudy that he is distracted by them. The grass in the infields has to be lime green, the dirt around home plate barely orange. Paul has been to Atlanta. Atlanta is nearly five hundred miles away, but cable picks up all the televised games. The Braves now call themselves America's Team. During the first week they had the set Paul waited patiently for a shot of the American flag flying out in center field; then he quickly locked in the flag's red stripes, its square field of blue, its crisp wrinkled lines of white, then marked each knob with a Flair pen so he could always return the colors to where they were supposed to be, clearly there on the screen, bright and true, but not so loud as to be distracted by them.

Maria doesn't care about the color. When she turns on the TV set, any colors are all right with her, even black and white. Maria is seven months pregnant. The color set was a pregnancy gift. Each day when she comes home from the university library where she works she watches "General Hospital," her favorite soap opera, usually in black and white. She calls the soaps "the dopes." She hasn't smoked any marijuana since she learned she was pregnant. Though the baby wasn't planned, Maria takes all the right vitamins and eats enough protein and vegetables to make herself so sick of doing things right that she wants to roll a fat joint and get high, but she doesn't have any grass in the house and she knows that drugs are probably bad for the baby. She drinks red wine instead. Seldom more than seven glasses a week. Paul drinks a lot of wine, mostly imported, now that they can afford it. He grew up drinking inexpensive homemade wine. None of the expensive imported wine is as good as what he remembers drinking. He thinks of himself as ethnic. At a Sociology Department party he joked the America was a Wonder Bread culture, soft and white, slickly packaged with pictures of colorful balloons. You think you're holding something of integrity and substance, but when you squeeze it you have mostly preservatives and air. Maria doesn't know what to think of herself. Her Spanish isn't fluent, and she has never been to Mexico, where her grandparents were born. She always feels peculiar checking the box next to HISPANIC on the equal opportunity forms. Paul is much less American than she, and he has no box to check. Today he comes home unexpectedly early from his teaching job at the university and sees Luke Spencer's worried face on the screen in black and white, and he adjusts the knobs, making darker marks with his Flair pen.

"Why don't you set this thing right?" he asks Maria. "Why do we have color if you don't use it?"

"You're blocking the picture," Maria says. She tries to stare past him. "You make a better door than a window."

Paul asks Maria if he can get her anything, if she felt O.K. at work, if she wants her feet or back rubbed. Maria waits until a commercial to tell him no, yes, no.

He checks the morning newspaper to see if the Braves have an afternoon game. Today is an off day. In the kitchen he pours a glass of apple juice. At the sink he rinses the evening's vegetables, then chops them at the table in the dining room. He sneaks behind Maria and kisses her on the cheek. He makes the salad and adds the imported black olives she hadn't seen him slip into the grocery cart. Paul likes doing things for Maria. He loves her, more than he knows, especially now that she's going to have a baby. This is a special, if tense, time in their lives—this spring, a year after the baseball strike, the year Paul is going up for tenure, the year Maria received a higher classification and a 5.2 percent raise at the library, the year they are learning Lamaze. Their afternoons together are cool and peaceful, and Luke Spencer is searching for his missing Laura, and the Braves are hot, on a winning streak. Yesterday the chairman of the department told Paul he needn't worry. Earlier in the week the obstetrician told Maria she was coming along just fine. The evening news won't be on for a few more hours. Paul readjusts the color of Luke's curly mop of hair as Maria chews a slice of celery and then closes her eyes and naps on the sofa facing the portable television.

Earlier that year they had a dog. Her name was Bingo and she was a dumb mistake. An impulsive decision made in a shopping mall the day before Christmas Eve two years ago. Paul and Maria paused before a pet store window and predictably Paul said, "Look at the cute puppies." He had never had a dog. He hadn't bought Maria's present yet. A toddler in a harness and leash pulled his mother toward the window, pointing with a wet finger he'd just taken from his mouth. Beneath the vague noise of footsteps and muffled conversation a Christmas carol was playing. From the doorway of the store a salesman in a doctor's white lab coat smiled at Maria, then caught Paul's eye and winked.

Maria and Paul sat inside a paneled cubicle, and the man in the white doctor's coat brought them the smallest of the puppies swaddled in a clean white towel. The puppy trembled, then licked Maria's fingers. "He's so frightened," she said.

"She," corrected the salesman. "But you'll see that in a moment or two she'll relax."

The dog did. Maria petted the pup's soft fur. Paul absently touched the checkbook in his sports jacket pocket, then stood and told the salesman they'd have to think about it.

Outside the store a Salvation Army volunteer rang a silent bell and held up a sign that read RING, RING. Shoppers rushed about. Paul and Maria shared an Orange Julius. "It's a lot of money," Paul said.

"She's so adorable," Maria said, her dark hair spilling over the leather collar of her coat. "I can't stand to think of her having to spend Christmas in that damn window."

There was nothing they could to. By the time Bingo was two years old she'd had kennel cough, bronchitis, seizures, and finally allergies. Paul and Maria sat in the waiting rooms of veterinarians. There was little the vets could do except mark the dog's chart and cash Paul's checks. The last vet was named Alonzo Scarr, and at a red light on the way home Paul joked that clearly the man had never had a future as a plastic surgeon. Maria held Bingo in her arms. She didn't smile. "So of course he became a veterinarian," Paul said, forcing his joke, hoping to make Maria laugh, to break the tension. "I mean, with the last name like Scarr—"

Maria said nothing. The car behind them honked. The red light had changed to green. Dr. Scarr had said with compassion and utter seriousness that Bingo was allergic to nearly everything.

This was after Maria and Paul had followed his advice and put the dog on a cottage cheese and vegetable oil diet. Dr. Scarr said, "Your dog has severe environmental allergies, and I could check her for sixty agents but she'll show positive on fifty-eight of them." Paul said, "Then she's allergic to life." The vet scratched his head and nodded. By then Bingo was a mass of scabs—an itching, bleeding mess of fur and nail, flesh and tooth—and nothing, not even the bimonthly shots, could heal her.

"It's a real racket," a professor in criminal justice told Paul one afternoon in the department mailroom. "See, they breed these poor animals in puppy mills in states where animal welfare regulations are lax. The pups are neurotic and plagued with genetic disorders common to their breed. The dogs are literally bred to death. My neighbors made the same mistake. Had to have the dog put down. Their kids really took it hard."

Maria was working the night shift at the library that semester. "We have to do something, " she'd tell Paul when she came home. She was just starting to show. She'd drink a glass of juice and sigh, then rock Bingo in her arms and say she wished she knew the answer. Paul watched television with the dog that semester. Their favorite show was "All Creatures Great and Small" on PBS. The set was new and Paul liked to make the colors bright, giving Mr. Herriot's face a garish redness. He talked to the dog when Maria wasn't home. "See," he'd say to Bingo, who'd squat beside him on the wooden floor, incessantly scratching her chest and neck, "Tristan's got himself in hot water with Siegfried again, but Mr. Herriot's sure to save the day."

Dr. Scarr was silent as he filled the large hypodermic. Maria's small hands held Bingo's trembling face. Really, it was the best thing; the dog couldn't even eat without scratching herself. "Relax, honey," Maria said. The first of her tears splashed on the stainless steel table. Paul was at school, teaching his seminar. Something about stratification. His specialty was something about stratification. It was all too complex. They could try another vet, but they'd already been to three and now Bingo's skin was badly infected and it wasn't even flea season and in five months if everything went well they'd have baby. Dr. Scarr stepped forward, then coughed. The night before, watching Bingo try to eat, Paul had announced, "I'm going to firebomb the pet store." "Is it the right thing?" Maria had asked. "You know, is it cruel to kill her?" Paul paced the length of the kitchen. "The only thing holding me back is knowing I'd have the blood of innocent goldfish on my hands." Bingo was licking her chops, then scratched open a fresh scab. "It's more cruel to let her live," Maria concluded. She stroked the dog's ears. Scarr withdrew the needle, and Bingo slumped. "Oh," Maria cried. He listened to the dog's sides with a stethoscope.

Maria would tell Paul what she'd done that afternoon at lunch. A person shouldn't have to kill his first dog. "It's O.K.," Maria said to Bingo, her voice thick.

"She's passed," Dr. Scarr said, not looking at Maria.

In his dark brown corduroy sports jacket, khaki shirt, and tan corduroy pants, Paul teaches aggressively and well. His peer evaluations say he is dynamic. Dynamic is their euphemism for controversial. Paul's methods are the subject of many mailroom gossip sessions. He knows the hush that sometimes falls around the white alphabetized boxes when he enters the room means that the old men were discussing him. What should be done with the young assistant professor? The consensus leans toward granting him tenure; his colleagues feel it will settle him down. Paul thinks of his colleagues as "the old men." He thinks of most of them as brontosaurus waiting to sink into the mud and die. They're a turgid lot, going through the same motions, reading the same yellowed lecture notes semester after semester. They are predictable and therefore safe. Students tolerate them. Paul is erratic, daring. Students either love him or hate him. His troubles with the old men and the higher administration began the day he threw the portable desk.

He didn't throw the desk very far—actually, he only shoved it—but the portable desk toppled and clattered and the noise woke his dreaming students and rang out through the silent halls. Paul shoved the desk for emphasis, to make a point, to drive home an idea. There is nothing safe and predictable about ideas, he believes. Sometimes ideas should strike you with thunder. He wants to make thunder, to knock the complacent off their high horse. He wants the exchange of ideas to firebomb the world.

The Dean called Paul into his office. The Dean said he was aware that any number of instructional techniques could, in the proper circumstances, be viable, but the abuse of university property was at best an unorthodox method that was untenable and certainly was not to be encouraged by administrative personnel. The Dean smoked a large cigar while he spoke. Hundreds of ceramic and mahogany toads covered his bookshelves and desk. The Dean had once been a biologist who led an excursion into South America in the search for new subfamilies of toads. Some of the toads' backsides were covered with bunches of ceramic eggs. On the Dean's desk was a plaque that read BUFO AMERICANUS. Paul reassured the Dean that his actions did not damage the desk. He said he chose an especially sturdy-looking desk to shove, aware of the appropriate respect university employees should afford university property. The Dean did not recognize Paul's sarcasm. Nevertheless, Paul said, the instructional technique would not be used by him again.

"Then we're eyeball to eyeball in this," the Dean said, puffing on his cigar and standing and extending his hand.

"Yes," Paul said. "Thank you for your counsel."

Paul wasn't unlike his students when he first entered college. But the climate of campus life was different then. There was an undeclared war in Asia, riots in the cities' ghettos, angry women who wore buttons that read OFF OUR BACKS. There were people who argued about DDT and ecology. Paul read *Silent Spring, One-Dimensional Man, Soul on Ice, Sisterhood is Powerful.* He listened to lunchtime debates in the boisterous Student Union. The ideas made a firestorm in his mind. When the National Guard invaded the campus, and students and professors went out on strike, and peaceful demonstrations were tear-gassed and scattered—legs tripped by nightsticks, heads, ribs clubbed—Paul felt a sudden spiritual manifestation, what he learned in Soph Lit was called an epiphany. He didn't have to be frightened. *He could matter.* So he became an active student radical. He helped coordinate teach-ins. He petitioned City Hall for permits to demonstrate, to march. He organized his thoughts. He felt he was a part of something and agreed with the student at Radcliffe who in 1968 said, "We do not feel like a cool, swinging generation-we are eaten up inside by an intensity that we cannot name." Paul read *The Guardian, Ramparts, Zap Comics, The Berkeley Tribe*. He was making decisions that would affect him for the rest of his life. He joined a group that put on guerrilla theatre. He rapped with guardsmen, lent them magazines to read, brought the coffee from Dunkin Donuts. After he was arrested during a demonstration in his senior year, the university attempted to withhold his degree. There was a month of hearings about all those who'd been arrested. Paul read Isaac Deutscher's book on Trotsky's early life, *The Prophet Armed*, during much of the hearings. A lower court overruled the university's findings to expel. Paul was graduated in good standing.

He returned to the city and for two years worked in factories. Then he went to graduate school. He met Maria. They fell in love. He completed the work on his dissertation.

The old men crabbed about growing course loads and static pay scales. They swapped stories about how ignorant their students were. Stories about absurdly ignorant students earned the loudest mailroom laughs. When one old full professor retired, he mimeographed a booklet of quotes from his years' worst student essays.

Paul didn't find it funny. "If they're so damn dumb," he told the laughing old men, "why in hell don't you teach them?"

The retiring professor scratched the side of his grotesquely large bald head. "That's why we hired you, you naive fool. Waste all your juice on the comatose shits. Gentlemen, I'm going fishing."

Paul wears the story like a badge. He tells it whenever the untenured faculty gathers to complain. The young assistants nod, sip white wine or Lite beer, repeat their stories, shake their heads.

Yet Paul cannot really empathize with his students. They seem hedonistic, concerned with copping highs and getting laid. Today's students are into escapism, he –, tells the young assistants. Their primary contribution to American society has been to make "party" into a verb. Where SIEZE THE TIME used to be written, now was scrawled PARTY DOWN. The students seem too close to the old men, Paul thinks. It's as if the students realized that the smorgasbord of good times was running out, but instead of working and struggling to replenish the tables they jostled only to load up their empty plates before it was too late. At his most cynical, Paul confesses to Maria that what the students need is a good taste of repression. The spur to the side of the sleeping horse. Then he immediately says, "No, I don't really mean that. Listen to me, I'm talking crazy. I must be getting old."

Maria was in junior high when Paul experienced his epiphany. World events bore her, though on principle she is against all forms of violence and war. She is glad she came of age when she did. She has an active imagination. She doesn't need to experience directly the burning of pepper gas to know it makes you sneeze and choke. Government plays for keeps, Maria believes.

Authority is brutal because brutality is endemic to authority. Maria doesn't like pain. She is wary of dentists, always polite to policemen. The major issues when she was in school were dress codes and whether the seniors could have a smoking lounge. Her ninth-grade class helped put together a rally for peace in the school auditorium; Maria neatly lettered a rainbow sign that read WORLD PEACE-LET'S TRY IT! She was attentive in class and did most of her homework, and each afternoon, after riding in a girl friend's mother's car to a girl friend's house where the girls sipped Tab and talked about clothes and boys and new records, she got high. Maria is an expert smoker of grass. She can smoke a joint down so close to her lips it resembles a half-moon sliver of fingernail, and that's not even using a roach clip. On the weekends she worked in a department store, selling mascara and lip gloss and cologne to large overdressed women who already used too much perfume and makeup. Maria seldom uses makeup. She is naturally pretty, with good cheekbones, her eyelashes naturally thick. when Paul met her at a party after a Grateful Dead concert, she smelled like Ivory soap and marijuana smoke.

Demonstrations frighten her, as do most overt displays of emotion. Why can't people be civilized and just talk things out? Maria thinks. War belongs to another world, like boxing. She cannot see any sense in people hitting each other, even if they are being paid millions of dollars to do it. It's stupid, she thinks, and the people who watch it and cheer are stupider, in most arguments she leaves the room or concedes. "You're absolutely correct," she agrees. But of course she isn't convinced; her surrender is only a ploy that helps her get past the time when someone else wants to argue. She knows that Paul finds her behavior irritating, but that is his problem. Maria loves Paul because of it, because she is what he isn't. Yin and Yang. Though she tells him to change, to see life as more than mere sets of social and political theories, she realizes that his personality is set as granite. If she were a nation she'd be Switzerland. Neutral. Protected by snowcapped mountains. Makers of watches, peace talks, chocolate. When Maria studied European geography in tenth grade she in so many extra-credit reports on Switzerland that her teacher raised the white flag and gave her a 101 on her report card.

In college she received a degree in library science. She is very serious about libraries. She finds them civil, even better than churches because in libraries you can move about. Everything has its place in a library. The Dewey Decimal System was as great an advancement as the discovery of the wheel. Everyone is equal in a library, and everyone knows it is improper to raise your voice. Whenever there is any unnecessary noise all a librarian has to do is say, "Shhh." People are usually grateful when you help them find a book.

The sole imperfection, Maria thinks, is the copying room. There the coin exchangers clank; The Xerox machines groan and whir. The copiers break the spines of books. The area is somehow impure, as sacrilegious as a Coca-Cola machine in a cathedral.

Maria is fond of sitting on a ladder in the graduate stacks, surrounded by books, reading. The gentle hum of the building's ventilation system is the only sound she hears. She imagines that she is the keeper of ideas, the custodian of civilization, and outside the walls of her fortress the barbarians wage war against the vandals, but the library walls keep her safe. All of the explosive issues rest quietly on their shelves. Sometimes Maria thinks of herself as a monk, sheltering the written word, in the darkest days of the

Dark Ages. Except for celibacy, she might have liked the life of a nun. She is often overwhelmed by the brash cacophony of life. In traffic jams, when others around her impatiently inch forward and blow their horns, she shifts into neutral and slowly idles, concentrating on the stutter of *r's* her engine continues to pronounce. Sometimes she smoked a joint in the library's third-floor ladies room. Marijuana pacifies her. Good marijuana puts a warm coat of varnish on her eyes. Then she is glazed, safe, protected by the haze the reefer gives her; the flow of life's madness is slowed down, and she can cope.

Maria accepts her Hispanic roots matter of factly, and she thinks that in a past life she once was Swiss. Though she claims she doesn't believe in organized religion, she wears a gold crucifix on a chain around her neck and makes the sign the Cross whenever she hears an ambulance. Maria believes in tarot cards, palm readings, astrology, the interpretation of dreams. Death always comes in threes and always knocks on the door or wall. One morning when she was sixteen she was brushing her hair, getting ready for school, when her grandmother rushed in to ask if she had heard the knocks. That afternoon her grandmother died. Then an uncle died, then Maria's cousin. Maria is proud of the story. When Paul hears her repeat it and criticizes her for not being rational, she says, "Paul, you're so limited I could laugh."

Maria is very aware of how tentative human life on the planet is. Secure on her ladder in the graduate stacks, she reads the predictions of Nostradamus. She studies the teachings of Edgar Cayce. She believes in good and evil, and she knows she has had many past lives. In at least one of them she knew Paul; that is why he seems so comfortable to be around. Their uncosciousnesses recognize each other. Maria can't remember any details of her past lives. The fact that she has lived before is enough.

People are born she believes, and they live and do good and evil. Then they're born again and again and again, until they do mostly good. Until they don't have to work through anything anymore. She knows she has many more lives to live.

She believes the body growing in her womb is just that, a body. It will become complete later, when a soul floating in the cosmos selects it. When a soul chooses her and Paul. So she and Paul need to be very good because many souls are judging them. Paul needs to fight against some of his rigidity. She needs more backbone, more courage to stand up, to define. She knows that this spring is a very special time, tentative as an interview. But if Nostradamus is correct, the world will end during the child's lifetime. This worries Maria.

Sometimes she sits by herself late at night, arms around herself, rocking, weeping. She weeps for the future of her child will see. What a bitter world, she thinks. What an obscene, violent, horrible mess. Don't come down to us if you're frightened, she tells the souls in the cosmos. We have very little to offer, so wouldn't it be better if you wait? If none of the souls choose to come down, Maria prays to God, let me miscarry. I'm not forcing you, she tells the soul of her baby. Choose me and Paul, if we are what you need. Come to us—we will welcome you—even though I know your death will break my heart when the world ends, when the ground is shaken by earthquakes, when the end comes and death falls like a rain of hailstones from the broken sky.

* * *

So Paul and Maria watch the evening news because it seldom fails to reaffirm their separate beliefs. Paul turns up the volume, adjusts the color, then settles on the couch. The best minds of the sixties had foreseen all of this, he thinks. But being right gives him little solace. He hopes the world can resolve its problems. He is tired and wants to grow old in relative stability and peace. Is that too much to ask for? he thinks. He knows the answer. Of course it's too much, because he and the rest of America are still so damn privileged, and because order naturally deteriorates into chaos and chaos makes fertile ground for discontent, insurrection, and war. The next war will be with nuclear weapons, he believes. Has man ever made a tool he didn't use eventually? It's the bottom of the ninth inning, he thinks, and there are no runners on base; the good guys are ten thousand runs behind, and the final pitch is on its way. Soon it will explode in the catcher's oversized mitt, and somebody will fire a nuclear warhead, and in a cloud of fire the world as we know it will be gone.

Even school children can recite the scenario, Paul thinks. No wonder they smoke angel dust and impregnate one another by the time they are thirteen. *Carpe diem.* He knows it is insane. It is is insane to sit in the faculty dining room of the student cafeteria and actually discuss with the young assistants how the world will end. His theory is that the planet itself will remain intact after the bombs are unleashed, but mammals, reptiles, birds, and most of the fish will be destroyed; plant life will be devastated, but some insects will survive, and some fish, so deep in the oceans that they continue to defy discovery. These forms of life will be left. So it will not really be the end of the world, Paul argues. Only the end of *us*. Then the analogy is humanity as dinosaur—human as extinct, lumbering beast. Our skeletons will adorn the insect museums of the future, he jokes, and future praying mantis larvae will ask their mothers what happened to the mammals, the reptiles, the birds, the large fish. Mommy, why did they become extinct? Oh, the wise praying mantis mother will say, we have any number of theories. They might have been destroyed by a supernova. Maybe large meteors fell from the sky and raised so much dust it erased the sun. Perhaps they burned too much fossil fuel and as a result of the greenhouse effect the polar icecaps melted. Some think man learned nuclear fission, but that's an extreme viewpoint. Even the ignorant aphids know not to experiment with *that.*

The ground ball skips back to the pitcher. He picks it up easily and scoops it underhand to first. Out. The ball game's over.

Maria leaves the room now that the news is on. She leaves, but cannot help listen. "Paul," she says, "do you have to watch it?"

"What would you rather I do?" he says. "Shut my eyes? Turn on 'The Beverly Hillbillies'?"

"Any thing," Maria says, pouring a glass of valpolicella in the kitchen. She touches her growing abdomen, is aware of the fullness of her breasts. Everything makes her think of the fate of her coming baby. The face of the Argentine widow staring grimly at the flag-draped coffin. The Irish children throwing back canisters of tear gas in the Ulster streets. Women wearing babushkas in food lines in Poland. The crack of automatic rifles on El Salvador. The very worst are the pictures of the starving children in Africa. Arms like wooden spoons, distended stomachs, flies crawling on their nostrils and open lips. Why can't the news limit itself to the weather? she thinks. Cars abandoned in ragged rows on a highway after a blizzard, homes that shouldn't have been built on mountainsides in the first place sliding down a lake of mud. These are things Maria can watch, can understand. Hurricanes. Floods. A tragic fire. Children playing with matches. Her baby will never play with matches. Already she has started to childproof the house.

Can the world be childproofed for her and Paul? she wonders.

They always end the evening news with a light note, a humorous touch. Exit laughing. A story about the grandmother in Florida who opened the house trailer to hundreds of foster children over the past thirty years—"There Was an Old Woman Who Lived in a Shoe." The Oklahoma cowboy who lived in a cage full of rattlesnakes for several months but who now wouldn't be listed in *The Guinness Book of World Records*. Pathos and irony. In Virginia Beach a man hacked his mother-in-law with a hatchet and claimed as his defense that he thought she was a raccoon.

Absurd. A commercial for something called Intellivision begins, and a shill praises it over other video-game systems because only Intellivision offers the total destruction of a planet. So their gravest fear is now a feature on a video game? The glass of red wine falls from Maria's hand. It shatters on the linoleum like a destructing planet. Paul rushes into the kitchen. And that's the way it is—

Later that evening, the television off, Paul sits on the couch with Maria. Her head rests against his chest. His arm hangs over her shoulder. They have sat like this since the room began to darken. Neither has wanted to disturb the other, to get up and turn on a light. The open window next to the sofa flutters the thin curtains that hang over it. From the even way he is breathing, Maria thinks Paul is asleep.

"Are you sleeping?" she whispers.

Paul's breathing stops, then starts again. "No."

"You never told me why you came home early today."

He lets out a long breath. "My three o'clock didn't read the assignment, so I told them to go to the registrar and withdraw from school."

"Why?" Maria asks.

"Sometimes the best way to get people's attention is to exaggerate."

Maria thinks about exaggeration. Then she swallows. "I can't tell you how much I want to get high."

"Let me give you a backrub."

"I don't want a backrub."

" Have a glass of wine."

"I'm sick of wine."

"I'm sorry." Paul doesn't know what else to say.

Her hand clutches his arm. The strength surprises him. "Are you sure having the baby is the right thing?"

"Yes," Paul says, too quickly. He isn't sure.

"I wouldn't do this for anyone else, you know."

"I know." His hand pats her hand. "It's the right thing, Maria." The hand squeezes her wrist. "Everything will be O.K."

She turns her head, trying in the darkness to look at him, but she can't see any of the features of his face. She can only hear his even, reassuring voice as he begins to explain that even though an event seems likely it is never guaranteed to happen, that it's useless to walk through life feeling depressed and powerless, that the birth of a baby is an affirmation, an ace of great courage, faith, and hope. For all we know, Paul continues, when things look their very bleakest we'll be visited by spaceships from a distant galaxy, and the alien life forms will help us solve all our problems. Maria scoffs at the idea, though it's tempting to believe. Paul softly laughs and says it comes from a movie, a classic, *The Night of the Living Dead*. Maria doesn't laugh at the joke. No, Paul says, it was *The Day the Earth Stood Still,* the best science-fiction movie ever made. Maria says she wishes the earth would stand still. It can't, Paul says, suddenly serious. He tries to think of something else to say.

"Sometimes when I come down here in the morning I still expect to see Bingo," Maria says. Paul's eyes dart in the darkness, looking for the dog. Maria sits up and faces him. She places her hands in his. "Why did she have to die?"

Paul feels on safer ground now. He knows the answer to the question. "Free enterprise. We were ripped off. We were suckered. We live in a country where salesmen can dress up like doctors and lovable little puppy dogs can grow up allergic to life."

"And we're not?" Maria says.

Paul reaches for all the hopefulness he has to offer. "No," he says. "Maria, we're the luckiest people in the world. Look at us. We're both alive and healthy. Our baby's on its way. We have a house, work, food. Ninety-five percent of world would give their arms and legs to have half of what we have." Paul's voice is high, speedy. "And maybe our baby will be the one who helps solve the world's problems. Maybe not. But if the child ever asks me why we agreed for it to be born—" He hesitates. His eyes search the darkness for the answer. "I'll say I though having a chance to live was better than no chance, even if we live to see the world destroyed."

Maria laughs, terrified. "I can just see it. The bombs will be falling down around our heads and you'll be explaining all of that to our baby."

"I'll be digging a hole, Maria. I'll wear a colander on my head. You and the baby bring the cans of beans. We'll do what we can to survive."

"I'll just stand in the backyard and hold my baby and weep."

"No, you won't." Paul shakes her shoulders. "We'll struggle. We're not cynics. We'll march in the streets. We'll influence opinion. We'll do what we must to survive." He takes her in his arms and holds her tightly.

Maria feels his arms around her and relaxes, thinking about her coming baby. Choose us, she prays, because we're not cynics. Choose us because Paul is so stubborn. Because I'll hold you to my breast until I die. The idea of holding her child gives her comfort, and Maria imagines that at this moment a very special and wise and trusting soul chooses the body floating in the warm waters of her womb. She believes she can feel the soul as it enters her body. Yes. The child within her stirs. Tears of wonder fall from her eyes.

Paul feels Maria's tears and thinks she is despairing. "Please," he says. "Let's not think anymore. Maria, please."

She cries freely now, rejoicing.

Paul goes on thinking. He gives full play to his doubts. Maybe this is the very worst moment to be alive, especially in America, the eye of the dragon, belly of the beast. Maybe this is the absolutely worst moment to have the audacity to give birth to an innocent. Maria's shoulders shake with what Paul thinks is great sadness.

He stares past her at the television squatting smugly in the corner of the room. Before the end comes, he thinks, everyone will see it, in living color, splashed across a hundred million TV screens. The multicolored maps, areas of greatest risk, perhaps even the warheads' trajectories. Certainly the assurance that the war is winnable. Certainly the glib warnings to stay calm. Maria is filled with joy. I'll make the colors so intense they'll blind me, he thinks. I'll turn up the volume until I grow deaf. He squeezes Maria so fiercely that she makes a squeak. Then I'll open all the windows, and I'll throw open the front door, and I'll turn on the water in the bathroom and the kitchen, and I'll flick on every light, turn on the stereo, the oven, the furnace, the air conditioner—then I'll wait in the backyard with Maria, with our baby. Paul's nightmare stops. His hand reaches down and touches the swelling roundness of Maria's belly. She is soft and warm, happy, in his arms. He feels the darkest despair he has ever known.

The curtains over the open window next to home billow suddenly like an enormous cloud.

A Curse

by Thomas Fox Averill

My ancestors landed first in Beverly, Massachusetts, more relieved than excited. When they left England under threat of persecution, they looked into the narrow horizon. The gaze of each eye funneled to a point so distant none could say what they saw.

They were only three: William, Ruth and Sarah. They were Puritans, though not puritanical, as people confuse those words now. William left behind a clerk's position. Ruth left the large family she came from when she married William. His family was spare: each generation mustered only one or two children, then raised them like difficult, vulnerable plants. Ruth wanted many children. Sarah was ten and an only child when Ruth finally accepted her small family life. She visited cousins and nephews and nieces. A huge number of them came to see her off on her journey to Massachusetts in 1686.

They were seasick rocking in that small ship those first days. Then they were heartsick and lonely. They took turns, each nursing the others through fevers and nightmares. William's journal is as cryptic as the man himself. At sea he wrote: "We are miserable pilgrims, all of us, cramped and filthy, as our innards come out through mouth and bowels. We long for strong legs to carry us up to breathe clean salt air. Never have I been so close to raw humanity, even in my own dear Sarah."

Finally, one day, thin, just able to stand, they saw land, the foreign shore where they would make their home. Relief swept through them, but not excitement. William did not know what he would find to do. Farming repulsed him. He was uncomfortable with animals. He was unused to physical labor. He stood on deck watching the land gradually loom in front of him and was almost overwhelmed. He was certain this new land would mean new trouble.

Ruth, too, felt smaller as America grew larger and larger on the horizon. They had heard stories of this vast continent, where people were lost and never found. The small family stood together. The unsteady boat bobbed beneath them. The new land drifted towards them. Ruth wanted to take William's arm to feel comforted, but she could not. She had never felt so alone.

Even Sarah was frightened: not by the slowly increasing land, not by the prospect of what might happen to her, but by her parents. She saw not only their fear, but how unable they might be to overcome it. They were two corks floating in the ocean.

Sarah made whatever came from outside an adventure: sky, bird, cloud, wind, storm. What was inside her parents, looking out at America, was something else, something foreboding. She wished they could turn it into adventure, too. For herself, Sarah wished for the land to come and take her quickly, to force her towards what her life might be, to turn her inside out.

William's journal reads: "Saw land today. By evening it swallowed the sun. We dock tomorrow. Captain and crew dancing like heathens. Ruth still not well. Sarah will be the first of us on shore."

The next day, William made his prophecy come true. They set anchor. They climbed the rope ladders down into the dinghy. They were rowed to the small dock. When some of the crew jumped out, William handed Sarah to them. She stood on the pier and looked back at the vast ocean. Then she narrowed her gaze onto her parents, sitting stolid in the dinghy. She could feel the tremble in her father's hands, see the tears in her mother's eyes. She leaped away, down the wooden planking. William and Ruth were too tired to call after her. On shore, Sarah knelt and hugged the first large rock, the brow of this new land. It was damp and cold, but she hugged it as though she could warm it up.

An old man watched her. He was sexton of the Beverly church, a stern fellow, hardened by years of failure in England and in America. He had recently lost his own daughter to fever. He tended the church grounds and building with great care. Passing Sarah, he prodded her foot with his cane. "Rise up, child," he said. "Set your eyes to God, not to the ground."

"I have taken a long ride on the ocean," Sarah exclaimed.

"As did I," said the old man. "But you did not come alone?"

William and Ruth walked on trembling legs up the pier. Even the old man could see they were the parents of this child: she had all their energy, all their hope, all that was washed from them into the ocean of their passage. He had seen it before: parents disembarking from the long journey, walking the pier like pale shadows, their children running ahead without restraint.

"You must be certain, " said the sexton to William and Ruth, "that the child does not remain undisciplined in this new land. The devil is everywhere." He looked past Sarah as though he could see under the rock she had clung to, under the earth, to the center of Hades itself. Then he tipped his hat and left them to find their way into Beverly.

They found shelter, and William found work. Sarah attended church school to continue her catechism. But the sexton was right: she lived without usual restraint. Her parents were unhappy, and tired, and unable to keep track of her as well as she could keep track of them. Much alone, she often retreated to the woods. So little sunlight penetrated the overarching limbs Sarah felt like she was exploring caverns, travelling inside the body of the new land, making it her own body. Sarah loved America, exactly as her parents disliked it.

Ruth spent much of each day writing letters to England. She often sat in a corner, a Bible on her lap, staring at the irregular line two walls make when they come together, her back to windows and light. She watched her shadow move across the narrow space before her. She prepared meals, but became alert only when Sarah and William brought her news and letters.

William spent long hours each day recording and checking the names of people and the kind and quantity of goods that arrived in nearby Salem Harbor. Always, he was amazed at how many and how much: He tabulated the abundance of persecution, despair, and the false hope of new lives. Stern and humorless, he watched people arrive on sea-washed legs and wished them, under his breath, to the devil. His journal reads: "Thirty more trembling souls on trembling legs. The Reverend Mr. Whitelock greeted them, but already they could not look him in the eye, so soon are they surrounded by the spectre of this place."

The first report of Sarah, brought to William by the Reverend Mr. Whitelock, did not surprise him. Sarah had been seen, past dark, in the woods. When called upon in the name of the Lord, she ran away. Her familiarity with the woods was unbecoming in a young, female soul.

Sarah denied going out past dark alone, ever, since coming to America. After a second accusation, again brought by the Reverend Whitelock, William questioned her closely. As always, Sarah told him the truth: She went into the forest by day, when her mother wrote letters. She had never been out at night. He understood her fear of the dark. He did not leave their small cottage by night, except on rare occasions.

The one time he did, he understood how people might think they saw something. The whole place was wilderness. Movement could be vegetable, animal, savage, or the devil himself: What was the difference in this untamed land where every night William felt hostage to sounds he could not fathom, to feelings he could not understand, in a small cottage so quiet he could hear wind, tree, animal, and the beating of his own heart. Next to him, Ruth sighed and shuddered in her sleep, as though afraid of her dreams. Sarah whimpered through first dark, then pretended she was in the dark, in the cave of the woods, which she understood from her daytime walks, and only that allowed her to sleep. William wrote in his journal: "Sarah speaks honestly as I question her, but she is secretive now. Her time for Youth is slipping away. I fear she approaches Womanhood, when she will be lost to me."

One day shortly after William's questioning, Sarah walked one of her large circles around their cottage, reading the random slants of filtered sunlight so she would not become lost. She saw, between the cracks of trees, over rock and under sky, the thatched top of a small cottage she had never seen before. She came as close as she dared, pausing from tree to tree, until she saw a woman, sitting in a patch of sunlight, no bonnet on her head, her black and white hair as commanding as a page of writing. Sarah moved closer to read it.

The woman sorted plants. From a large bag she took a leafy top, then a root, then a plant pulled whole from forest floor or meadow. As she worked, she spoke to herself, or to the plants: Sarah could not tell what she said, or to whom. Even though she had heard William speak of the old women on the edge of Beverly, their minds overrun by the devil, Sarah was not frightened. After all, Ruth sat facing a corner, muttering to herself as she wrote long letters home. William came from Salem each day, downcast and stern, opened the Bible and read to himself in frantic whispers.

So when the old woman turned from inspecting a plant and said, "Sarah, you must come help me, " Sarah went immediately to sit in the warm sunlight near the door of the cottage. She looked at the woman, and the woman looked at her. And smiled.

For the first time since coming to America, an adult looked Sarah directly in her eyes and held her gaze. Sarah did not feel rude staring back, finding clarity in the gray and blue of the woman's iris, despite wrinkled flesh and wilted eyebrows.

"So many plants," said the woman. "Some to eat, some to drink as tea; some to heal, some to poison. Some day I will know them all. See." She pointed to where plants fanned around her on a circle of sun.

"How do you know my name?" asked Sarah.

The woman laughed. "Goody Highsmith knows everyone's name. We are a small group. I know the people. And I know the plants, their properties, their names, from the most common to the most delicate and rare." She reached out her hand, still dirty from digging and handling roots, and touched Sarah's cheek.

Tears sprang to Sarah's eyes, and she looked down. "I must go home," she said.

"Certainly," said Goody Highsmith. "But you are often alone in the forest. You are like me, you want to explore. When you come back I will teach you." She stood up. She was the tallest woman Sarah had ever seen. Sarah stumbled to her feet. Still, Goody Highsmith towered over her. Sarah ran into the woods, and did not look back until she was certain she would not be able to see the woman, nor the woman see her. Then she made her slow way home. She said nothing about Goody Highsmith.

The next day, after William left for Salem Harbor and Ruth positioned herself in her chair, paper and pen in hand, Sarah moved slowly to the door. Just as she put her hand to the latch, Ruth, who never challenged her, said, "You are your father's child, to leave me alone each morning. Is it any wonder I do not manage well?"

Sarah stood silent. Any other day, she might have welcomed a call to her mother's side. Today, she felt an urgency: She had to go into the woods, to see if she could see, just see, Goody Highsmith. Though her mother's voice called her back, she suddenly burst out the door into the air and light.

She moved so fast William could barely keep pace with her. In fact, several times he lost sight of her and moved blindly into the unfamiliar woods. Fear gripped his heart: He was not taking his bearings, not noticing landmarks; he was counting on Sarah to know where she was going, counting on her to appear, and to reappear, so he might not be lost. So he forged ahead, hoping to see her slight form moving delicately through rock, bush, tree. As for himself, he cursed every obstacle, wished it to the devil. He talked to himself so pointedly he almost didn't hear the voice nevertheless stopped his feet.

"How nice, to see a father and daughter in the woods together." William looked forward, towards the voice. Sarah was ahead of him, looking behind. William followed her gaze to a large woman, tall as a tree, bareheaded, smiling, a sack slung over her shoulder. He watched to see what Sarah would do.

"Come," said the woman to William. "We have both found the one we are seeking."

William approached, heavy-footed and scowling. He did not raise his hat. "Why do you seek my daughter?" he scolded. As William approached her, he felt smaller and smaller, just as he had when their boat approached the American shore. He stopped some distance away. "What are you doing in the woods?" he shouted at Sarah who moved towards him from the other side of the woman.

Goody Highsmith answered as though William's question was for her. "I gather plants. To learn their qualities. I met your Sarah and asked her help. She is young, and nimble, with strong hands. She can climb trees, and narrow herself between rocks." She stopped speaking and moved towards William. She walked comfortably, like William had seen no grown woman walk before. Like an animal, he thought. He almost gasped when she leaned against a tree and spoke again: "We are all so much alone here. We have all lost our mothers. We are all orphans. Even the young."

As Goody Highsmith spoke, Sarah circled back to her father. She stood as far from him into the woods as Goody Highsmith did, on the opposite side of a huge tree. "I didn't come here to find her," Sarah said simply. "I only talked to her once. I have only done what you have done. I stopped and questioned her. I want to go home."

"Home?" asked Goody Highsmith, her voice raised. "And where is home? And how shall you find it?" William followed her eyes into the vacant woods. They were as deep, dark and incomprehensible as his heart. He shuddered. He turned and left, Sarah following behind.

His journal reads simply: "Met in the woods a bareheaded woman, a collector of herbs and plants. She speaks without knowledge of the Heavenly Father. I have rescued Sarah from consortion with her dark soul."

Sarah stayed home then, and helped her mother as she could. She sat staring out the window as Ruth wrote letters. Although Sarah was inside, safe from Goody Highsmith, her heart swelled into the woods, wandered there, ranged towards what she did not know and could not see. Sarah sat inside through a changing season, through the flaring of leaves, the curling of ground plants, the withering of so much life. She envied Goody Highsmith. The woman was mad, her father told her, but she came and went as she pleased. She reached high, dug low, burrowed into the new and strange country. Sarah wondered what the woman found in winter.

Soon, Ruth began to send her on brief errands. Sarah lived to breathe fresh air, even the cold air of winter, the powder of snow crunching under her swift feet, her breath billowing around her, snapping like a sail. She soon ventured farther than any errand. She looked for Goody Highsmith's cottage, watched the plume of smoke from her chimney rise among the pine trees. One day she knocked on the door.

"Child," said Goody Highsmith, "I have expected you." The old woman seemed even bigger than she had been in the woods. She was bundled against the cold: heavy coat, legs wrapped in blankets, feet in oversized boots. She filled the doorway, then quickly stepped aside, like an agile tree, saying, "I've made tea. American tea. From the wild rose, the bark of the elm, the gentle camomile. You'll see how it warms the heart."

Sarah took the chair offered her near the small fire. The teapot, on a hook above glowing coals, exhaled a cloud of steam. Goody Highsmith poured the pink liquid into a china cup. "Let it cool, dear," she said when Sarah put it to her lips. "We want to warm your heart, not burn your tongue."

Sarah blew across the cup and waited. Goody Highsmith told of her work with the plants. She was busy, even through the winter. "Nothing dies," the woman said, "though it may dry and wither. Within it still is a power, waiting to be released. It might be soaked and made into a dye. It might be ground into a paste and put in food. It might be boiled for a tea. It might be smoked as these Indians do. It might be a seasoning, to lend spice. It might be a poison, to bring life to an end. Winter is a time to find out."

Sarah's eyes widened to include the room., full of hanging branches, stalks, leaves, bundles of roots. Small sacks, bulging with plants, lined the wall. Sarah sipped the tea, bitter and astringent, but warming to her insides. At one moment she wondered if the tea might make her sick, or even kill her. Then she looked at Goody Highsmith, whose hair shone, whose blue-gray eyes were gentle, whose mouth smiled even as her lips explained the plants. Sarah had never seen anyone so intense except in matters of religion. It was wrong—Goody Highsmith's abandon to worldly plants, like the heathen sailors' dance at the sight of land—yet Sarah, too, felt such abandon, to everything, inside and outside herself. She sat uncomfortably in front of the fire with her own recognition, desire, dream. And when she finished her tea, she hurried away.

Ruth waited, sitting in a chair staring at the door. "I have but one child," she said as Sarah took of her coat. "And she wants to belong more to the world than me."

Sarah went to the fire to warm her hands.

"Where have you been?" asked Ruth.

"I stopped when questioned by the Reverend Mr. Whitelock in the catechism."

"He held you in the snow to talk about your mortal soul? You're lucky not to have frozen to death."

"Yes, mother."

"You do not seem cold."

"I ran home to warm myself after he let me go."

That night, William questioned her as well, so closely each knew she was not telling the truth. Yet they did not say so. Her lie was simply a presence in their cottage. And as she went back to the woods, to sit in the warmth of Goody Highsmith's compact fire and tea and breads and eyes, and as William and Ruth knew it, the presence of Sarah's deceit grew familiar, palpable as a piece of broken furniture they hoped to someday mend. They let their first winter go by.

In spring, everything budded, bloomed, and grew toward rankness: root, stalk, plant; vine, bush, tree; branch, stem, leaf. Sarah did, too, budding out of her girlhood. She was twelve. She became shy, especially of William: Their small cottage afforded her no privacy just as she wanted to hide her new body most from him.

She talked less, became more secretive in her manner, until William felt shunned.

"What is it, child?" he asked one morning as Sarah hid herself under the blanket again, waiting for him to leave for Salem Harbor.

"Nothing," came a muffled reply.

"You must look at me when you speak," William insisted.

Sarah peeked out from under her cover. "Nothing," she repeated again. "I am just waiting for you to leave."

"You are being a foolish little girl," William said. "Get up, now, and help your mother prepare the morning meal."

"It is fine, William," said Ruth. "I will take care that she helps me later this day."

"Now," William insisted. He stalked to her bed. Though Sarah burrowed under the blanket, trembling, and Ruth inhaled as though to speak, William did not stop. He ripped the blanket from his cowering daughter. "Up," he commanded.

Tears in her eyes, her face pale, Sarah stood up, then sat lightly on the edge of the bed. She looked behind her on the sheet, and saw what she had been hiding.

William saw it, too, a stain of blood as large as his hand. He went pale, and left the house without eating his meal. "The curse," he wrote in his journal, "has overtaken Sarah. Her womanhood comes too early for us in America, where we might have remained our small family sometime longer. This place is accursed, where everything grows too quickly for thought."

After William left, Ruth helped Sarah to clean up. Sarah was frightened. Ruth told her that she must expect and accept the blood as she prepared for womanhood, but she told her no more. She could not embrace her daughter. Like William, she felt she was losing a child.

As soon as she could, Sarah left the cottage, to roam the woods, she told herself, though she went straight to Goody Highsmith. The walk in the cool air made her feel unwell. Her stomach was in knots, her face pale. She did not sit in the chair offered her, afraid she might bleed and stain it. Pain stole her liveliness. She tried to talk. She tried to drink tea and eat the bread offered her, but she could not.

"You are ill, child?" said Goody Highsmith at last.

Sarah and been sick before. This was different. She shook her head.

"You are not sick, but not well. You have pain, but do not know why. You bleed, but have no wound." The woman stood up quickly and went to her shelve. From the stone jar on the highest shelf she took a spoonful of powder. She carried it to Sarah's cup, and stirred it in. "This is your bittersweet time. You are neither girl nor woman. This powder is bitter to the taste, but sweet in its results. Drink."

Sarah drank, forcing herself to swallow the bitter cup. She tried to smile at Goody Highsmith through her puckered lips.

"Hurry home now, " said the woman, standing tall over Sarah. "Lie down. Soon you will feel well again."

Sarah ran home, lay down, and slept. She was still sleeping when William returned from Salem Harbor. She awoke to his anxious talk, though she could do nothing but smile dreamily.

The Massachusetts Bay Colony had lost its charter, William muttered angrily. The Puritan Saints, from the Reverend Mr. Whitelock to Cotton Mather to

Endicott himself, would no longer exclusively control the people: their lives, laws and liberties. The Church of England they'd escaped could reach its baroque and corrupting fingers into the New World. William was full of the rhetoric current at Salem Harbor. "We have enemies," he said. "Even as I speak, they plot against us. There is the Savage in the woods. There are those who have covenanted with the devil. There are those souls teetering on the brink of their own destruction, and ours."

William's voice filled the small cottage. But once he stopped his fervent speech he became suddenly and acutely aware of how quiet his home could be: Ruth, her back to him, looked first at the page of the letter she was writing, then out the window; Sarah stared up at the ceiling, her eyes unfocused, uncomprehending. William felt he hadn't been heard, then had the strange feeling his words had been sucked away, out the window, that by some enchantment his speech had disappeared. At the same time, he remembered the morning, and Sarah's blood.

"Ruth? Sarah?" he asked.

Neither turned to him.

"Ruth!" he shouted, but before she responded a knock sounded the door.

The small family turned. William strode to the door and flung it open. Taller than the door frame, Goody Highsmith stood on the step. As always, her head was bare. She stamped her man's boots as though to force her speech. William though she might curse him, or accuse him, or laugh at him. Instead, she reached into her coat and gave him a small sack. "She should take this, too," Goody Highsmith said. "It will help." And then she was gone.

William slammed the door. He looked at the sack in his hand, then pitched it against the wall as though it held a snake. "Too?" William shouted at Sarah. "What did that woman give you?" He took a few steps to where she lay, still staring dazed at the ceiling. Sarah tried to look at her father, but she could not focus her eyes. Instead, he was a blur, and his voice only an urgent sound, like the sea slapping the shore during a storm.

When he slapped her, first on one cheek, then on the other, so that her head tossed from one side of her pillow to the other, Sarah saw him clearly, his face twisted under his black hat, his hands red, chafed, his eyes hot and red.

Sarah sat up. She screamed, and her scream filled the cottage. Sarah began to tear at her dress, scratching at the collar, the buttons, until her frail but budding chest was exposed. "I hurt, " she wiled. "I am going to die." She ripped at her lower buttons, but Ruth ran to her and threw her back on the bed.

"What did Goody Highsmith give you?" Ruth asked. She covered Sarah with her own body. "Please tell me, Sarah."

"For the pain," Sarah whispered to her mother. "Some tea. I was frightened. Now it hurts again. Worse. I want to die."

William recovered Goody Highsmith's sack and removed a small vial. He held it to the window. Inside was a small draught of blue-gray liquid. "And she would give you this, too?" William uttered. He threw the vial into the fireplace, where it shattered. The liquid vaporized, took on what looked to him like the shape of Goody Highsmith herself, and disappeared up the chimney.

61

Ruth and Sarah were not watching. Sarah smelled flowers on the salt air, a morning after storm, the woods after being cooped in her small cottage with her mother's back. Ruth saw nothing, smelled nothing. Her eyes were filled with tears, her nose clogged with mucus. And through her tear, she, too, saw her husband's form, twisted, hulking, frightening.

William approached them. Ruth moved to cover Sarah. "Button your dress, child," she whispered urgently.

"Why did you have dealings with Goody Highsmith?" William shouted. "You must tell me why!" He stood above them, and raised his fist. "We must speak with the Reverend Whitelock of this."

Sarah did not answer. Ruth kept her back turned. Again. William felt unheard, unseen, unknown. His anger swelled so huge in him he knew he must leave, before he, too, was poisoned by the very air of the cottage.

Outside, he was lost. He wasn't ready to speak with anyone. He went to the woods, which he hated for their shadow, for how the temperature fluctuated from light to dark, as though he had suddenly been lowered into someone's well. As he walked, he began a rhythm of words in his mind, then on his tongue. He began by cursing England. Then he cursed those in England who had persecuted him. He cursed those saints who influenced his emigration to this new land. He cursed his parents and his cousins, all of his family and all of Ruth's family, who had not resisted his plan. He cursed the sea captain and sailors, those devils who had delivered him to this horrible shore. He cursed Salem and Beverly and Boston for their small and pitiful grasp on the shore of this expansive new land. He cursed Endicott and Mather and Whitelock for losing the charter of the Massachusetts Bay Colony. He cursed Salem Harbor for its activity, for what he saw in people's eyes as they approached new lives in this new country. He cursed his wife for not adjusting, for neglecting him and the child. He cursed Sarah, taken now by something incomprehensible. He cursed the woods, too, the branches, bushes, boulders and stones. He cursed his own steps even as he walked.

Then he saw her, bent over in the middle of the path, and he realized he had not been cursing these things in his mind, nor muttering them under his breath, nor whispering them to the wind. He had been shouting them, kicking stones and cursing to the heavens. William turned to hurry away from her, but at that moment he heard her voice, and he stopped.

"William," she called, and he wondered how she made her voice the same shape and sound of his mother's voice, which he heard clearly in the air. "William," she called again, this time in the voice of Ruth. "William," she said a third time, in a new voice, which he did not know, but which started his feet towards her.

As he neared her, he was amazed: Her head was bare as always, but her graying hair was now rich and black, almost floating around her head with the spring breeze; with each step he took, her wrinkles disappeared; her old body, stooped from bending and digging, straightened as he came to her. Before his eyes, her tall figure became lithe, her face winsome, and when he was close enough to take her outstretched hand, he did. His flesh thrilled, then went weak.

"Come with me, William," she said. She turned onto a path William had not travelled before, and they walked into the forest darkness.

When William returned home, having stumbled along the path unknowing until he found himself facing his door, he was trembling, perspiring, nauseous. He had a terrible cramp in his abdomen. Sarah and Ruth were at the hearth, speaking in droll voices, as though they had suddenly become old friends. The cottage still smelled of the vial, which lay broken in the back of the fireplace. William went there, brushing abruptly past Ruth and Sarah, and picked the glass out from the ashes. Just as he had it all, he stumbled slightly in his weakness and one of the shards cut his hand. He shuddered with the pain. He held his hand up to look at the blood seeping out of a large slit. Unconsciously, he wiped his hand on the front of his waistcoat, leaving a smear of blood. He went to the door, threw the pieces of glass as far from the cottage as he could, and went to lie in his bed, his hand pressed hard on his stomach.

"Let me help you, Father," said Sarah.

"No," he said. "Haven't you done enough already?" He moaned, and held himself.

"What is it, William," said Ruth. "You are sick."

William nodded. Large beads of perspiration forced their way onto his forehead, beaded his lips. His body stiffened, and he pressed his hands against his stomach so he looked as though he was trying to hold himself down. He mumbled and groaned. Ruth brought him a blanket, and he shivered and perspired under it. When he became delirious, Ruth sent Sarah to the Reverend Mr. Whitelock's home for guidance.

Sarah reported her father's trouble dutifully. As she returned home she heard her name whispered softly. She knew who called her, but dared not acknowledge the voice. She moved on , slowly, purposefully. "Sarah," she heard again, and she hurried her pace. "So you are well?" Sarah saw Goody Highsmith in the bushes near the path. "So you wouldn't take the second draught?" Sarah paused to listen. "So you see your father?" the old woman spoke. "He is a man, Sarah.

He will curse everyone but himself, when he might be most cursed. Don't curse me. Don't curse me." Goody Highsmith's voice rose, until it seemed she would shout, and Sarah ran from the voice home.

The Reverend Mr. Whitelock was just behind her, listening. When he reached the small cottage, he spoke: "The ears of a minister of God hear sin where sin lies, unbeknownst to those mortals who do not suspect the devil in his strange coupling with those weak souls who bid him in."

Sarah was unsure of his meaning. Ruth moved against the wall, for it was the first time anyone had been into her home in months. William tried to sit up in his bed, but the stern grimace of the Reverend Mr. Whitelock's face pinned him down. He moaned.

"Your daughter," the minister said, "has consorted with witches. You, sir, are suffering the awesome power of a witch's cursed work. She is close by. She must be found, and made to stop."

William moaned again. Sarah was afraid. She had heard of witches: they took the forms of animals and disturbed the dogs of good souls; they entered the pens of livestock and drank the blood of cattle and sheep, leaving some dead, their eyes eaten out; with a spoken word, they turned milk sour and honey bitter; they caused warts and rashes, disease, madness, even death.

Sarah sighed and fainted to the floor, overpowered by the sudden fear that she, herself, was a witch. She had eaten and drunk with Goody Highsmith. She had bled from her body. She had weakened her mother and subdued her father. Before she lost consciousness, she looked at the Reverend Mr. Whitelock, pale, his hands trembling. Even he, she thought, is afraid of me. She bared her teeth at him. Trying to speak, she hissed.

Ruth moved quickly to her daughter. "She is ill, Reverend. I should not have sent her to you." She pulled Sarah from the floor and helped her onto her bed.

"She ran to me, and back again," said the minister. "Perhaps she is now overcome by her own evil."

Ruth looked at her daughter, now and suddenly a young woman. She thought of her own difficulties at that time, how hard it was to understand, how awful and yet exhilarating to be in the grip of such a thing: to know there is a future that cannot be stopped. She knew the temptation to shame, the association with illness, wrongdoing, sin. She remembered her own mother's gentle help and explanation. She remembered her mother's touch as though the woman were in the room with her, massaging her temples, rubbing her back, smoothing the tight knot of her young womb. She looked out the window, away from her daughter and the minister. She thought she saw a shadow, a woman's shadow, disappear into the woods. Was it Goody Highsmith's? Was it her own mother's?

Suddenly, Ruth hated how Massachusetts had separated her from those she knew, from what she held dear. Homesick and lonely, she wrote letters, thinking only of home, while in her own cottage her husband was sick, grim, muttering, begrudging, as dark and dense as woods and rock. Her daughter, too, lay sick, suspected by the minister of evildoing. How strange, Ruth thought, to look into the heart of a twelve-year-old girl and see evil. What must the Reverend Mr. Whitelock think of the rest of them?

Ruth looked at the minister, a pale, quaking Saint in this new land. He was not so different from her, living between the English past and the American future, fearful and uncomprehending in the grip of what was larger than him. He was no different from Sarah and William. Everything, she thought, is subsumed in what is larger and stronger, be it good or evil.

"The girl is not sick," Ruth said finally. She looked at Sarah, and found her daughter's body suddenly precious. She turned and glared at the minister. "She has her time of the month. She is a woman. This is her first time, and she is frightened."

Ruth watched her frankness strike the minister like a blow, watched him grimace, and turn from her daughter. As the Reverend Mr. Whitlock gripped the door handle, Ruth said: "That's right. Go to the woods if you will find your witch."

Ruth attended Sarah and William. The Reverend Mr. Whitelock did not return. Nor did Goody Highsmith. Within several days, Sarah was well, the redness returned to her cheeks. She flew to the windows like a trapped bird, ready to fly into the woods.

As Sarah recovered, so did William. Like Sarah, he went to the windows. Unlike Sarah, he was afraid. At night, as Sarah and Ruth slept, he reconjured that day in the woods when the old woman became young, and tempted him. He had given in, but it was like a dream, something in the darkness of his own mind. He kept it like that, and never spoke of it to Ruth. His hand, though cut deep, closed without suppuration, leaving a long pink line parallel to, but longer than, the life line on his palm. He was surprised to heal so quickly, and without pain. Perhaps, he concluded, he was not one of the unrighteous after all.

Once well, the family left their cottage. All three walked to Salem Harbor with William. The day was crisp, but promised warmth. The cloudless sky made the ocean shimmer as it swelled towards shore and ran back again into itself. Sarah skipped ahead of Ruth and William, though they did not let her from their sight. They passed their fellows as they neared Salem, but were neither hailed nor acknowledged. Once they reached the harbor, William approached the Custom House with dread. Another man sat at his desk, writing with an intensity, even a flourish, William had never been able to muster.

William did not go in. Instead, he turned to Ruth. "The Reverend Mr. Whitelock has seen that I am replaced."

Ruth felt a thrill, and her heart leapt across the ocean. She imagined the same people greeting them who saw them off.

Sarah was on the pier, watching the gulls, fascinated by the large ships docked and bobbing in the harbor.

The sexton was nearby, watching: Ruth stared out into the ocean as though her eyes could transport them home to her memory of the Old World; William, as always, looked to his boots, at home only in his rationalizing mind; Sarah ran along the pier, up onto the shore, then back again, careening like a gull, the only one still alive in this New World.

The sexton went to them. "William," he said, "your best opportunity is to book passage for New York, to the South."

"Why do you say so?" asked William.

"The Reverend Mr. Whitelock has asked me to," said the sexton.

"Yes," said William. He turned to Ruth. "From there, we will decide how we must proceed."

Sarah was the only one in the family to make a last journey into the woods.

"My Sarah," Goody Highsmith greeted her, "I hear you are not long for this world."

"We leave soon for New York. Will it be like it is here?"

"How should I know, child? I only hope it is not. For your sake."

"Do you not like it here?" Sarah asked.

"This place is overcome with evil," said Goody Highsmith. "The men here stand frightened of their own hearts. Their own minds. A New World is too big for them. They are like stock grown comfortable in a narrow pen. They are afraid of all that is outside. Given freedom, they still nudge each other at the same filthy trough.

"But you, and me? We are like birds. We fly, unafraid of what our hearts can hold. I know that. I see it in you." Goody Highsmith reached out and touched Sarah's cheek with the same tenderness as at their very first meeting. Sarah did not flinch. "You and this country shall be one," Goody Highsmith said. "I am in danger. Woman's blood will be shed. But blood will consecrate this New World and make it ours."

Sarah thought Goody Highsmith was speaking now like the witch she was increasingly accused of being. "What will you do?" asked Sarah.

"I?" asked Goody Highsmith. "I will be the blood. You will be the wings. Fly, my child. Fly."

Soon, Sarah and William and Ruth, my ancestors, set sail for New York. William wrote: "Sarah is now a young woman. She is the one of us who looks forward. We will nourish her in spite of our misgivings. She will be our hope."

69

A year later, New York had news of the Salem witch trials. Goody Highsmith's was among the names of those executed. William said nothing. Wrote nothing, either. He silently watched Sarah bud and bloom.

We Tried to Stop the War

by Marvin Bell

We tried to stop the war by standing up.
We emptied files and broke official seals.
We used skeleton keys on the closets in old houses.
Then we turned on a lamp to study the darkness.

We tried to stop the war by shutting our eyes.
The blast tore the retinas from oaken knotholes.
The blast ripped the ears from young guinea pigs
So we turned on a lamp to study the darkness.

We tried to stop the war by going to war.
Our loyalty at night shocked even the owls.
We tried to stop the war by shining a light on it.
Then we turned on a lamp to study the darkness.

Poetry & Politics – A Poet's Impressions

by Christopher Buckley

In the third edition of his creative writing text, *Three Genres*, Stephen Minot offers some advice to the beginning writer. Essentially, he says that if you visit New Mexico you many have some material for a piece about a tourist in New Mexico but you should not try to write about the life of a Navajo on the reservation. I, then, can only write about my impressions of the former Yugoslavia as a tourist—a guest of the state to some extent, and a guest of poets for six weeks during the spring and early summer of 1989. I was awarded a Fulbright grant in Creative Writing and my primary function was to exchange views of poetry and writing with writers throughout the country and to attend, as the U.S. representative, the two major writers conferences, Sarajevo Poetry Days and the Solvene PEN Conference. I had, only in the few years previous to my trip, become familiar with Yugoslavian poets and knew little about the politics of the country at large and the countries within. I was perhaps a sophomore in the college of Eastern European poetry and certainly a freshman in the political realm.

At first, I encountered poetry more than politics, but both were equally on my mind after only a week in the country. In the few months preceding my trip, there had been a number of reports about "unrest" in Kosovo, the southwest portion of Yugoslavia that has a high concentration of ethnic Albanians. The National army, under orders from Belgrade, had gone in to put down demonstrations. There had been some Yugoslav Albanians shot. Although I occasionally asked about this situation directly, my impressions came mainly from what I overheard in conversations, and also from what many poets and writers simply wanted to avoid discussing. By the time I left the Split airport in June, I had a view of the political climate via the Serbian centralized government in Belgrade, and the Serbian aggression during the last months of 1992 and into 1993 has substantiated that view or impression. I would have preferred my views to have been wrong; I would have preferred to concentrate on poetry.

I had heard wonderful things about the Fulbright Program in Yugoslavia as early as 1984 from Diane Wakoski and Susan Ludvigson who visited the same year. Later, Larry Levis and Philip Dacey, among other well-known writers, went over, and it seemed like an interesting and energetic program. From reading and conversations, I knew of the beauty of the Dalmatian coast, the intriguing Stari Grads of Sarajevo, Dubrovnik and Zagreb as well as the many fine poets in Belgrade and Slovenia, the warmth and hospitality of the Writers Center in each city, the week-long poetry festivals. Certainly, the climate for poets and writing in Yugoslavia seemed to far surpass anything in the U.S. I applied to the program twice and was accepted on the second application, largely, I think, due to the influence of Richard Jackson. I really got to know him at Bread Loaf Writers Conference in 1988 when he and

I were paired to respond in conferences to a dozen or so manuscripts by contributors. By that point, I had read Vasko Popa and Ivan V. Lalic in the Simic translations. Jackson had been recently to Yugoslavia on a Fulbright and had been back since. As editor of *The Poetry Miscellany*, he had published a special feature on Yugoslavian writers and was passing out copies at the conference. He also had the *Ecco Selected Poems of Tomaz Salamun*, the great Slovene poet, along with him, and over the two weeks showed me many poems by Tomaz. I found all of the work exciting, especially Salamun and Lalic—they seemed so much more accessible than Popa, who was the Yugoslavian poet most Americans knew. There was still myth and a little riddling, still the elliptical imagistic sequence. But to my reading, the psychological and personal motivations for the imagery seemed clearer and more moving in these poets than in the more medieval context of Popa. Also I started to read newer poets, such as Boris Novak, Veno Taufer, Aleksandar Petrov, and Mario Susko. Rick had become something of a transplanted local hero in Yugoslavia. He had published this special issue, was going to publish some chapbooks in translation by Yugoslavian and Slovene poets and was returning for a third summer in a row there, bringing students along with him, presenting demonstration poetry workshops at the University in Sarajevo and PEN conference in Slovenia, and arranging for visits of Yugoslavian poets to the U.S. My upgraded familiarity with the poetry and poets of Yugoslavia, coupled with a letter from Jackson, turned the trick of the award for me, I think.

Moreover, Rick was instrumental—no, essential—in setting up an itinerary for me during my visit. Despite numerous cables, letters, forms, etc., there seemed to be no actual communication between the Fulbright offices here and in Belgrade. Rick knew when the big conferences were, was in touch with the organizers, let them know that I was the poet selected for the program and would be attending. In between the two major events, I was on my own, to arrange transportation around the country, visit with writers, readings and such. Rick was bringing a group of students and attending the same conferences. I arranged travel with him and set up my schedule accordingly.

It was communicated to me that I should be in Belgrade by the end of April, something about presenting myself officially to the Fulbright office there and the writers behind selection. So I arrived, after 37 straight hours of travel, to find no one at the airport to help find the correct bus into town, the hotel, which had a room reserved for me. I found the Hotel Kasina after a half hour of walking around the downtown area and was shown to a small, spartan, proletariat type room. This was a state-subsidized hotel—you could stay across the street at the charming Hotel Moscova—you could pay for it yourself. Up 37 hours straight, about four words of Serbo-Croatian, I stayed put. I went down and sat at a table on the sidewalk as the late afternoon light dusted down over Belgrade. I drank slowly a tall beer and went up and slept until midnight, when I woke up, read a while and went back to sleep until nine the next morning. I had no idea what would come next.

I had arrived with only one day left to contact the Fulbright office—half a day, really, as the director, Bojan Drndic, was leaving early to drive to his house on the coast for the holidays. It was May Day and Easter weekend, and everything would be closed for days. Jackson would not arrive with his crew for a week. I did finally receive a call from the Assistant Cultural Affairs Officer who said she would try to put a dinner together so I could meet some folks, but it was a bad, long holiday weekend to arrive in town. She had worked out a schedule for me but had never sent it. I told her that by this point I had my own schedule set up as they never responded or got in touch, and I would keep to that. I did manage, however, to add a reading and presentation at the Old Library in Dubrovnik toward the end of my stay, which was very rewarding, but I could not manage to coordinate with some interested people in Zagreb. But for Belgrade—we were in luck in that a number of writers remained in town. At a very nice dinner at the very nice home of the Assistant Cultural Affairs Officer, I met Ivan V. Lalic, Sasha Petrov, and a number of other interesting writers and local Belgrade people.

Lalic was a modest but exact man and wore a conservative business suit and tie. He was generous about my poems and relaxed speaking about his own—but, again, very modestly. Petrov was very outgoing and personable and had a sheaf of his recent work he was handing around. He and his wife, Krinka, a prolific translator, invited me out to their home in the suburbs for dinner later that week.

For the next four days, I wandered on my own around Belgrade. It was a cold late April and May, and I was lucky that the bars remained open; most of the other shops, especially all those along the great pedestrian mall in the heart of town, were closed for the holidays. With all of the locals, I promenaded up and down the mall looking more at the people than in the windows. I checked when the museums were open and visited the painting and architectural exhibits. I walked out of town across the river over to the Museum of Modern Art, but it was closed. Mostly, I walked up and down the mall and out and back to the great public park in the old Roman fort of Kalemegdan, watched the grey waters of the Sava and Danube converge below the grey sky and found a new route around the park each day.

A portion of the park was filled with WWII displays of cannon and tanks, one boat, and I began to notice something else—a preponderance of young men in army uniforms everywhere. They all had good shoes and the same olive wool uniforms whose cloth had the thickness of blankets. They were everywhere in groups of three to six or seven, young men 19 or 20. It seemed that they were all on furlough for the long weekend in the same place. Each day at 4:00, the time I made myself stay out until, I headed for a nice bar overlooking the small square at the end of the mall and ordered a lovely great bottle of the local Belgrade beer and a Slivovitz. I'd make a note or two in my small book, sip the Slivovitz and half the beer and then order one more Slivovitz. The chill disappeared, I did not feel sorry for myself there in a foreign city all alone, unable to speak with much of anyone besides hotel clerks, waiters and workers in the bar. The soldiers crowded the tables and shared drinks—two or three to a beer or Coke and seemed to be having a fine time. They all smoked the government-subsidized cigarettes, and when finished drinking would go for another stroll up the promenade or stand in line for the one theater. One day I walked in a direction away from the park and into the business district as I heard one or two small groceries would open for a few hours around midday, and I needed a bottle of wine to take to Sasha and Krinka's. Even walking away from the mall, I ran into groups of soldiers on almost every street. I assumed that they were all stationed in Belgrade and could be out all day for Easter and May Day.

I had met Lalic, which had been one of my hopes, and some other very engaging writers. No poets and certainly not the Assistant Cultural Affairs Officer had mentioned Kosovo. I had the example of the soldiers everywhere around me, but no one spoke of politics. On May Day, I was walking through the hotel section of the city and heard some booming choral music next to the main Marx/Lenin square there. I stood on the edge of the park with a few older people—for all I could tell, the only tourist—and watched what was going on over at the government building. One camera was set up on a TV truck across the street from the entrance to the building, black cables straddled the street and the road was blocked off. Banks of speakers were installed on each side of the steps out of which what was surely a grand chorus of the Peoples' Odes to the State burst. After about five minutes, the doors opened and groups of teenagers waving flags and apparently singing, rushed out and ran to two flatbed trucks on either side. The TV camera held its one unwavering position as the energetic teenagers climbed upon the beds of the trucks and were driven back and forth in front of the camera waving flags. This was orchestrated to look as though a large celebration of the people was taking place. The local people there, like me, had perplexed looks on their faces which soon changed to indifference as they hoisted their shopping bags and headed off through the park or down the sidewalk. This official posturing would, of course, turn up on the one TV channel that night as news. Across the square, four large flags hung down the face of the government offices—one with the face of Marx, one with Lenin, Engels, and one with Tito. Few people looked up. I walked through the park wondering about the Communist Party here. Who belonged? No one appeared to really much care. The teenagers had obviously been hired and the TV crew, though instruments of a socialist state, knew how to produce commercial TV.

I acquired a better idea about politics from my dealing with Bojan Drndic in the Fulbright Office when things returned to normal the following Tuesday. He was dressed in a stylish suit and had had a wonderful holiday at the coast in his second house. His office ran with a computer and copier, secretaries, an accountant behind closed doors, and a nice coffee machine. He had learned his English in Washington D.C., son of a diplomat. His idioms were so swift, exact, and up-to-date. He was so slick, he could have sold a used car to Richard Nixon. He was in charge of the Fulbright program and my visit, but he had done next to nothing about it. I had to talk to him about itinerary, formal requirements, hotel reservations, my stipend for travel. Nothing was arranged, not much information available, but he assured me that it was all "no problem." He did, in fact, secure two airline tickets for me for upcoming trips at the Yugoslavian rate instead of the tourist rate (three times the cost), but that was about the end of it.

Luckily, the Assistant Cultural Affairs Officer at the U.S. Embassy had made a reservation at the hotel in Sarajevo for me, as that part of my itinerary and her belated one coincided. Drndic had whisked me along saying he would take care of all these reservations, etc. I was in and out of the office in twenty minutes, my official presentation of myself to the Fulbright commission and Party done. He went into a back room and came out with an envelope stuffed with bills, Dinars, and though it was thick enough to choke the proverbial horse, it was about one-fifth of what he was supposed to provide, what would be necessary for expenses. No problem. He would wire the rest to the hotel in Stan, or Dubrovnik, or Sarajevo—it kept changing each time I talked to him from a public telephone office, and the calls were not cheap. Drndic put me off a week at a time. Finally, he would mail or wire a portion—just enough to get me out of one town and on the road to the next—at the previous week's exchange rate, thereby pocketing any difference for himself or his office, and, taking up a good portion of my time in each city I visited chasing around after his bureaucratic paper trail. Lying—diplomatic speak—was part of a daily business routine for him, and time and again, I was told my stipend would be at such and such a place, and it would all be sent. It never happened. In Ljubljana, I received some help from the American Center there, and the Slovene woman called to Belgrade to find out what had happened to my stipend. I was sent to a post office across town—no money. I came back the next day, apologized for being a nuisance, and she called again. This time another post office—only a partial amount again. I returned, she made a third call, looked at me and pronounced a phrase in Slovene which translated as "Serbian Business." At the hotel in Lake Bled, no stipend had been wired as promised. Three more phone calls, daily checks with the desk clerk—nothing. On the last day, a message regarding the last of my stipend; without it, I would not be able to pay the hotel bill. I had to hire a cab to take me over to the next town and go through three offices and interviews to pick up the bit remaining. This cost me about $25 and took up most of my last morning at Bled.

Drndic made a good profit off me and was no doubt chuckling to himself each time I called in. Ah, the prerogatives of power, political privilege. Drndic was fairly high up in the Party, and as I learned, only about 20% of Yugoslavs belonged to the Communist Party. Yet, it could give you an easy job you could do or not do, two houses, a car, nice suits and the ability to skim a little off the top. They seemed like congressmen or appointees in the Republican Party to me. But I get ahead of myself.

In Belgrade, though I enjoyed a cordial and stimulating evening with writers and poets of renown, no one mentioned Kosovo. At the home of Aleksandar and Krinka Petrov, I enjoyed Sasha's homemade lemon and hot pepper Vodka, wonderful Serbian cuisine, and talk of poetry and translation—a wonderful evening with generous and gracious hosts. Still, all the boys in uniform all over town—I wondered. No one was much concerned with the Albanian question. Perhaps they felt there was nothing they need be concerned about. Perhaps, it was just small and far away, and the army would, of course, keep order. On the other hand, no one was eager to embrace or espouse the outward political trappings, the official "lines" of the state—the May Day "Celebration" was hardly that. I found more people attending the rich and sonorous Easter week ceremonies in the Russian Orthodox church.

Rick Jackson and crew arrived the next day, and we rented vans and headed for the town of Stan on the coast, not too far from Dubrovnik. Stan was a small village founded to support the frontier wall of the old kingdom of Ragusa which stretched south to Dubrovnik. The wall still worked its broken way over the considerable hills and some students one night fearlessly walked its vestigial reaches. Every one walked along the wall around the old city of Dubrovnik. It was a wide and wondrous view from almost anywhere, and you paid a nominal amount to climb up and take the path at the top of the walls that surrounded the old city. The small harbor was tucked away from the sea in the back of the walls and you could easily see how in feudal times this was well-protected from invaders by land or sea. At this point, we were really tourists, enjoying the sights and seacoast and wonderful food and wine, a wonderful chamber orchestra concert in the Baroque Church there, featuring Bach, Albinoni, and Mozart. We visited Split and Trogir, and then made a long drive to Mostar for the old city or Stari Grad there. In Mostar, we visited the bridge, the Mosque, and at a wonderful outdoor restaurant whose food was somewhere between Greek and Turkish. We did not meet any writers until Sarajevo for the week-long Sarajevo Poetry Days.

This was the 27th annual poetry festival, and most countries were represented. Rick and I read a poem each at the international reading. Poets read in their language, then an actor read the poem in Serbo-Croatian, or Croatian-Serbian, as they referred to it there. There were late evening readings from individual countries as well—evenings of Italian poetry, Austrian, German and one evening, our host, the poet Mario Susko, organized a bilingual reading and discussion of American poetry. But by far the majority of the poets were Bosnians and Croatians. One night, in order to show respect for our host, Jackson and I sat through an hour and a half of poetry all in Bosnian, though between us we knew only enough words to order beer and ask directions to the hotel. None of the Yugoslavian poets spoke of the political unrest. There were no Serbian poets there, no Slovene—in retrospect, one absence was the result of political tension, I suspect, and the other probably poetic. Nonetheless, it was truly refreshing to see how much good will there could be between so many different poets from different countries. There was a poet from Cypress, one from Egypt, Poland, Czechoslavakia, Austria, Italy and more. Not all was perfect, however—the Russian poets were, for the most part, distant and formal and read in the old, very stentorian mode. The poet from Iraq was arrogant and egotistical. There were surprises, too. We met the poet Vyacheslav Kurpianov from Russia, leader of a new free verse movement there, and the Cuban poet Exilia Saldana, who had a great lyric and imagistic gift. Still, we did not discover much political discussion. If we poets were legislators, we were certainly unacknowledged. We did get some discussion going when I worked with Jackson and his students to present an American-style poetry workshop at the University in Sarajevo. The professors were a little skeptical but interested.

Frankly, I think the writers and professors were a little skeptical in that in Yugoslavia, as in most of Europe, if you were a writer you just got on with it and wrote. At some point, you either made it, or you didn't It didn't appear to me that anyone was eager to critique each other's work. The circle of writers was much smaller, each city having its own group. And one of the things I found most heartening about all the Yugoslavian cities were their Writers Unions. Each major city had a building dedicated to nothing but the writers. There was often a restaurant, a bookshop, a general reading room, and rooms for seminars. Visiting writers were brought there to meet with other writers and the director. You could have a glass of juice or a beer and talk about your work. The Writers Union published books by local writers. This was really the most civilized support for writing and for art I have ever seen at the state or societal level. We could do well to learn from that example.

Once or twice in Sarajevo, aside from all the official readings and gatherings for poetry, I asked a writer connected officially with the festival and the Writers Union about the government in Belgrade, about Kosovo, and the response was, very politely, that this was not a subject that they wished to or would profit from discussing. I got the clear impression that some were worried about what they might be heard or understood to say—there would be those taking names was the impression I received. Moreover, it was not good manners as a visitor to press this question about the government. I let the matter go and enjoyed the poetry and the mix of international poets.

On the road heading for Ljubljana and Lake Bled, the lead van pulled off the main road after we had been in Slovenia about an hour. No one seemed to know where we were going except Rick. We drove up a side street to the edge of the town and into a large circular car park and got out. We had anticipated stopping to find some lunch, but Rick had taken us all to the Muzej Talcev V Begunjah. This place was now partially preserved as a memorial to the partisans murdered and tortured by the Nazis in WWII. Next to a large two story hospital-sized building was a row of small motel-like units all whitewashed. Originally, this had been a women's prison institution and then the Nazi's took it over. In the seven or eight adjacent rooms there was all the grisly documentation of the methods and equipment used by the Nazis on the Yugoslavs. Still preserved beneath plexiglass were the wall carvings by the prisoners, carved no doubt with only their fingers and the blunt ends of their wills. A candle burning inside a heart, names of loved ones and the name of freedom. Three large metal poles or spikes which would be fixed together in the yard and from which prisoners would be hung took up most of one cell. Ten partisans were routinely machine gunned here every time one German soldier was assaulted or killed in the nearby town, and one room showed the photographs of the dead in mass graves. It was sobering to say the least and even more eerie in that the main building was again being used for an asylum and many of the patients would wander into the museum cells—silently moving about, in and out in their bathrobes and slippers, a lost look in their eyes.

On the way out from the museum, walking up the path, feet echoing in the crunch of gravel, I stopped to admire a bed of pale violet irises, and as I did so Rick pointed out a circular cement bunker half buried in the dirt. It was, he said, a pillbox for a machine gun, also hidden for the most part when the Nazis occupied the place. Their favorite trick was to leave the end cell door open late at night as if there were a chance of escape. Then, as the partisans tried to run across the field and climb the hill into the trees, they would cut them down with the machine gun. It was a brutal and chilling reminder. This was mainly a shrine to the Serbians, as the Croatians, to a large degree, had collaborated with the Nazis during the war. At the time, visiting each cell and its attendant horrors, that thought never crossed our minds. Brutal and chilling also was the fact that once the war was over, the communists, the Serbians, executed a large number of Croatians to retaliate for Serbians and partisans lost in the Croatian collaboration.

At Lake Bled and the PEN Slovene Conference, I met many wonderful poets, and at the same time I could see the political climate rise a few degrees in temperature. The Slovenes have for centuries been an independent people, with their own language, culture and art—a small country which various larger countries with armies have overrun. It became quickly clear to me that these people were defiant when it came to Belgrade, and it seemed justly so. The GNP of Yugoslavia was disproportionally provided by Slovenia. I met a number of writers who had spent time in jail at the hands of the Serbian-run government for nothing more than poems they had written. Homes were broken into by the police, writers carried off in the middle of the night—the usual oppressions by the state. It was no wonder that certain poets, some well-known, and one would think beyond reprisal now, would still not comment politically for publication or reprint even in the states. But there were other outward manifestations. The conference agenda was not concerned with aspects of the craft of writing so much as with signing documents to protest the imprisonment of some writers and to support others. There were headphones with three languages—Slovene, English and French—no Serbo-Croatian. An honored guest at the conference was one Hungarian playwright who had not left his country in 19 years, and there was a woman from Lithuania who spoke openly of independence from Russia. Even then it was clear that the political situation was starting to loosen up somewhat in the Eastern Bloc countries. This was the first conference I had been to at which the Albanians were invited, and they were eager to speak out about the oppression by the Serbian government in Kosovo. The Slovenes felt a good deal of solidarity with the Albanians knowing for many years the repressions the Albanians were recently undergoing. I met a charming intense man from Kosovo, Ibrahim Rugova, a poet who is now the Leader of the opposition party in Pristina Kosovo. We had no common language but at a reception in one of the rooms one evening there were so many people speaking several languages that we easily found someone who could make a bridge between us. I learned that at that point 80% of Kosovo was ethnic Albanian and they were not allowed to use their own language in government or in documents. That, in effect, laws were made and enforced by Belgrade and the army. That they had no real self-determination. Ibrahim could also talk poetry and knew a number of contemporary American poets. In such a situation, an American is made to feel the poverty of his linguistic background—especially Slovenes have many languages—Slovene, Serbo-Croatian, English, French, and often German and

Russian. There was not only my poverty of languages but now here was a man who knew my poets and I knew none of his. This was a wonderful experience to be exposed to so many poets and poetries, to exchange views with so many different nationalities, but it was also a very humbling experience—humbling in that it made me realize the parochial nature of my view of poetry as well humbling in the political freedoms one take for given.

The same evening, I was talking with some Slovene poets and mentioned my stay in Belgrade, all the soldiers everywhere all the time. The point, one of them said, was a calculated one. Over that holiday weekend, Easter and May Day at that time, what was wanted was for the people to feel the presence of the state, on all corners and in all places—to realize, if only subconsciously, the power and effect of the government. And so soldiers from many areas were given their furloughs in Belgrade.

Though I learned about some of the historic animosity between Serbians and Croatians, the oppressions historically of the Slovenes, I came away feeling a present oppression little related to traditional ethnic motivation. I saw a government that would imprison writers for writing. As the events of the Serbian war on the Bosnians and Croatians has unfolded, my impressions have been reinforced. We have heard the old ethnic complaints brought up, we have heard the proffered disputes over an edge of land between Serbia and Bosnia. I cannot remember a war, an aggression that was without some ostensible "rationale." And while there is no doubt that atrocities have been committed on both sides, the objective news agencies have reported for months now that the preponderance of atrocities have been prepetrated by the Serbians. The Navy bombarded Dubrovnik for weeks and destroyed substantially the old city—a city and Old Library that some very fine and generous writers in Dubrovnik showed me around and made come alive for an evening of literature and discussion. There was no strategic purpose of threat in Dubrovnik, especially in the old city. The "National Army" has for months shelled Sarajevo and killed, starved and frozen the people there. This is not a civil war. A few people in power over peoples who wish to be independent will not give up that power. The rest is half truths and smoke screen. My feeling is that if Slovenia had not taken a step back on its independence when it did, it would have been bombed before Sarajevo. Before long—as the U.S., U.N., NATO and other European nations will not involve themselves—the Serbian army will again put down "radical elements" in Kosovo and then in Macedonia.

I was only a tourist but I listened to the writers and people in the individual countries who had felt the heel of the government. You don't have to be an expert to see that this is a central government propped up by guns, tanks and a few planes. The other people, the other countries, will go along or they will be bombed, killed, raped. There is no rationale that will support that. I am not schooled in the historic, national and ethnic difficulties of the area. Yet, perhaps, even a tourist, a poet, can see beyond the language, propaganda, and nationalism proffered from the barrel of a gun to understand that perhaps the world has had enough of this "politics."

Lines to King's Cross Terminal

by Janet Burroway
for Eleanor Bron

Across from me, a gentleman under thatch
Thick-trimmed against the weather at ear-high eaves
Sets his mouth ajar to admit his pipe,
Reproducing the outdoor mist, producing a wince
In the smoke-green eyes of the lady in the pince-nez.
It must be his wife between them. She shuffles through
A tattered Home Show shopping bag, and spades
Up the dry leaves of her adverts. On this side,
Beside me, a Cambridge undergrad going home
Plants noughts and crosses on the frontespiece
Of a Penguin, with a man in a pudding-bowl hat.
The East Anglian faces are mostly flat,
Their furrows plowed orderly downward, skirting the bumps.
 What vegetable seeds of talk I fling
Fall into the ruckle, not affecting the look of the land.
As: 'Isn't it cold for March. And dull for noon.'
'More so than others,' says the woman next to the man.
And: 'That castle must be older than anything
Still standing in my home town.' 'You're not from here,'
The man with the pipe explains. They introduce themselves.
Their names are the Stoates, John Gallow and Lady Lindle.
The other, intent on rightly placing his nought,
Only tilts his brim down toward the seat
At the delta of green velour between his knees.

91

Above us over the wife's head and the boy's
Identical mirrors set in black wood frames
Exchange flat looks, and mirrors of mirrors of mirrors
Recede backwards into the length of the slowing train.

Coming to a halt takes time in England.
A muted screech, a minor lurch, a sign
Announcing, and then another, and then another,
Announcing that this is one of a score of milk-stops
Before we achieve the King's Cross Terminal.
Lady Lindle, with a dull eye on her emerald,
Is making little hillocks of her hands,
Which gambol, rear and romp upon the hide
Of an inverted black-dyed kid. How such
Cultivated ladies come to travel

Second class is no longer the subject of much
Discussion in England. In the green square of my window
The sheep abound. It is somewhat early for lambs,
But the ewes have cropped the fist-like hills as short
As my lady's youth, no longer the subject of much
Discussion in England. I am doubly struck
By the emerald fallow lying left and right.

All halts are like this. Death succeeds decay
And birth is happening in the silt most fallow.
False springs deceive the bud, and the fruit comes thin.
Lady Lindle shrugs off her tartan Mac;
Her belly rounds like the boll of a blighted tree.
We are off again among the lucious hills,
But she is tired, and will tire with every milk-stop
Before we achieve the King's Cross Terminal.

The Last Bear

by Andrei Codrescu

The first piece I ever wrote for *All Things Considered* was a lament about the fate of the bear. I mourned the passing of that great animal for the forests where he had once lived into the captivity of zoos and thepages of children's books. But I refused to believe that the end of the bear had truly, truly come. "Where could all the bearness go if not in us who so delight in it? It is possible that at any given time, in any gathering, a number of us are bears." That's what I wrote in the bittersweet optimism of a decade ago when nasty as people seemed to be there was still a hope that something natural and uncontaminated still lived in them. But I believe it no longer! We have killed whatever redeeming bearness still attended us. Listen to the news: A bear, the last survivor in the Sarajevo zoo, died of starvation. He died after eating his mate, as did all the other animals, the eagles, the leopards, the lions, the tigers and the pumas. They each ate those closest to them, their mates, the members of their own speciae and then starved to death. The bear held on the longest waiting, perhaps, for some bearness or at least some pure animal nausea to put an end to the shelling. Of all the horrid news coming out from Bosnia these days this seems to me most poignantly criminal. It brings home what the pictures of murdered children, raped women and executed civilians have failed to. Namely, that nothing of the sense of fairness, justice and yes, compassion that prevails among animals exists in us any longer. There is no pure hate among bears. They do not kill each other because they do not like each other's way of eating, singing or living. They do not destroy each other in the name of ideologies, there are no hate mongering Nazis, nationalists and communists among them. And no members of their speciae stand by watching the slaughter of their kin on television without lifting a finger. The last surviving bear of Sarajevo accuses Europe and the United States of what used to be called inhumanity but which is, I'm afraid, humanity at its barest.

The Neighbors

by Philip Dacey

Ask yourself who you would prefer as a neighbor—Saddam Hussein or
George Bush." Mary Jane Laub, *Christian Science Monitor* Feb. 25, 1991

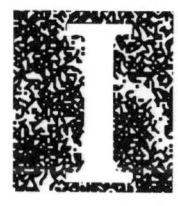

I walk out my front door
to enjoy the summer evening,
the silk hand of a breeze.
Immediately eastward,
Saddam is watering his lawn.
He sees me and waves absentmindedly,
absorbed in the sound of the drops slapping grass.
On the west side, George reclines
in a lounge chair, a newspaper folded on his lap
as he looks at nothing in particular,
a car passing, a bird hopping at a distance.

They're good neighbors.
It's true I worried when they moved in,
one right after the other.
I had heard stories.
And there I was between them.
But I have seen them pass each other on the street
with an acknowledging nod
and even sometimes chat for a while
before they part with smiles and touches
on the arm, the back.
From time to time I borrow things, too,
a ladder from Saddam, a drill from George.
As I said, they're good neighbors.

Only occasionaly
a small hand pushes up
from the ground their lots enclose,
breaking the level green,
the fingers uncurling
toward the light
and moving with an appearance
of great expressiveness,
and then only briefly
before a small engine starts up
and low blades
whirr quietly, restoring
the uninterrupted
and peaceful expanse
of the neighborhood
we take such pride and pleasure in
on summer evenings
like this one.

On the Murder of Two Orphan Children by Sniper Fire, Sarajevo, 1992

by Robert Dana

Sick shimmer of migraine;
a narrow rain falling;
and news of their deaths
stuck in our throats
like a bowlful of vomit;
the stink of it clinging
to skin, clothes, hair;
lush green country
rolling to the horizon,
cornfield and beanfield.
Here are the babies
in their bloodied dresses.
Here are their mourners
mortared on their knees
in the old cemetery;
a mother, her arm blown
away while cameras roll.
Where do the birds go

when soul shrivels to
brute cinder? Their small
calligraphies of dust?
And how many hundreds of
years to sweet mercy? To
these cheap, black tears.

Marie Antoinette Ocean

by Connie Deanovich

Wearing heavy chunks of silver
and carrying a basket
they venture to Marie Antoinette Ocean

her eyes came here first by letter
when she wrote for reservations
requesting an ocean view

could all be contained and marked
in elegant gilt script
RESERVED

his eyes were wrecked, hidden behind red lenses
which made him look decidedly tense
as if his demeanor were of the finest Swiss
   craftsmanship

his headache   was gone   as soon   as they   lowered
   themselves onto
the sand, taking pains to treat their lower backs
with the same care owners of rare foreign cars use in
   parking

they wore heavy gowns underneath their heavy chunks
   of silver
and they ate butter with tiny forks and dug out little
   bits
of pomegranate and shared these with one another

tied turning always made them want to read of
   discoveries
so she extracted a letter from the basket and made him
   see
corn fields fertilized by diamonds as seen by their
   correspondent.

She

by Helen Degen-Cohen

She gave me a pin once, which caught the light like diamond or steel, as we passed in the corridors. I didn't know what to do with it, whether it was meant to be put in the hair or on a gown, or had a more meaningful use. I walked in our door this way, puzzled yet grateful somehow. My mother was greasing a chicken, she had on her full apron and was sweating. She said, "You can set the table." The place smelled of greasy chicken and sugar, something sweet. She pointed to the dishes I should use, thinking I might forget to use the better set, her ancient, yellowed dishes, as if one set were better than another, as if she wouldn't have to fill in with another set anyway, since there wasn't a complete set of anything left. The wrinkled white tablecloth was already on the table and I tried to smooth it.

She would pass through the corridors without knowing me, at first, tall, thin, and stately. Many of course were tall, thin, and stately, but she was taller than the rest, even more aloof, extending higher into the air, tapering up to the sleek, turbaned head, taller than a model, taller it seemed sometimes than Highrise City itself, though she was under its roof. She never passed as if she didn't know me, she only passed without acknowledging me, passing, moving. She was always, as long as I remember, moving, on her way to or from somewhere, passing, moving. Of course everyone was, but she seemed more of everything than everyone, more purposeful, more on the move, passing swifter and surer, without any loss of pride or grace, without ever bending her head or lowering her eyes.

Then one day as she passed, she looked at me, without moving an eyelash (or any line of her face), without judgment, but seriously. I didn't know what to make of that look. The looks of others were haughty or superficially friendly—smooth, polite glances. Nor had they ever drawn my attention.

My mother was vacuuming quickly around things, the smells grown thicker and more aggressive. One had to want to eat these smells, one's hunger was aroused as if it were a solitary instinct, unrelated to the others. She looked at me as if to say, where were you—you always go when you could help. "Skim the soup, here," she said, giving me a large stainless steel spoon. I walked over to the steaming pot and skimmed what she called dirt off the top of the soup, and threw it in the sink. The whole house was steaming. "When are they coming?" I said, not as if I couldn't wait. She kept on vacuuming before she answered. "I don't know. I told them at four." They always came at four, for all the holidays, I don't know why I bothered asking. She would stand at the window of the two-flat watching for their cars between the trees, never noticing across the street the orderly borders of red salvia and other early fall flowers, installed on the periphery of the eye, like the trees, the parked cars on both sides.

Her gowns were elegant and straight as gleaming cones, tall thin teepees, topped by her glossy turbaned hair—I could never remember what antiquity the style reminded me of, something to do with knights maybe, though of course she was taller than the Ladies of Yore, and we were in the latest New Era. Have I lived in all Eras by now? At any rate, she began to extend her look at me, as she passed. I don't remember how we ascended or descended in those days, it seemed that she simply passed through walls out of the building, into air miles above the ground, and descended however, in her own way, though of course we had conventional means of descending, as well as bridges at one-mile intervals of height, from building to building, which I used myself. I admired her at various distances. Her perfection in carriage, in dress, her indifference. As if the world were meant to serve her, and not vice-versa. The persistent looks she sent my way surfaced a longing I had owned at some unreachable depth, placed it before me, as if on a silver tray. I averted my eyes.

My mother's house sweated with aromas of food. She was pulling clothes out of a closet in the bedroom, I could see her through the open door, could smell the odor of clothes as it drifted into the living room and wandered curiously among the food smells. She made a face, pulling shut the sliding door of her closet and came into my room, opened the door to my closet and surveyed the contents critically, then returned to her closet. I followed her. She pulled out two blouses and two dresses. "That blouse is mine," I reminded her, "but you can wear it, it's all right." She gave me a look. She tried it on. It had large red polka dots and a red bow, and was snug around the bust. "No, I don't want it," she said, and I hung it back in my closet. She tried on a skirt and a blouse and looked lumpy in them; then a dress. I said, "Wear the dress." I thought, we should get you a long sleek gown, under which you could hide. "Do you need something at the store?" I asked. It was oppressively pungent in the house.

Once I saw her look not quite behind her but rather off to the side—it would have been presumptuous to think that she was looking at me, since I was behind her, but still I had that feeling, as if she were looking off into the distance on her left side, through several layers of glass buildings, but also at me. But she walked on and disappeared, as usual. The corridors melded into one, I felt myself living in them, between sleek others of various heights, all in the moot, metallic tones, smoothly covered from neck to toe, all stylish and alone. And while her gown was loose and not fitted, spreading down and out like a tent, a svelte cone of elegant shine, she too moved through corridors stylish and alone, confident, passing through. I never saw anyone do anything but move. I never saw anyone speaking to anyone. The buildings shone as silent as sun on steel, the sun was as remote as the childhood I could never remember.

I told my mother, who was so much shorter than I was, so much closer to the ground, to wear the beige and brown striped dress. She ought to deodorize herself somehow, though the smell was not of armpits but of her general self, the mild, acrid aroma of cooking and sweat like a halo around her, blanketing everyone who walked into the house. "These are my colors," she said, reminding no one, holding up green and beige. "Wear the beige," I said. The blanket was closing in around me, like the doubled-up scarf around my face during that childhood I could never remember. The suffocating feeling was not quite death, not that bad, yet I too found myself walking to the window, looking for our guests to come, guests who were hers, not mine, who would ask questions of me and admire me, and whom I would have to flee, one way or another.

I found myself watching for her now, in the corridors, waiting for all things foreign to me, journeys, straight and narrow as her sharp height wherever it was she went, I waited to see her again, hoped to understand, to communicate with her at a safe distance, somehow, I couldn't imagine how. No one spoke in the corridors. I wanted to look like the best in the corridors, I wanted to leave my house. She looked like the best, without noticing others. Nor did they care about her; they passed, absorbed in themselves. Her perfection must be for herself alone, or some undefined something in the air. They were all always coming and going, I grew tired of their coming and going, as if it were myself; though of course it wasn't. Then one day, she stopped to look at me. It was as if I could fall into a long, indefinite sleep.

My mother was taking off her apron, looking out the living room window. The house was ready, the food ready to burst, a damp cliche rousing the nostrils to eat, eat. I couldn't wait for them to come in and eat, I stood in the kitchen pulling scabs of meat off a bone, sucking a cooked plum into my mouth, pulling golden crust off a piece of egg twist, pulling more meat off the bone. "Wait for the others," she said, not meaning it, proud of the hold it had on me. I went in the bedroom and lay down, then sat looking out the back window, at the little yard, its big tree shedding slow, fated leaves.

I stopped in the corridors more often, pulling into myself, snail-like, the silent, sparse parade passing by, the pretended knowing looks, the silver-gray shine in the windows of other silver buildings, the air itself gray, the color of eternity. I would freeze to some spot and could not move. It seemed I didn't exist, I was one of the buildings. The lack of sense didn't disturb me. The motion in the corridors was the motion of time, unseeing, transparent—I would have liked to have seen through the walls of buildings, the layers upon vertical layers, to something else, but there was nothing to see, nothing to hold onto. When she came by. Came along, even though I didn't exist. And gave me the pin. Without words, of course. Diverted her eyes toward me for a moment, and handed it to me, a present. A straight, beautiful pin, as I said, of diamond or steel, which sleamed saberlike in all directions, like a diamond in a darkroom. She had pulled it out of the shadows, a small bag in her hands. She looked serious, almost benevolent, even without a smile, as she handed it to me, waited for it to take effect, then moved on, taller than as a goddess. The oppressive tallness of steel and glass, the corridors, spread and loomed. I turned away with my pin. I laid it on my human hand.

My mother was ready. She smiled at me and wiped her hands on a towel, took a drink of water. She kept walking around the house, then to the window. I was trying to remember all the things I had to do. The holiday would be over tomorrow. I wanted to run outside and take a bath in the air. The odors hadn't permeated yet to the outside. I laughed. "What are you laughing at?" she said suspiciously, turning around from the window. I really didn't know. Suddenly I went over to her, and without much fuss, took out the pin and stuck it carefully into her thin, graying hair.

The Lessons of History (Yugoslavia, 1992-3)

by Emilio DeGrazia

Here in this land the curse
Is crescent-crossed,
All shreds of the argument
Hung up on Truth.
Rivers, clotted with cleansing
The bones of the dead,
Have nowhere to run,
And memory is so vengeance-gorged
It has completely lost its mind.
Where the Sign of the Cross
Has a left and right wing
Chained to armored divisions
Blasting equally to hell
The catholic orthodox infidel;
Where still the male is master
When mounting the slave,
Woman and child—then
Assisi, Mecca, and Sarajevo
Are equally the shrines
Of Death Squad saints.

Crows

by Stephen Dixon

She went outside, came back in, pounded her head with her knuckles several times, went outside again, looked and looked, nowhere to be seen, couldn't imagine what had happened, yelled "Henry," and he appeared, his voice did, from the cellar. "Yes, what's up, I'm down here." "Thank God," she said and held onto the doors folded over and then the walls as she went down the stone steps. "Don't leave me like that anymore, please." "Leave you how?" he said. "Like that, like that," pointing upstairs. "Like what, like what?" he said, painting a lawn chair, looking up at her for a second. "Like leaving me. Tell me next time. You know how I am." "No, I really don't, or not exactly. How are you? You're fine, I can see. But you were worried. Don't be." "I was worried. When I call for you, look for you, go up and downstairs and outside and down the road and around the house for you? Well, I only called that one time and I didn't go down the road looking for you, but I almost did." "Did you by chance ever think to call for me earlier or to look down here? When you see the cellar doors open, assume I'm down it." "You could have been elsewhere but airing the cellar out." "That's true," he said, painting; "you're right. I forgot that's what I do and it's just the kind of day for that."

She looked around. "I think we should build a staircase inside the house to the cellar. Then you could go up and down with ease, even evenings if you'd like,

for there'd be a railing and light. And also not get wet
in the rain if it's raining when you want to come here,
or have to put boots on if it's snowing. And I wouldn't
be searching frantically for you. I'd open the door to
the cellar in the kitchen, let's say, and know by the
sounds or the light on that you're down there." "Then
we'd call the cellar a basement. I never want to have a
basement to this house. Then we'd fix it up, put in a
convertible couch and lamps and fixtures on the walls
for more lamps and insulate it so guests would come, or
for when they came, and a place to dump the grandkids
when they were being too restless or loud. And fancy
windows and then bars on the windows to protect our
valuable lamps and grandkids from vandals and
thieves. And the walls would have to be plastered
smooth and then painted bright to cheer up the room,
and the furnace would have to be concealed because it's
an eyesore. And a drop ceiling to make believe we
have no overhead pipes, and pictures in frames and so
on. A mirror. A dehumidifier. A wine rack instead of
the boxes the wine comes in I now use. Never. My
parents had that right down to the bar with two stools
and a carbonated water tap and it was disgusting.
They had to clean it every other week. The floor—I
forgot the floor—which was linoleum and when we left
scuff marks on it we got reprimanded for it. I like the
way it is. I open the cellar doors—clement or
unclement weather, who cares? Climb down, do my
work, single bulb dangling over the table, furnace like
a furnace, no electrical outlets but the extension socket
the lightbulb's in , my sweater or vest or both if it's
damp or cold, and once a year I use the old broom to
brush away the spiders and spider and cobwebs." "But
I get worried for you." "Then I'll tell you what, ask
yourself why you do." "Because if I can't see or hear
you I sometimes think something awful's happened to
you." "Ask yourself this then: What could happen to

me? I'm healthy. A heart attack? Hell, I could have got one when I was forty or fifty, and statistics say there was a better chance then, or is that just with a stroke? And I know my way around and don't risk injuries and accidents. If I got pains someplace that might seem unusual, and I know where those places are, I'd recognize the signs. So from now on, if you want me, look for me further. Upstairs, downstairs, outside, in. That's not much looking. Down the cellar—now that's looking, or down the road." "But you weren't down the road." "I was, this morning, for the mail." "Was there any?" she said. "Nothing useful. Ton of junk mail as usual. And a letter from Nina. I read it and tore it up." "You didn't." "I didn't," and pulled it from his back pocket and gave it to her. "That was unfair holding it from me this long." "I got disoriented. Distracted, I mean, or involved in something—that's it. Came back, had read it on the way back—there's absolutely nothing new in it by the way. Jeremy Junior's fine, hiccupping more often, that's all. Jeremy's busy at work and thought he was getting the flu. Sunny weather, stormy weather, a film dealing with values and serious moral questions that we also might want to see on VCR, and her book's going well. But then I saw the cellar doors, opened them because I thought of painting the chair. Now I'm finished," and put the brush down. "One thing we can use down here is running water so I can clean my brushes and hands, though not at the expense of converting this dungeon into a shaped-up basement. Bringing down a pail of water and leaving the liquid soap here does the trick just as well." He cleaned the brush, then his hands, dried everything on his pants. "Maybe a paper towel roll would help too, but not a rack for it please. The pail was from a few days ago, if you're wondering." "I'm not, " reading the letter. "Is what she says in it any different than what I said? I tend to miss things, and not read between lines. Oh, this is getting us nowhere. Let's go upstairs." "What's getting us nowhere?" she said. "I don't know. I just said it to get us out of here," and shut the light.

He grabbed her elbow and moved her to the steps. They went up them, she holding onto his arm till she was able to grab the edge of one of the folded-up cellar doors. When they reached the top, a bird swooped down on them. "Duck," he said, pushing her head down till she was on her knees with him. The bird came a few inches from hitting them. "That crow was aiming at us," he said. "Where's my gun." "You have no gun," she said. "I don't, huh?" He pointed his finger at the crow, which was circling about fifty feet up, followed its movements with his finger for a while and then said "Bang bang, you're dead, you bum." The crow's wings collapsed and it dropped to the ground some twenty feet from them. "I don't believe it. Did you see that?" "I saw it," she said, "and I don't believe it either." "With this gun," holding up his finger. " Do you think if I pointed it your way and said bang bang, I'd knock you off too?" "Why, you want to? Anyway, don't try." "But it's ridiculous. Just by going bang bang, I killed that bird. And I had a bead on him too. 'Bead' is the word they use for it—out West or in criminal or law enforcement circles—right?" "You're asking me?" "Bead, a bead, or maybe it's 'draw a bead,' but like you're aiming." "The beads I know are little stones and ornaments around the neck and droplets and so on. Of sweat. I still can't believe what you did though." "Neither can I. I aimed my finger at it—like this," and he pointed his finger at her, "and then when it seemed to be closest to me and my hand wasn't shaking so much, I fired. Bang bang. I didn't pull any trigger, though, meaning, use another finger as if I were pulling one." He still had his finger on her. "Maybe I should move it away from you just to be safe." "Don't be silly. We both are. It was a coincidence. The crow died of a heart attack, but not one brought on by you, or something like that when you pretended to shoot it. Pull it if you want. Shoot it. Go bang bang, even bang bang bang. Three shots for the price of two. Suddenly today I'm feeling very brave." "Bang bang," he said. Her face got distorted, hands sort of stiffened into claws, and she fell to the ground. "Darling," he said and got on his knees. Her eyes were closed. She was on her side and he put his ear to her chest, and moved it around above her breasts, her back about where he thought her heart would be behind, then her nose and mouth. He didn't hear or feel anything. He did it again: chest, back, nose and mouth and then put his mouth on hers, kept her mouth open with his hands, and breathed into it, took his mouth away, took in a mouthful of air, breathed into her again, pulled away. "Oh Christ, what have I done? —What have I done goddamnit?" he screamed out. He stood, forced his fist into his palm, screamed "What the hell have I done? I've killed my wife. It can't be so." Got on the ground, listened to her chest, mouth, put his hand on her neck where he thought her pulse might be, was none, felt around her neck and temples, didn't try her wrist because he was never able to find it there, turned her over on her stomach, straddled her, did what he thought was the thing to get someone breathing again. Pushed down with his hands, sat up, pushed, sat up. Lay down next to her and put his ear to her mouth; turned her over and put his ear where he thought her heart was. Nothing. He pointed his finger and pressed it into his forehead. "Bang bang," he said. "Bang bang. Bang bang." I'm not shot, he thought. Not even hurt. "Come on, sweetheart, you got to be kidding." He sat her up, held her while he listened to where he thought her heart was. Thought he heard something. Touched her neck. He felt something. Forced her eyes open. They looked alive. She smiled. "You," he said; "you nearly gave me a heart attack there." "You'd kill yourself for me? I peeked. Oh my dearest," and she hugged him. "Yes I would," he said. "I was so full of guilt and everything else. Sadness. I suddenly believed . . . well, who wouldn't after he shot that bird down? The bird," and he stood up, helped her up and ran to where the crow had landed.

It was still there. "I don't want to put my head near its heart or beak, for those things can bite. No wonder I hit it. Look at its size." "Kick it," she said, walking over. "You mean nudge it with my foot. Okay. But if it jumps it's going to startle me." He touched it with the tip of his shoe, then jabbed it. The crow moved but didn't seem alive. "Think it's alive but just pretending?" he said. "I wouldn't doubt it.

—Seriously," she said, "I don't think so. I think it got that heart attack or the cerebral equal of one—a flying stroke or something winged animals get only when they're flying, and not particularly when people below are shooting their fingers at them, but that's all. Your bang-bang and its fatal heart failure or stroke are only coincidental, one chance in a million, and it came up today." "I hope so. Because I wouldn't want to personally kill anything living like that. But come on, crow," he said to the bird, "move, move, get up, fly or walk away. Do your messy garbage-bag biting and picking, your squawking, keeping us up when we want to take afternoon naps or sleep late. Do what the hell you're supposed to and don't make me feel bad, because the one-in-a-million coincidence I can't prove."

The crow began fidgeting, stood up—they backed away—flapped its wings, seemed to be testing its feet out on the ground, flapped some more, tried to fly, looked at them, walked backwards away from them a few feet, flapped harder while it walked frontwards even farther away from them and took off, flew a few inches off the ground several yards and then up to the sky. He pointed his finger at it, held his wrist while he got a bead on it. She said "Don't chance it; not today. Maybe you did kill it and then your little entreaty before brought it back to life, and you won't be so fortunate the next time." He said "Just a test to prove my supernatural or whatever-you-want-to-call-them powers—powers I never had that I know of but am now naturally curious to see if I do. —Hold it. Steady, steady. I've got it. Bang bang. And bang, just in case." The crow flew on, settled in a tree. "Maybe I missed." "Or you wounded it," she said. "Well I'm not going to find out. In fact, no more games or tests like that. In fact, I'm throwing away my gun," and flicked his hand to the side. They heard a clump in the grass about ten feet away in the direction he'd flicked to. "You believe that?" "It must be a rabbit or squirrel," she said, "or a mouse." "Probably a mouse." "But then again, who knows?, though we should try to find out."

She went over to where they'd heard the clump. Nothing moved. "Maybe it's already gone," she said. "Or it could have been something that just went down a hole, didn't need to go through the grass. But we won't tell anybody about all this, okay?" "I don't know," he said. "It's a good story to tell, raises lots of interesting questions, puts what you didn't think you think right out there, right? And we're having dinner with the Chamberlains later and they're so dull that they're wonderful to shock, so why not?" "It might be somewhat off-putting to them. They'll think we're getting loony and they'll tell people, and then everyone will think we've become peculiar." "Let them," he said. "If they don't like it, let them ostracize us too. Then we won't have to return the dinner invitation to the Chamberlains and all our other dull neighbors who sort of force us to socialize more than we like. Let the whole town know, for all I care. It'll give us more time to ourselves and what we really like to do. Like reading, for God's sake. I'm going in to read. Like a good cup of hot tea, or a drink?" "I'll make it for you," she said. "No, it was my suggestion, and what I want to do, and you put up and will probably still have to put up with all my antics today, so I'll make it for you."

A crow in the tree their crow flew in, crowed. "It doesn't necessarily have to be the one you shot at," she said. "That's a favorite resting and gabbing place of theirs," he said. "In fact—I just figured it out—I bet it's nesting there, or protecting a nest of another crow there—that's why it swooped down on us. Because I've never seen one so aggressive, except with dogs and cats." "It could be sick," she said; "distemper, or whatever crows get." "No, it looked too healthy on the ground. Children, wonderful, just what we need around here, more crows. But I like the idea of an animal protecting its young or soon-to-be young or someone else's." A crow crowed from the tree. "See, it agrees with me. We won't tell the Chamberlains this part because it's getting too silly. But this, yes," and he aimed his finger at the tree and said "Bang bang bang, bang bang, bang bang bang bang," moving his finger around to different places in the tree. He imagined several crows dropping out. "Ah, wonderful, a longer sleep tomorrow morning, maybe even after that caw-free afternoon nap. Actually, I'm glad I didn't hit any. Some of them might have been young. Let's go in before we truly get silly." "Did we shut the cellar light?" she said. "I don't remember. I'll see you inside. Put up the water, or take out the ice tray," and he headed for the cellar. A crow crowed from the tree.

"That a boy," he said, "or that a girl. Whatever you are, crow, crow." What I'd like to know, he thought, peering into the cellar and seeing it was dark, is why I didn't hear her breathing or feel her neck pulse or her heart beat when I checked. The pulse, even in the neck, can be a little difficult to find, and I was nervous. Even her heartbeat, but her breath? He flipped the cellar doors closed with his feet. They made a loud double bang and she yelled from kitchen window "What's that?" "Just closing things up," he said, "and the light was out. You do it? Because I don't remember I did," and he went inside.

What the Woman at the Origami Village Remembers

by Jim Elledge

1. A Hand-Stitched Prayer on the Wall
Father Air, Mother Dirt:

Bless me now.
Hours tick, drop through a well.
Echoes gather at my shoes, rise chin-
high, threaten.

Father Thunder, Mother Waterfall:

Spare me now.
So many fictions spin—Mars burns over
mountain peaks, black holes throb, tornadoes tear
across landscapes and pierce tree trunks
with blades of grass.

Father Star, Mother Diamond:

Silence the racket of clock
chime and bird twitter, of interstate
semis and drunks vomiting around the corner.
Quench my cotton mouth. If the wine's
run out, Jack Daniels will do.

2. What Her Uncle Said Just Before He Slammed the Front Door

"If you have a problem with that, I'll be out in the driveway. But I've gotta warn you: I boxed in jail." The other men and women laughed.

They'd arrived at dusk, a storm of boots clunking on the wood floors. They put the burlap sacks on the table, bottles inside clinking together, and I saw how they rolled their eyes in their heads, how their lips, glistening with the sweat from the stifling heat, went *Whew!* all over their faces. And *Whew!* again when they saw me. And other things, I think, but I can't remember that. Men and women.

Mother said, "Time for bed" to me in a voice lilting more than usual, as if we were used to company that time of the day, that many at once, and all strangers to us. She pointed to my bedroom door, and once I closed it behind me, I heard her pull a chair up to it—the scrape of the legs along the floorboards—and the woosh of air from the seat cushion as she sat down. It was at least two hours earlier than I usually said good-night. The chair legs threw their shadows under the door

crack—sentinels or bars.
Too much noise for me to sleep with that many people—
all the sizes and shapes and colors a mishmash now.
They looked too much like the rest of us, grimier
maybe, maybe more gaunt, but
dressed as we. Of course, they had weapons.

A scent filled the dining room first then spread
through the house, a *staleness* that seeped in, a tide
rising so slow you didn't know it was there until it'd
filled the space.

I must've begun to fall into sleep because my body
jumped at a door slam. I lay there in the sudden
silence that was so thick I was afraid, my mind revving
like one of the old beaters he always tinkered with. I
knew I was alone, not just in my room but everywhere.
Terns and grackles twittered in trees outside my
window where the sky had turned a peachy grey. The
shadows of the chair legs were gone, too, although the
lamps were still on, and I couldn't hear my mother
moving over floorboards nor the clanking of pots had
she been making breakfast.

His voice came back, clear as if I'd been awake and
wrote the words down when he said them, "The bitch
stabbed me for the last time."

3. Her Dream of Capture

The sky spits ash downdown in waltz-time. We sit in
chalky dirt, she in my arms, on my lap, facing away

from me, her shoulder blade jabbing my right breast. Neither guard interrupts me unkotting her gag. She turns, and by turning, her breasts nuzzle the soft flesh on the inside of my arms.

I see her face for the first time. No one I've ever known.

Her nipples smile and lick my arms. A sweat bead slips from her navel, glides over her flesh downdown. I hold her tighter and keep my hands in sight, on her shoulders. Her breath drops in chunks, clinks against path stone. She cranes her head, eyes squinting, boring into mine.

Both guards shift their weight, left to right foot and back again. Their eyes flit from me to her, to one another, back to us.

I remember how to say *please,* botch the words for *knife, pistol,* then draw pictures in the bone-like dust. I hold her tighter, knowing what I'll do if they figure out what I'm asking.

One guard points, calls the knife "tongue," the pistol "hitchhiker hand."

I understand. She doesn't.

They laugh, slap their thighs, discuss how the blistering sun paces through narrow walls with never a thought of mercy, the wide brims of their hats casting shadows like wings, and I wake long before dawn again, my heart flip-flopping against its cage.

4 The Message in Lipstick on the Medicine Chest Mirror

I could teach you how to divine water—
  the way to hold a switch and walk without tripping over field stubble or dirt clods, how far
    far from Earth to hold it, what switch to cut from a branch on which tree, the type of
    tree, what we name it and what it calls itself.

...what herbs to use for washing your hair—

  whether to look for them in forest or field, how to lift them from Earth, how to carve
    their leaves into perfect O's, to snip their stems into straight I's, how to press them with a
    prayer into cloth, whether to use burlap or silk, which prayer to whisper, how to fold the
    burlap or silk, under what phase of the moon, how long to let them soak in a stoop of
    rainwater, what we call them and what they name themselves.

...how to shape your nails with a kitchen knife—

  how to whetstone the steel sharp as sunlight through a jug of creek water, how to angle the
    blade and pare away the cuticle along the sides and base, to round the tips into moon
    crescents like the one brightly rising over Earth

—but not how to dig blood out from under your nails.

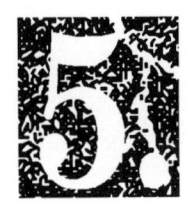

5. Her Mother Reading Aloud from The Home Companion

"15. If you shake the egg and you hear a rattle, you can be sure it's stale. A really fresh egg will sink and a stale one will float."

"392. These hair rinses will remove soap film and shine hair: For blondes, rinse water containing a few tablespoons of lemon juice. For brunettes and redheads, a few tablespoons of apple cider vinegar in the rinse water."

"47. Keep tomatoes in storage with stems pointed downward and they will retain their freshness longer."

"404." For tired eyes, place fresh cucumber slices on your eyelids to rid them of redness and puffiness."

"254. To remove blood on the rug, rub off as much as you can at first, then take a cloth soaked in cold water and wet the spot, wiping it up as you go. If a little bit remains, pour some ammonia onto the cool, wet cloth and lightly wipe that over the spot, too. Rinse it right away with cold water."

...Try, try again.

"215. To remove blood from clothing, pre-soak in cold or warm water at least 30 minutes. If stain remains, soak in lukewarm ammonia water (3 tablespoons per gallon water). Rinse. If stain remains, work in detergent, and wash, using bleach safe for fabric."

Try, try again, I thought. I thought, *No hint about what to do with the scraps arsonists leave behind. The wounds rapists gouge beyond flesh. The vacuum the militia blasts into the air.*

6. A Story Her Father Told After Dinner

"Their friendliness fooled us at first. The militia's. That's what they called themselves. *Militia.*

"And they called themselves Citizen This, Citizen That.

"They banded together years before, when all the trees hereabouts stopped leafing. This male, that female from a parish elsewhere, someone's daughter or aunt, someone's nephew or grandson. Desperation their bond, 'Nothing Left to Lose' their motto.

"Once we got back on-line, we had some contact with other villages. The keyboard clacks like tom-toms telegraphing parish to parish or traders arriving, pulling their wares behind them in carts. The story's the same.

"Oh, they'd walk single file into sight, ragged as us but friendly-like—weapons holstered or slung on their backs, polite as you please, smiles smeared all over their faces like a child's drawing of family. So many of them they gorged the village. They gave the kids chocolate; we butchered some lambs. Wasn't long before they'd be burning incense and making speeches all hours day and night on every corner about a better day to come and rewards in heaven for those suffering now. "We didn't take long to figure it out, couple of days, no more. A boy or girl would disappear, then another, and another. Or a newly-wedded couple. Then *anyone*. Twenty, more or less. Someone's mother or son, someone's uncle or niece.

"If wrinkled or deformed, you thanked your lucky stars the first time in our life and went about the day's business. If not, you prayed. Too late to hide. We let them in. Gave them a seat. Why not? They were smiling.

"We learned to listen close at night, the wind no longer wind but knives ripping through clothing, the screams of boys and girls, of women and men, and the cheers and groans of Citizen This, Citizen That.

"Sometimes, we would find a body nailed to a tree limb like laundry on a line. Or a flag.

"When they left, they swarmed down Main Street. They waved like football stars and beauty queens to us behind doors we locked too late. They yelled thanks and praise-be's for our hospitality."

7. Her Parents' Pet Names for Her

Sometimes when I speak, it's my mother's voice. Sometimes, my father's. The timbre of hers thread-thin; the syntax of his wax-thick. Hers a castrati melody, pitched pure in the April air. His opera's oboe gracing

Earth's brittle grass.
She would call, *Buzz... Buzz... BuzzBuzz*, out the window over the kitchen sink. At noon, when she called me for lunch, I'd stop pouring imaginary tea for imaginary guests. I imagined her antennae flexing, gossamer wings folding the air around her, and more arms than she'd a birthright to. At dusk, when she called me for bed, I imagined her abdomen lit a blue-gray, blinking a code I'd never understand, some incantation or prayer or gossip that filled the room a moment, disappeared, returned as if fighting off the flood of darkness.

Out the front door at noon to give him his injection or dusk to play cards, he would call, *Ann... Ann... AnnAnn*, and I'd drop wrench and caliper and slide out from under the junk heap up on blocks and feel his loss, the lack of what followed his name for me and what could have introduced it, what it could have concluded, what it bridged between what he never said before and after, and I thought of myself as the least needed word in a series and the only word of the series that he spoke, and could speak, and wanted to speak, and had the courage and naivete to speak.

A Story For Young Moderns

by S. P. Elledge

On a gloomy Sunday. The art museum. We go there with the children, all of them. The guards appear to be the only things on exhibit. We admire their new royal blue suits, the gold braiding, the epaulettes. They are extremely suspicious of the children; afraid of being defaced? Surely the brats would scrawl mustaches across their faces, but they (the guards) are already mustached.

The children are monsters. Want to know what's happened to all the paintings (they are of course wrapped up and stored away during the occupation). Bloody little beasts, I say to you, not being in a paternal mood. Do not touch the guards, I tell them (the children) one by one.

Outside it is snowing. The city police have thrown themselves into the streets, body to body like biscuits in a tin, blocking the route of a proposed protest march. In the distance you can hear the protesters chanting - but they are in the trees, throwing snowballs at one another. On close inspection one sees that they are mere children, none over twelve years old. The headlines in the Sunday papers read: CITY FEARS MORE TERRORISM.

Your children are in fact monsters. We drive them home, send them off to the woods behind the house.

The wolves, I have heard, have come down out of the mountains this year, lean with hunger. Imagining their howls of pleasure, I am driven by a mad desire to make love to you.

Belinda, I say, ravish me, and I shall ravish you. Make me feel like anyone but the humble but still frightfully witty art historian I am. Make me feel like Frederick Church (1823-98) of the Hudson River School as he stood before the yawning chasms of the Orinoco and painted his masterpiece, "Rainy Season In The Tropics."

These are modern times, you say, and we live our lives in fragments. To make sense of anything is like piecing together tiny shards of Etruscan pottery and then trying to read the inscriptions of a dead language.

Always the philologist, I say. One fits one's metaphors and allusions to one's occupational framework. No wonder you are a professoress at our largest university and no wonder I love you like money. And I simply don't care what they say about your first three husbands.

But I am, you say with a bit of a wheeze, a specialist in sub-Neo-Platonics. You are at the window. The snow is still falling. But really did I ever really love you and all your monstrous children, really?

Many days later. At the movies. A documentary of the life of Marinetti, Italian futurist (1874-1935). The kids are enthralled. I am bored and restless and bite your shoulder playfully. This movie has been playing to full theaters for months, the critics have raved, sequels are in the works, yet all it arouses in me is a great nostalgic hunger for your flesh.

Outside it is raining. I've left you all back at the cinemahaus. The city has strung colored lights and tinsel between the trees on either side of the main boulevard and the effect is dismal, the appearance of a festival that is no longer celebrated except by government officials in need of a holiday. I feel very sad and gaze upon the monumental statue of Renee Branson, French actor and art theorist (1931-1969) in the city square. Graffiti has been scrawled across the base of the statue: NO GODS NO MASTERS.

I notice a rat dragging a child's torn red shoe into the gutter. The rat is bleeding as if it has just escaped a cat, and when I run after it, it drops the child's shoe and disappears down a drain. The shoe, I see when I pick it up, is a very expensive designer shoe, and there is a bit of a torn cloth nestled in its mouth: a child's tiny ruffled sock. All at once I begin to cry. It is the seventh and last year of the plague.

A year or so later. After the occupation. Your children are all grown now and away at college studying medicine and law and journalism. They are still bloody monsters and write only to ask for money. You have borrowed against your inheritance like the tragic character in a melodrama and yet you continue to send them more. They are all working for revolutionary causes and claim to need the money for ammunition, though I suspect they are spending it on records, clothes, comic books.

Belinda, I am fond of saying to you, we are old now and no longer truly love one another and your children are grown and we live in a police state now the war is over. Don't you think it's time we took a rest?

This year we do. There is rioting in the south, and we go there with our video equipment, hoping to catch something saleable to the five-o-clock news. One must earn a living somehow. The train down is crowded with religious separatists fleeing the country. They are a very amusing lot; we all drink too much and wind up sleeping with each other's wives.

The woman I wake with is fat and smells of polyvinyl chloride and she is wearing the blue uniform of a museum guard. Aha, I say, fondling her epaulettes: thematic repetition.

You wait until we are leaning over the Bridge of That Sinking Feeling into the Questionable Alibi Gorge to tell me that you are pregnant once again - this time with my child. I wonder whether to kiss you, smack you or knock your body into the raging waters below. We go out dancing instead.

A little while later. A Monday afternoon, terribly hot. Some hotel room with no running water or clean towels. We have just finished reading Sir Thomas Mandeville's Jacobean restoration play, "1688!" to one another in a torrent of emotion. I have never seen you look quite this way, with your hair down, your makeup smudged with tears, your ears red as poppies.

Outside we hear submachine-gun fire. Nothing to worry about: just the reactionaries fending off the post-reactionaries. There is also a children's choir practicing scales in a nearby church, one that had its roof torn off in the war. It is a very melancholy but somehow anesthetic sound. They are singing "O Brave Souls of Canaan," an old spiritual I learned at my mammy's knee.

There is also a parade somewhere - but no, I think that was another day just like this one. The past can overlap in that way: sometimes, especially since the children left, I don't know where I am in time. Sometimes I don't know whose story I am telling.

Maybe this is just senility's way to make things more interesting.

Manuel, you whisper to me, half-asleep, let us go tomorrow to the exhibit of Renji-Moro tribal totems on the village green. It is perhaps the most romantic thing you have ever said to me. Call it animal magic, but we were made for one another after all.

An hour later. I have been called before the local magistrates, representatives of the Bilateral Commission; there is the snout of a rifle tickling between my shoulder blades. The gig is up. They want to know what I have done with the body. They want to know where the stolen documents are hidden. They want to know what our beloved leader said to his mistress the night of the inauguration. They want to know just exactly how Egon Schiele, German artist (1888-1930) revolutionized expressionist art.

I will tell them nothing. Just then I see a very large black rat scampering across the straw in a corner of the disused cattle barn. It is dragging - no, not a child's red shoe - but a heavy cassock of an East Anglian parish priest, of the sort used between the years 1919 and 1937 (I know, because I once wrote a graduate theses on this subject.) This is my chance for a very cinematic escape.

A minute or two later. In a raging downpour. The last I remember you and I were lolling on a local greensward, kissing each other's nether regions, talking of God and men and the children of men. In the distance we could hear the changing of the guards outside the queen's summer home. No, it was the drum and bugle corps of the county war veterans. No, it was a child singing in a tree as below him mollydancers cavorted, dressed as bullocks and beefeaters and giant flower-bedecked phalli. Yes, that was definitely the sound I heard as you sunk your teeth into my earlobe and tore it clean off.

And tonight, chere ami, I said, we shall go dancing in the grottos of the gods the way young childless lovers have always done. We were that happy.

One second later, and they have begun to drop the bombs, the big ones. They explode in the air like crimson flowers and we watch and applaud from our ziggurat - discovering there is a certain recherche artistry in annihilation. As the Dadaist Francis – I begin to say when you clasp your palm over my mouth.

No, not again. Not at all. Nothing doing. Nononononono. You are blithering, you are tearing your bobtails from their roots.

So, we choose to survive, like the new Adam and the new Eve. It's a changed world, and it will become a better one. We shall carve our initials in the Parthenon. We shall host a popular daytime series. We shall dabble in chromatism and fin de siecle theosophism. We shall revive vaudeville. We shall run for office. We shall write the children daily. We shall become famous and arrange car-bombings, apartment ransackings, and wiretapping. In the end we shall of course sell out and agree to a movie adaptation for briefcase after briefcase of sweet sweet money. *On n'a rien pour rein*, which means nothing is had for nothing, not even me

Dear Dagmar, Wie Sagst Du Denn Heimat?

by Lucia Cordell Getsi

1970 German was a weight
our tongues worked to lift. Your Czech
bowled the gutter of your throat better
than my lazy southern consonant that left
a hole in the word. My lips pursed
the umlaut *ü* like Monroe mugging
the camera, yours went slack. We joked
it took both of us to speak. But no jokes

the day you held up a letter from home,
every phrase between *My dear Dagmar*
and *Love, Mother* censored. Hard to read
across the scissored gaps Your brother
was killed in a wreck. Piled on your dresser,
other letters like a stack of doilies—
Your brother has died of fever or
Mikhail was killed in an accident at work,
each letter a different death for Mikhail,
so many deaths you thought your mother had cracked
or that this was a code. Activists,

you had travelled out before Prague Spring,
he had stayed. There was no returning
even to lay a wreath on his grave

if there was a grave. Foreign coffee stiff
in our cups, our jaws stiff with new
language, we groped for words to fill in
the missing things—your brother dead, mine
fighting not to fight in Vietnam; home;
our mothers, yours cut from your life
absolutely as a word from a letter, mine,
one bullet through her heart. We explored

the aisles of the München *Wertkauf*, you as broke
on your resettlement stipend as I on a Fulbright,
my two-year-old prancing between us, babbling
two languages at once, German words strewn
across her English syntax, and later,
the reverse. You worried which language
you would raise your children in, if
you would have a choice. Somehow, choice
was something I still believed in, knowing
also I could go back. *I am losing my language*
you said in German, *even my memories are falling
silent*, and I understood those Soviet scissors
had cut a gorge through you, *before* and *after*
two edges you crossed with every thought.
After more than twenty years, I've lost touch,
lost the fluency to remember a clear passage
back to you, I find myself searching
newspaper photos for your face
among the thousands
of waving arms, banners.

Dagmar, that phase of our lives was like tunneling
out of the wreckage of old worlds, those new words
like unfamiliar digging tools. We gripped the edges
of language, startled
like Abraham at yet another world
spread in front of us, the weight of our old selves

pulling down to remind us we would not speak
or think the same ways again, even if we chose,
or events allowed us, to fall back into the same
place, which had changed, as Czechoslovakia
has, yet again, as my Tennessee home has,
Dagmar, so that my questions
are falling far short of you, the pieces
of syntax dislocated like the *Flüchtlinge*
rushing the borders to fill both eastern
and western cities with a language that shouts
at itself in dialect. But what I want

to know, before everything changes again,
is where are you now, dear Dagmar?
Have you lifted your arms in triumph above
your head? What is the language
of going home?

almost always

by Alvin Greenberg

birds feeding on the highway almost always
fly up in time, but you, when you come over
the rise at sixty five with a semi on your tail,
where will you go? the etiquette of the road
says you can leave the table anytime you want,
anytime you feel the world bearing down on you
to heavily, but you've got to have somewhere to go.
people die from not knowing where to go next,
from slow reaction time and two-lane blacktop gluttony,
in their fragile vehicles of feather and bone.

so talk to yourself, to your foot on the brake if you
must, but make it quick or you'll have a back seat
full of truck and never know the scatter and squawk
of a flock of blackbirds on the road's dark track.
remember: birds feeding on the highway almost
always fly up in time. they know some things
you don't: hunger for the road's a relative thing,
there are other directions than straight ahead,
it pays to have an eye on each side of your head.

so: that semi and you and the birds: everything
either behind you or before you as you come up
over the rise on this winding two-lane blacktop
country road at ten miles over the speed limit,
just the way you've traveled all your life, only
slightly out of control, wondering if it's true,
wondering if it's really true that birds feeding
on the highway almost always fly up in time.

Heart Tones

by Dan Guillory

You'd be fifteen now,
combing back your hair,
Dreaming of the mysterious
Whiteness of women's thighs,
Borrowing my shirts and socks,
Shyly avoiding the subject
Of love lost or unattainable.
    You'd have the sensitive ears
    Of a fox: the miraculous small
    Music of longing would flow
    Into the pure instrument
    Of your heart, breaking
    The silence of our lives
    With unmistakable tones.
On the day of your birth
(Also the day of your death)
I watched pathetically
As the nurse put radar
To your mother's belly
Panicking, shouting
I cannot hear the tones—
Where are the heart tones?
    My big red dream becomes
    A car and I give you the keys:
    We follow the river, the light,
    We're cruising into the globe
    Of sunset, flooded by the oldest
    Sound waves in the universe,
    The smallest crumbs of stars

    Igniting, resonating
    From the sonic zero of space.
I'm awake again at sunrise:
It's snowing, and the landscape—
Glazings of rivers and trees,
Brown birds bracketing the roadway—
Hangs together, moving in time
To the broken music of heart tones.

The Border

by David Jauss

The morning sun slants
    through the kitchen window
as I drink my coffee and listen

to Respighi answer the birdsong
    in the evergreens.
It's easy, sitting in the light

of a day not yet spoiled by failure,
    to forget the country half a world
and half a life away, where night

is just beginning, the sky
    over the Mekong River
bruised black as the border on a map,

dividing the world into darkness
    and light, the two
countries we're all citizens of.

But by the time I come home from work
    the border has crept up the yard
toward the hedge of honeysuckle
and I sit in a lawnchair at the edge
    of the shrunken light,
drink sweating in my hand, and brood

over the lie I told at lunch, the wrong
    I did a friend, the right gesture
that was too late to do anything

but hurt—all the petty failures
    of an average day—
until, for comfort, I call up

the larger shame that soldier felt,
    when I was him,
to see the light leaving

the eyes of the dead. I remind myself
    I have killed no one
today. But still the sky

darkens like a map drawn
    and redrawn on the same
soiled paper, each gradation

of darkness a further border,
    complicating location
and fear. To play music now

would be one more betrayal
    so I sit in silence made larger
by the cry of crickets. Then

the light is gone
    and I'm in that other country
where nothing is clear, where the border

is everywhere.

True Crime

by W. P. Kinsella
Chapter One from a novel in progress

The telephone call to 911 at the Amalgamated Six Towns Area Sheriff's Service and Emergency Response Center in Doreen Beach came in at 9:53 P.M. on Tuesday, March 31. The response office was located in the only brick building in the Six Towns area of Seven Towns County, Alberta, about sixty miles more-or-less west of Edmonton, Alberta, the capital of the province.

The only brick building in the Six Towns area of Seven Towns County had originally been the Doreen Beach Grocery Store, a store that had never been very successful, one of the reasons being that Doreen Beach, in spite of its name, was not a resort town, or even on a lake, as many surprised visitors found out each summer. In the days when there had been a railroad, Doreen Beach was named by the first station agent, R. Ebeneezer Beach, for his daughter Doreen.

After automobiles, and television and first graveled and then paved roads made small towns and villages obsolete, and made hamlets, which is what most small towns and villages were anyway, veritable anachronisms, and after seven consecutive would-be grocery store owners went broke, including a Bosworth from near to where the town of Fark used to be, a fellow who wore lavender scarves and had long, pale fingers, and male visitors who drove large, clean luxury automobiles, and arrived for the weekend carrying wine coolers and Judy Garland tapes, the brick building sat vacant for nearly eight years, being overgrown by blackberry vines, and becoming a home to raccoons, and sparrows, until Seven Towns County decided to use the building which had been seized by the county for back taxes, as its Emergency Response Center.

The final would-be store owner, a Cambodian refugee and her extended family, which comprised so many people they could have extended all the way back to Cambodia, cooked evil things on the stove in the back of the store, the odors driving away what few customers might have been inclined to deal there.

The Cambodians rapidly depleted the colony of wild cats, that had been started some fifty years before by a strange woman named Loretta Cake who lived in an abandoned cabin a mile down the road from Doreen Beach with about one hundred cats, and seemed to live off the land. The Cambodians not only ate the wild cats but all the stock in the store, and when everything was gone but a few pairs of work gloves and several cans of smokeless tobacco, they filled the gas tank of their beat-up car with the last of the gas from the single tall pump that had once been brightly painted but had now been weathered to a seagull-gray by the mean-spirited Alberta winters with their freeze-the-balls-off-a-brass-monkey blizzards that occurred with great regularity from September thru June of every year, and headed off in the direction of the Edmonton-Jasper Highway, never to be seen again.

That highway had, over the years, progressed from badly graveled, to fully graveled, to partially paved, to fully paved, to twined two lane fully paved in both directions, in all but a few stretches where the road was plain old two lane risk-your-life-on-the-curves, don't even think of driving Saturday night, two-way traffic, where in spring, which in Alberta is any day after June First when it doesn't snow, frost-heaves would shoot chunks of asphalt the size of a politician's ego, as high as four feet in the air, crushing the grill of many a car, and occasionally cracking a windshield.

* * *

When the emergency call came in, Tammy Oxendyne, the dispatcher for the Amalgamated Six Towns Area Sheriffs Service and Emergency Response Center, was engrossed in watching a rerun of *Dallas* on her portable TV. She was concentrating, a scowl on her face which was only about three feet from the surface of the TV set, on a scene where J.R. Ewing was just about to hop into bed with a pretty, young, starlet-looking bimbo. Tammy Oxendyne was wondering if the rerun was going to turn out the same as the original, because in the original when J.R. Ewing turned back the covers there was a snake there all curled up and hissing, a snake planted by his nasty wife Sue Ellen who just didn't appreciate J.R. one iota, and was unwilling to make allowances for the fact that men as rich and powerful as J.R. Ewing generally made their own rules, especially when it came to hopping into bed with pretty, young, starlet-looking bimbos.

Since Tammy Oxendyne had seen the original episode of *Dallas*, she knew for a fact that there was a snake under the covers, all curled up and hissing, or at least she strongly suspected it was there. You just couldn't always trust TV, Tammy had learned. But if that snake was there she sure wished she had a phone number where she could call up J.R. Ewing and give him a friendly warning. In fact, Tammy Oxendyne was so busy imagining that she did have that magic telephone number, and that J.R. Ewing was just now going to turn away from the bed and answer the telephone, that she could actually see him doing it.

"Yeah," J.R. Ewing said, and his eyes got wider and showed genuine worry as he listened to Tammy Oxendyne's warning.

"Well, I declare," J.R. went on. "I do thank you for saving my life. Just leave me you name and number and I'll send you a Cadillac first thing in the morning, and if I ever get to, where did you say you were callin' from? Seven Towns County, Alberta, why I will stop by personally to show you my gratitude, and you know how I generally show my gratitude."

"Oh, that would be wonderful," Tammy Oxendyne said to the TV set.

J.R. Ewing made a note of her address and phone number, then turned to the pretty, young, starlet-looking bimbo. "Don't go near that bed," he said to her. "That was Tammy Oxendyne from Seven Towns County, Alberta, and she says there's a snake under the covers there. I reckon Tammy Oxendyne just saved our lives."

Tammy Oxendyne was so engrossed in *Dallas,* and in her fantasy of saving J.R. Ewing's life, that the 911 Number rang six and a half times before she could tear herself away from the TV in order to answer it.

"Nine-one-one," said Tammy Oxendyne.

"Help! Help!" yelled a woman's voice. "I'm bein' murdered. I've been shot..."

"You just hold on a minute. I've got me an emergency here," said Tammy Oxendyne, who hadn't really heard the caller, being so involved with *Dallas,* and whether or not there would be a snake under the covers in the rerun like there had been in the original.

Later on, when the Royal Canadian Mounted Police reviewed the transcript of the 911 tape, there would be an interval of one minute and fifty seconds before Tammy Oxendyne came back on line. There had indeed been a snake under the covers in the rerun just like there had been in the original. Tammy Oxendyne couldn't help but wonder why a smart man like J.R Ewing wouldn't know that the second time round. It seemed to Tammy Oxendyne that finding a snake in among your bedclothes was some thing you'd be likely to remember. Only when a commercial came on featuring some Mexican golfer selling either hot sauce or potato chips, Tammy Oxendyne wasn't too sure which, did she remember that she had a caller on the 911 line.

"Now what can I do for you?" Tammy asked.

"Help! Help! I've been shot. I've locked myself in the bedroom but someone's trying to cut through the door with an ax."

In the background, Tammy Oxendyne could clearly hear loud pounding noises. She listened for a few seconds and decided that the background noise might indeed be the sound of an ax chopping at a door.

"Okay, now you give me your address, honey, and I'll send somebody around to check it out."

Tammy Oxendyne was known as a woman who always kept her cool. In fact that was the way Sheriff Claude Bopkin described her anytime someone asked how she was getting along as dispatcher for the Amalgamated Six Towns Area Sheriff's Service and Emergency Response Center.

The widow, Mrs. Beatrice Ann Birkland Stevenson Rasmussen, the elder stateswoman of the Six Towns area, said she thought there was a very fine line between always keeping your cool, and being stupid, and she said on more than one occasion, she suspected that Tammy Oxendyne fell on the stupid side of the line.

The reason Tammy Oxendyne had been appointed to the job of dispatcher for the Amalgamated Six Towns Area Sheriff's Service and Response Center was that the alternative was placing her on welfare. Seven Towns County, in which the surviving five of the original six towns were located, didn't have much of a welfare budget, and in Tammy Oxendyne of the Venusberg Oxendynes it had a separated woman with more children than someone of her intelligence should be allowed.

Seven Towns County also had no social service investigative personnel, and no one with any idea of how to track down the fellow who fathered Tammy Oxendyne's children, or at least most of them, a red-headed Ostapowich from over near Wildwood, who sometimes drove a school bus for Muskeg County, when he wasn't occupied by stealing from summer cabins along Purgatory Lake and the Pembina River.

If they didn't appoint Tammy Oxendyne to the position of dispatcher for the Amalgamated Six Towns Area Sheriff's Service and Emergency Response Center, why her welfare payments would have to come out of the snow plowing budget, and they would still have had to hire a dispatcher.

"What's your address, Honey?" Tammy Oxendyne said.

"1516 Nine Pin Road," the woman screamed.

Tammy Oxendyne wrote down, 1560 Nine Pin Road. Tammy wrote carefully, putting curlicues on the numbers and dotting the i's in Nine and Pin with hearts.

"Now is that the part of Nine Pin Road over by where the town of Fark used to be, or is that the part further north?"

"You're supposed to know where things are," the woman cried. "I'm just visiting here."

"You visitin' anybody I know, Honey?"

Tammy Oxendyne realized the sounds of the ax were getting louder.

"Just get somebody out here. I'm being murdered."

"Well, no need to get snippy," said Tammy Oxendyne. "We'll have somebody out there in a jiffy. Soon as I can locate somebody to answer the call and figure out which part of Nine Pin Road you're on. Y'all take care, now," she said cheerfully and hung up.

"You catch more flies with honey than with vinegar," said Tammy once the phone was back on the hook.

Tammy Oxendyne turned her attention back to the TV. As she watched "Next on Dallas." she decided she would definitely write to J.R. Ewing, just to let him know that beady-eyed little weasel, Cliff Barnes was planning to steal Ewing Oil right out from under him, if he wasn't careful.

Tammy Oxendyne pressed down on the microphone button and said what she always said when she needed Sheriff Claude Bopkin or his deputy Morgana Sigurdson, who was part of the Red Sigurdson clan from over by where Fark used to be. Morgana Sigurdson, as far as Tammy Oxendyne knew, was the only Red Sigurdson in Seven Towns County to hold a job for our generations.

"Is anybody out there?" Tammy Oxendyne said.

And, as usually happened when Tammy Oxendyne asked that question, she didn't get any answer.

Tammy Oxendyne knew that this time of night, Sheriff Claude Bopkin would be in the Donut Shoppe in Sangudo (pronounced Shop-pay by local residents), drinking coffee, eating chocolate-coconut donuts, and flirting with whatever waitress was on duty, unless it was Jeannine McClintock, who looked like a bulldog and wasn't quite as friendly.

And since it was after nine o'clock, Morgana Sigurdson's boyfriend Eddie Lakusta would have finished work at the potato warehouse in Venusberg, and would now be riding along with Morgana, and they'd be parked somewhere on the beach of Purgatory Lake, both of them probably mostly naked, and by now some parts of their writhing bodies had probably turned down the volume on the police radio.

The TV show starring Jane Wyman was coming on. Tammy Oxendyne didn't like that one; it was about grape growers in godless California. Jane Wyman should have quit while she was married to that nice man, Donald O'Connor who made all those movies with the chimpanzee, or at least after she made the movie *Johnny Belinda.* Now there was a movie.

Since she couldn't raise Sheriff Claude Bopkin or his deputy, Morgana Sigurdson, Tammy Oxendyne picked up the telephone, not the 911 line, but the Sheriff's Office line, and after trying for several minutes to find the Sangudo Donut Shoppe in the white pages of the phone book, gave up because she couldn't remember its exact name, though she tried looking all through the D's. She then looked in the yellow pages under restaurants and after five minutes or so discovered that it was called Al's Donut Shoppe, which Tammy decided was reasonable since the owners name was Al Rasmussen, one of the sons of the widow, Mrs. Beatrice Ann Birkland Stevenson Rasmussen, the elder stateswoman of the Six Towns area. She dialed.

"Al's Donut Shoppe."

"That you, Jeanetta?"

"No. This is Holly."

"Holly Chalupa?"

"No. Holly Dwerynchuk. Who's this?"

"This here's Tammy Oxendyne down at the Sheriff's Office in Doreen Beach."

"Oh, Hi," said Holly Dwerynchuk. "Gee, it's a coincidence you should call. Ben Ostapowich was just in here. He's your old man's brother isn't he?"

"Yeah. But him and my old man haven't been on good terms for years. He got drunked up one night must have been seven, no, let's see, my Imogene was just a baby, so six years ago, and drove our car off the pier into Purgatory Lake. Say, by the way, does the Sheriff Bopkin happen to be there?"

"Yeah," said Holly Dwerynchuk, "but you better give him a minute, he's in the john. Besides I just refilled his coffee."

"Well it's kind of important. But, say, what was Ben Ostapowich doin' in there? I thought he was workin' the oil fields down Drayton valley way."

The sheriff, Claude Bopkin, wasn't exactly a sheriff, though he liked to be called sheriff, and there was nothing in his job description to stop people from calling him sheriff. In fact there was hardly anybody in Seven Towns County who didn't refer to Claude Bopkin as Sheriff Bopkin, though if someone wanted to be nasty about it, and throw something up in his face, maybe because they'd been given a traffic citation for driving too slow, like the widow, Mrs. Beatrice Ann Birkland Stevenson Rasmussen, the elder stateswoman of the Six Towns area ("Land sakes, I'm eighty-four years old, how fast do you expect me to drive?"), could cause him genuine humiliation by referring to him by his official title, which was Town Constable.

Everybody in Seven Towns County, except real sticklers for detail, the kind of people who would correct your grammar at a house party, referred to Claude Bopkin as Sheriff Bopkin.

The widow, Mrs. Beatrice Ann Birkland Stevenson Rasmussen, the elder stateswoman of the Six Towns Area, who was the widow of Earl J. Rasmussen who, at least before she was married to him, lived alone in the hills south of New Oslo with about six hundred sheep and was known to recite *Casey at the Bat* at the top of his lungs at any gathering of more than two people, even if one of the two was Earl J. Rasmussen.

Earl J. Rasmussen especially enjoyed reciting at box socials, sports days, whist drives, or ethnic weddings, in the days before box socials, sports days, whist drives, and ethnic weddings became obsolete as small towns, and box socials and whist drives disappeared altogether, while sports days became something attended once a year by athletically inclined high school students, and ethnic weddings went high tech and were generally held as far away from the Six Towns Area as Onoway and Devil's Lake, where, since the bride and groom were most likely young, they generally hired a band made up solely of percussion instruments played by long-haired screamers, who set the Onoway High School Gymnasium, or the Devil's Lake Pavillion to shaking right down to its foundations, so that the people old enough to know what a schottische or polka, or the *Blue Skirt Waltz* was, or who loved a good, fat accordion player, and knew the twang of a dobro, went home as soon as the foundation started shaking, which is what the young people wanted anyway.

Claude Bopkin had been hired as town constable and Morgana Sigurdson as assistant town constable for Seven Towns County, which was located sixty miles more-or-less west of Edmonton, Alberta, the capital of the province of Alberta, a city of three-quarters of a million people, with an oil and agriculture based economy.

Seven Towns County, which was described, no doubt by a bureaucrat with too much education, as rhombus-shaped, was very much a backwoods county, one of the poorest counties in the province of Alberta, sparsely populated, with land too stony and worthless for successful farming, and with too little timber to be of any value to logging companies, so the land in Seven Towns County was generally occupied by people who ended up there by accident and stayed on because they feared the next place they moved might be worse. Some of them bought land from a leafy-green brochure that appealed to city people who had the vague and ill-conceived idea that there was some pleasure in country living.

Seven Towns County was also occupied by the descendants of the original immigrants, who by the bad luck of the draw, had been assigned to the stony and worthless land around Purgatory Lake and the Six Towns area, instead of the rich, black farmland of Eastern Alberta, or the timber-rich land further north and west, where they scratched out a living grazing a few cattle, raising a few pigs, and generally withdrawing into poverty and everything that goes with it.

The original immigrants had come, many from Norway, a few from the Ukraine, the odd one from Germany or England, and many from the United States, some via Norway or Sweden. Many landed in the Six Towns area during the great Depression, where they endured not just financial misery, but total poverty pinned them to the land like insects to a slab of cork board.

By the time the great Depression ended and the economy of the Six Towns area improved from total poverty to just plain financial misery, most of the residents had put down as deep a roots as was possible in that stony and worthless land, and they either couldn't afford to move, or simply found it too much trouble.

Sheriff Claude Bopkin had no experience with law enforcement, but he had from his earliest childhood a fascination with uniforms. He had grown up in Edmonton, Alberta, in a section of the city known as North Edmonton, underneath a huge green water tower that looked like the cloud that rose over Hiroshima after the atomic bomb went off, only the cloud-shaped water tower was painted apple green.

His mother, Flavella Bopkin worked as the gate guard at the nearby Swift's Packing Plant. Flavella Schwartz Bopkin had her own private little booth behind the twelve-foot chainlink gates of Swift's Packing Plant. She unlocked and opened the gates personally every morning at 7:00 A.M., and all day she sat on a tall stool in her little gatehouse and checked in and out every commercial vehicle that entered or exited Swift Packing Plant property: the farm trucks loaded with pigs or cattle or sheep that entered and drove around back to the livestock pens, and the big red trucks with white lettering that pulled out every day filled with fresh meat for the grocery stores, butcher shops, and department stores, as well as packaged bacon, ham, wieners and lunch meat.

Flavella Bopkin's favorite drivers were the ones who, on the way out, their trucks packed full of fresh meat products, took time to slip her a package of wieners, or a pound of bacon, or a package of macaroni and cheese loaf, saying as they did so, "You feed those growing boys of yours good now."

The drivers knew that Flavella Bopkin was a war widow, whose husband, Bob Bopkin, had gone missing in action toward the end of the Korean War. Not exactly killed, just sort of misplaced, was how the apologetic Canadian Army described what had happened to her husband, Bob Bopkin.

Bob Bopkin had been stationed in Korea, and had seen some action from which he survived unscathed. He was due for a furlough, the apologetic Army explained, but there was no record of him ever going on that furlough. Private First Class Bob C. Bopkin just sort of vanished from Army records, as well as from the face of the earth, the apologetic Army explained. Since there was no indication that Private First Class Bob C. Bopkin was dead, and since he wasn't officially classified as missing, and since there wasn't any place to desert to in Korea, and since the apologetic Army didn't have any classification for Misplaced, the apologetic Army kept on paying her husband's pitiful Army salary to Flavella Bopkin, who wasn't exactly a widow, but certainly didn't have a husband.

Even now, some forty years later, the long-retired Flavella Bopkin still received Private First Class Bob C. Bopkin's pitiful salary from the apologetic Army. Even though Bob C. Bopkin, if he were alive, would now be 72 years old and retired from the Army about thirty years, the army was apparently too embarrassed over misplacing Private First Class Bob C. Bopkin during the Korean War, and also afraid that there might be some legal repercussions if they tried to alter the situation, that they though the best thing they could do was continue to pay his pitiful Army salary to his wife for her lifetime.

As far as Claude Bopkin was concerned while he was growing up, the best thing about Flavella Bopkin's job as Gatekeeper at Swift's Packing Plant, even better than the free wieners and bacon and macaroni and cheese loaf, was that his mother got to wear a uniform.

Claude Bopkin thought he remembered, though he wasn't too sure, his father standing over his crib, a cigarette in the corner of his mouth, his army uniform the color and consistency of weather stripping, staring down at Claude. There wasn't much to like about his father's uniform, but Flavella Schwartz Bopkin's uniform was another matter. It was made of a fine, brown shiny material, with dark red epaulets on the shoulders, and a beautiful cap with a brim that made her look like an airline pilot, and brown boots with two-inch Cuban heels and a dark red stripe down each side.

When he got old enough to travel by bus after school, Claude Bopkin would ride one of the cream-and-red Edmonton Transit System trolley buses up a diagonal street called Kingsway, a street that originally had another name, but got renamed in honor of the visit of King George and Queen Elizabeth in 1939, to the Edmonton Municipal Airport, where he would stand around the small waiting room and watch as the pilots in their shiny blue uniforms would get out of their taxis and walk across the lobby of the airport to a mysterious door marked Personnel Only. Little Claude Bopkin would stride along behind each arriving pilot, mimicking his walk.

Sometimes when he came home after school, with his mother at work and his older brother Gunther off playing hockey at the North Edmonton Community League rink, he would lay out his mother's extra uniform on the floor in the living room of their small apartment, then lay down on it, his arms and legs appropriately spread–eagled. As he grew older and larger, he eventually tried the uniform on, enjoying the exhilarating warmth of it, enjoying the thrill of illicit contact, experiencing his first sexual awakenings.

Little Claude Bopkin kept a scrapbook full of pictures of people in uniform, military, police, milkmen, firemen, mail carriers, crossing guards. He was particularly impressed with a photo from a travel brochure of a Bahamian; it was unclear if he was military, police, of just someone playing dress-up for the tourists, but the starched white uniform with the white military cap, and the ice-blue sash that ran diagonally from shoulder to waist, made Claude Bopkin's blood scamper like hamsters through his veins, and his not-quite-understood sexual longings cry out like small animals lost in the night.

Back at Al's Donut Shoppe, where the owner, Al Rasmussen, and most of the customers pronounced the *pe* at the end of the final word, though they pronounced it *pay*, Sheriff Claude Bopkin finally emerged from the john.

"You need to call you office, Claude," Holly Dwerynchuk said, as he was making his way back to his favorite table by the window.

"I'll head out to the car as soon as I finish my coffee," said Sheriff Claude Bopkin, who was dressed in a powder-blue uniform without a blemish on it, the trousers creased until you could scythe your weeds with them, whether Sheriff Claude Bopkin was in them or not.

Sheriff Bopkin loved to have a style-your-hair, pick-the-lint-out-of-your-sideburns shine on his genuine right-out-of-the-catalog, police issue boots, but he found the shine difficult to maintain without often getting stains and blemishes on his powder-blue uniform, a uniform he'd had custom made, at his own expense, using as a model a tuxedo Elvis Presley had worn in the movie *Blue Hawaii*.

What Sheriff Claude Bopkin eventually did to solve the stains and blemishes problem was to go to a shoemaker in Sangudo, a Cambodian, probably but not certainly a cousin of the unsuccessful storekeeper at Doreen Beach who, with his extended family, made the cat colony first started by Loretta Cake over fifty years ago an endangered species. Sheriff Claude Bopkin had that Cambodian shoemaker cover his genuine right-out-of-the-catalog, police issue shoes, with gleaming black patent leather, which the sheriff maintained by wiping them down with lemon-scented Handi-wipes each time after he had to walk through dust, or mud, or dewy grass. In order to cut down on the frequency of maintenance on his shoes Sheriff Bopkin tried to spend most of his day in his office at Doreen Beach, or at Al's Donut Shoppe at Sangudo.

"Tammy said you should hurry it up," said Holly Dwerynchuk, "She says some woman up on Nine Pin Road is yelling bloody murder about a prowler."

Sheriff Claude Bopkin washed down the last of the chocolate-coconut donut with the last of his heavily creamed coffee.

"I reckon I'll be off to do my duty," he said.

In the patrol car, after settling himself behind the wheel, wiping traces of dust and grime off his shoes, fastening his seat belt, starting the motor and releasing the hand brake—Sheriff Bopkin wanted to be ready to take off, wheels screeching, rubber burning, in pursuit of whatever evil lay waiting out there in Seven Towns County—he picked up the microphone.

"Hey, Tammy, was you trying to reach me?"

Sheriff Claude Bopkin was thirty-five years old, 5'9" tall, and weighed a solid 180 lbs. His black, well-oiled hair supported his powder-blue military cap, and kept it a full inch from any part of his scalp at all times. Sheriff Bopkin had deep-set eyes and a button nose. He imagined that he looked considerably like Elvis Presley, and he even fantasized sometimes that Elvis Presley was his real father, that his mother, Flavella Schwartz Bopkin had come in intimate contact with the King. To that end, Sheriff Bopkin always made a point of saying Ma'am and Sir, softly and politely, especially when his was on police business, the way the King, or any proud relative of the King, or even a fantasized relation of the King would be bound to do.

For once Tammy Oxendyne was paying attention to the radio.

"Yeah, Claude, we got a call up on Nine Pin Road. Some snippy woman wantin' rush service. You know what these city people are like, they figure they can order us around just 'cause we live in the country."

"Gimme the address and I'll go take a look," said Sheriff Claude Bopkin.

Tammy Oxendyne read him the number she had written down, 1560 Nine Pin Road.

"She didn't even know whether it was on the part of Nine Pin Road over by where Fark used to be, or whether it was on the stretch further north. Said she was visitin' someone. But when I asked who, she got downright unfriendly."

"Well, I'll take a look."

Sheriff Bopkin had, while struggling with his pen, trying to get the dome light in the patrol car to stay on, and listening to Tammy's conversation, written down 1516 Nine Pin Road, an error which turned out for the moment to be fortunate, for that was the correct address.

Sheriff Bopkin knew that the 1500 numbers on Nine Pin Road, were on what Tammy Oxendyne had referred to as the stretch further north. Nine Pine Road had been named by an original Norwegian settler, because there were a row of eight pine trees along the road allowance in front of his property, and even in Norwegian Nine Pine Road sounded better than Eight Pine Road. That Norwegian settler's relatives in Norway either didn't see or didn't recognize the "e" at the end of Pin, and addressed the Norwegian settler's mail to him c/o Fark Post Office, Nine Pin Road, Alberta, Canada, and either the postmaster at Fark or some other bureaucrat in the post office somewhere entered that address in some sort of official Post Office record book, and before the poor old Norwegian settler knew it, he was living on Nine Pin Road and there was nothing he could do about it. Sheriff Claude Bopkin, when he thought about the Nine Pin Road story, always recalled a motto which he thought belonged to either Alcoholics Anonymous, or the Six Towns Area Sewing Circle and Temperance Society. Though he could never recall the whole motto it had something to do with *accept the things you cannot change*, which was certainly the right attitude to have when dealing with the Post Office.

The north fork of Nine Pin Road was a pretty isolated area, which had been abandoned by its few resident farm families shortly after the end of the second world war, and with good reason, for the stony and worthless land was barely suitable for grazing, let alone raising crops for generating any appreciable income. Also, each spring, after at least nine months of winter, something called Jamie O'Day Creek flooded every spring for several weeks, making the north fork of Nine Pin Road more inaccessible than it was already.

On the one of two farms in that area the farm buildings slowly rotted back into the earth, and Nine Pin Road, which wasn't a real road anyway, but only a trail with a name, filled up with aspen and birch saplings, and the beginning of red willow clumps.

The farm houses, which were generally built stronger and sturdier than the farm buildings, weathered and sagged and became sanctuary for raccoons, and skunks, birds of all ilks, and bats, while the houses themselves remained relatively unscathed because they were so far back in the bush they couldn't be conveniently reached by vandals.

Mother

by Ted Kooser

She says she sleeps so little,
three hours a night, no more than that.
It troubles her. Sometimes, she says,
she lies in bed all night
and listens to the call-in talk-shows
though the people who phone in
are mostly stupid and upset her.

She doesn't say the early morning hours
are like her sewing basket,
chock-full of spools of every shade,
a rainbow of silk. Once she selects
a thread she may then begin
to unwind her way into the past,
a different memory at every inch,
until, somewhere, so many years ago,
there is that perfect peace
like sleep, a naked spool.

Interrogations

by Paul Lake

I

Let's start with the noisemaker's fife:
Trumpet, trombone, or oboe shaped,
It looks festive almost, like a horn,
Though your fingers are kept in their place
By a close fitting grip, and screwed down
Till they're locked into the fingerboard.
Imagine walking though your hometown
With that collar locked under your chin
And your fingers clamped in its vice
And the neighborhood children all laughing
And dancing as if to the tune
Of a vagrant Pied Piper too gay
To stop twiddling the stops or remove
The brass instrument from his mouth,
whatever his current condition
Or the mood of the gathering crowd.

II

What droll imaginations men had
To carve stocks out of iron and wood
In the shape of an instrument and
Then call it a neck violin
Or shrew's fiddle, to lock women up
So it looked like they fingered its strings.
What a jig those old girls must have stepped
At the end of a chain when dragged home.

Or should one give too much rein
To her tongue, she might suddenly find
Her head slapped in a cast iron mask
In the shape of a bird's or boar's head,
An iron bulb forced between her teeth
Like a bit in a horse's mouth,
And the shape of her world metamorphosed
By that grillwork to something grotesque.

III

What did men think a body was
To be treated like that. Where was soul,
So much spoken of, if not somewhere
In the fleshes interstices
They burned, flogged, or pierced with suc
pride,
As if rooting out of its lair?
How trivial, how undignified
Even death must seem in a broze bull
That's heated until, roasting inside,
A voice cries out in agony,
And bronze lips, to the frenzied delight
Of the crowd, howl, belch, bellow, and bray
Like a tormented animal.

IV

Death wasn't their object, nor pain,
Nor confession, whatever they said,
Those doctors and inquisitors of
Our being's dark underground chambers.
Why string a man upside down
To saw him in half through the groin
If not to assure that some blood

Might to continue to flow to the brain
To let him perceive all he can?
Why stake a man down to the ground
And then open him up with a knife
Just enough to clamp viscera
To a drum and then slowly turn,
If not to let mind reflect on
That unraveling knot, human life?

V

Rack, screw, Judas cradle, cat's paw-
The whole Medieval science of pain
Now seems paradoxical,
Recalling how such things were born
To crush the heretical doctrine
That matter and spirit remain
Locked in perpetual war
And the body's so radically evil
That the soul must annul each dark cell.
What could those good fathers have done
To convince a heretical soul
Of God's love of his perfect creation
Except crush his bones under a wheel
Then weave the pulped limps through its spokes
Before hoisting him up on a pole
To survey all His wonderful works?

VI

God himself set the precedent for
Every future inquisitor,
Argued one Ludovico, when He
Tried our first parents secretly,
Expelling them both from the garden,

Thereby seizing their worldly possessions,
Then condemning then always to wear
Fig leaves, like a green sanbenito,
Before handing them over to hell
To be purified in its fire.
St. Thomas himself theorized
That the purpose of man's resurrection
Was to make both out sorrow and joy
More intense, since in order to feel
Either pleasure or pain to perfection,
Souls need bodies as sounding boards.

VII

What could such a God mean to us
From his throne in impregnable heaven
Looking down on the torturer's prod,
Slaps, questions, the gun to the head,
And the victim's inscrutable writhings,
As He hovered above the world,
Sole witness, secure in the knowledge
Of his own immortality?
What hasty theological shotgun
Wedding of the spirit to flesh
Could effect a reconciliation
Of such a One to this variable world
He's supposed to have made and called good,
Unless mocked, beaten and crucified,
He were finally, irrevocably left
Nameless, faceless, staring up at the sky,
Without credence, credentials, or creed
Among the other abandoned dead
On the road to the torture house.

Mabel: A Life in Four Scenes

by Jean C. Lee

Portrait of Mabel and Bernice,
Found in a Blue Velvet Family Album

Sepia, formal, posed: Mabel is head and shoulders taller than Bernice, eleven, maybe twelve. She is rounding into womanhood. Bernice the mischievous one, the sly darling, coy and cute, appears about to toss her chestnut curls and run away, tethered only by a trick of light to her bland sister. Mabel wears a white waist, a black velvet ribbon winds about her neck. Not ugly, but homely: pale colorless hair, face and features broad and round. Her eyes small, undistinctive; lips large, too soft somehow. Placid as a cow.

"I always tricked her into giving me the hair ribbons I wanted," Bernice would twitter years and years later. "Aunt Fanny always thought Mabel should wear blue. 'I want the pink, I want the pink,' I'd say. Then Mabel would say, 'Let her have the pink,' and Ma and Fanny'd think me greedy, so they'd give me the blue, which is what I wanted anyhow."

"Oh that old story," Mabel once laughed. "Bernice never knew I really wanted the pink."

Christmas, 1952

Two clear glass jars of mints: one white, one pink, marked xxxx, like kisses. The white are Esten's, the pink Mabel's . Mabel grabs a pot holder, pulls open the oven door of the big black cookstove. The chickens she slaughtered and dressed for Christmas dinner are sputtering and golden. Mince pies perch on the warming shelf. "Please, Aunt Mabel," her grandniece asks, "can, *may* I have a mint, a pink one?" Mabel goes to the side cupboard, opens the jar, gives her one. She watches the copper-haired girl skip away. Bright as a penny, Mabel thinks. She's made her a pink dress for Christmas, trimmed with pockets and tatted lace. Whoever said redheads shouldn't wear pink?

Nearly her entire family is here for Christmas: Bernice and George; their daughter, Ardythe, and Ardythe's two kids. Her brothers, Raymond, Paul, and Harvey. Raymond's stopped his traveling, opened a hatchery on the home farm. He takes care of Paul and Harvey now; she doesn't have to do that anymore. Esten doesn't much care for her family, but he doesn't say anything. He's gone out to do the evening chores. Her grandniece has laid aside the set of doll china and plays with her brother, with his new toy tow truck. They wind the winch up and down, up and down. She no longer wonders what it would be like to have kids of her own. She watches Paul, hair graying now, still happy and innocent as a child. He fingers the shirt she gave him, smiles shyly at her. Sometimes when just the two of them are alone, he'll talk to her. Harvey, only forty-two inches tall, a man as small as a child.

He sits in the lowest chair she has; his feet still dangle. He enjoys the children, even when they ask to see how tall they are compared to him. He looks happy, too. It has been a good Christmas; she is thankful for her family.

Mabel Wins First Prize at the Chippewa County Home Extension Art Exhibit for Her Painting of the Clark Family Sugar Bush

Mabel is embarrassed, disgusted almost. She'd only entered the painting because it was the only new one she'd done in the past three years. And here were the judges exclaiming about how it was a real find, some sort of primitive, like a Grandma Moses. Foolish college professor talk. Grandma Moses, indeed. She'd painted it from memory, couldn't get the perspective right. It was as if the perspective, like the memory, kept slipping away. And the colors were wrong, muddy, the paint too thick. They should see her paintings at home, the woodland scenes, the soaring mountains, the ones she'd copied from books. They wouldn't call her a primitive then.

She dipped her brush back into the cadmium blue. A pretty color for the baby doll's eyes. Her grandniece watched attentively. "We'll make your dolly's face like new again," she told the girl. "But you'll have to let her dry for a day or two." Her grandniece picked up a blue crayon, drew two small circles on the paper in front of her, then picked up a black crayon, drew a smaller circle toward the top of those, an arch over both. She held the paper in front of her, scrutinizing her marks. She turned it toward Mabel. "Is this how you draw eyes?" she asked. Mabel looked into four big, very blue eyes. Maybe the girl would be an artist. It was too early to tell; no one should push her.

The Workhorse Fails

Workhorse, Mabel thought, that's what her sister, Bernice, sometimes said. He only married you so he would have another workhorse on the farm. And what did Bernice know? When Ma died, it wasn't Bernice that had to give up her life; she'd had a beau. Bernice has a beau, Aunt Fanny and Pa had said. She'll be getting married soon. So Mabel, good old dependable Mabel, she'd cancelled her classes at the Normal School in Menominee, stayed home to take care of Pa and the boys: Raymond beginning to wander; poor Paul, an idiot since that accident in the barn, hardly able to take care of himself; and Harvey, a dwarf, trying to take care of himself by signing up with a sideshow. And Pa, that sickness he'd take, not able to see anyone, not able to talk. Well, she reminded herself: it was only right. She wasn't bitter then, not much, and she had no reason to be bitter now. She'd been foolish then, thinking Floyd was going to be her beau. She'd cut the pages out of her diary, and she'd cut the possibility out of her mind. She took care. And after Pa died and Raymond came back and started the hatchery, Esten took her on, took her as his wife. Bernice had said, you got to watch out for those old Norwegian bachelor farmers, they're stingy as the dickens. But Bernice had George, two nice kids, grandkids down the road. How could she know? Mabel was too old to have children, but she sure could use the company. And maybe Esten was a little stingy sometimes; nothing wrong with being parsimonious. She lifted the handle of the hay wagon. Sure is hot today. Must be the heat is giving her those dizzy spells. She pulls on the handle. Blasted wagon is heavy. She pulls harder, harder, trying to budge the load. She feels the blood rise like a song to her brain. Workhorse, workhorse, a chorus of angels, she imagines. The clouds are like ribbons. A soft explosion: gray and pink and cerulean blue.

An Arch of Birches

by Joseph Maiolo

As Ingrid answered the telephone, she had a moment's premonition when at first she could hear no one on the line. Then she heard a word—"Mom?"—like a sound from her usually meek self, and her inner voice wanted to say, Hello, you.

"Chris?"

The small voice cleared on the other end. "Yes."

"What is it? What's wrong?"

"Yukon went out this morning, and he hasn't come back all day."

There was no fear in his voice, but since he seldom spoke his mind she knew better than to trust the absence. "Did you go looking for him?"

"I've looked all morning."

"And you didn't see him at all?"

"No."

"Well, try not to worry too much. He'll probably show up. You know how he likes to run around the edge of the lake. He's probably chasing some animal or something."

"I think a hunter shot him."

She felt the hairs on the back of her neck move. "What?" Then what he had said registered. "You mean they're hunting out there?"

"Deer season started this morning."

She gripped the telephone with both hands. "Now, I want you to listen to me, Chris. Please. Are you calling from the inn?"

"Yes, but I want to go back to the cottage now."

She thought about the men out there with guns. "No. Wait there. I'll be right out."

"I want to go back."

She heard that unsaid thing in his voice and knew that staying there was no good. "Well, walk the road. Don't go looking for the dog in the woods."

There was no answer.

"Chris? Do you hear me? Will you promise me that?"

"Okay."

There was a bare click on the other end, and she saw him in her mind walking the mile along the road, alone in his green jacket. Only her last-minute insistence that Chris take the dog with him...but now the dog was lost.

She dialed Mark's number and let it ring several times before a demure voice came on: "Yes?"

"This is" –she hesitated–" Ingrid. Is Mark there?"

"He's outside or in the garage."

"Please get him for me."

"Is anything wrong?"

"I must talk to him."

"Just a minute, please."

She waited, thinking of the trim-figured...girl, padding barefoot through the living room and out patio doors to the deck, calling Mark, it's for you. But then Mark was on the line before she could complete the picture.

"Did you know it was hunting season?"

"My God, no, Is Chris–?"

"He's all right," she said. "He just called. The dog is lost. He says he thinks a hunter might have shot him."

"What!"

"He didn't find it dead or anything, but he hasn't seen it since this morning. He says they've been shooting out there all morning." She waited, as if she had put a question to him.

"I can't imagine a hunter shooting a *dog*." He paused. "I guess I'd better go out there and see about it."

"No. I want to bring him home myself." She began to twist the telephone cord around her finger. "Did you know they were hunting out there?"

"No, I didn't, Ingrid. I don't always know everything."

"But you encouraged him to go out there alone for the night."

"He asked me if he could, and frankly I thought it would be good for him." There was a muffled cough. "I thought he didn't want the dog with him."

"He's only fourteen," Ingrid said. "I thought he needed company."

"Well, maybe he knew hunting season was starting today. I certainly didn't."

She didn't want Mark in on this anymore just now, and she certainly couldn't deal with his take-charge manner about to surface. "Did he have a gun with him?"

"Just his pellet gun."

"Would he go hunting with that?"

"A pellet gun!"

"Whatever."

"You can't kill a deer with it, Ingrid."

She started to ask him how he knew so much if he didn't even know it was hunting season; instead she asked him how he got to the phone so fast if he was in the garage.

He sighed. "It's a cordless. I keep it out here with me."

"How nice." And she pressed the button to kill the line.

One day last year Mark had come home from his dental office and said that he was tired of looking into other people's mouths for a living. Ingrid was in the dining room, trying to write a paper in linguistics, one of the last barriers to her degree. She'd just had an argument with her daughter, Karen, about watching television when she was supposed to be fixing dinner.

"I wish you'd have thought about that a long time ago, before you invested eight years in school while I invested six in trying dresses on middle-aged women." She laughed, trying as an afterthought to deflate what she'd said.

"I didn't say I was going to quit. I just said I was tired."

She watched as he walked into the kitchen and began joking with Karen, who after a while began to laugh. Ingrid bristled as she heard Karen say something about

"Mom's messes," and the two of them snickering. But she kept silent and went back to writing her paper.

A week later, a Friday, he didn't come home after work but called, saying he was having a few drinks with some friends and would be home later.

When he got there, Ingrid was sitting at the kitchen table, stacked with books and papers.

"Where are the kids?" he said.

"Karen's staying with a friend. Chris is in his room." Then she added, "And I know the house is a mess."

He said a few things not amounting to much, and then he said, sighing, "I don't know. Sometimes it just gets to be too much," and he looked out the window, letting his weight fall against the counter.

"You ought to try doing this...this *algebra*," she said, referring to her linguistics paper she was proofreading at last and had come to loathe. But it didn't work to lighten the moment, and she felt compromised that she'd tried. So, slamming a book closed, she stood up and asked him what he really wanted to say.

He told her that she had become slovenly, always in jeans and sloppy clothes, always going to school, to meetings. She'd even stopped wearing make-up. His voice rose to a shout, as he berated her even for things he had seemed before to enjoy.

A fury rose in her, and she screamed at him. Slovenly! Make-up! When at long last she had found out how to relax, when after all the years of treating his profession as the main, the *only*, thing in this family, she thought that she could at last just be herself.

"Self, self, self!" he'd said. "I'm sick and tired of the word. Do you think my profession defines *me* ?"

By then she was crying, screaming and crying, and she hit him, hard on the face.

It was what he wanted, of course, for then the truth began to come out little by little, until he spilled everything about him and his receptionist and left for good. It was an argument she'd read so many versions of over the last few years, she felt almost silly that they had had it. Her life had become a magazine cliché.

But then it hit her hard. She felt like a woman lost, lost and drowning in a lake with no shore.

***

At the Loon Lake Inn, a beer-and-eats joint where the blacktop ended, she saw the trucks, already loaded with the carcasses of deer whose eyes were frozen sad, tongues lolling out of their mouths like sausages, their bellies slit and empty. She passed other trucks and their jolly, serious men on her way in, their kill strapped to their trucks' hoods and the inevitable gun rack behind them. Hunters walked the road and woods on each side, holding their guns in the crooks of their arms, stalking wearily in the snow in their Day-Glo orange suits.

When she arrived at the cottage, which they'd agreed to use on alternate weeks until Mark could buy her out ("I've given you the house; the cottage ought to be mine," he maintained), and with strict rules about leaving it devoid of the other's belongings, she found Chris idling with a stick at the edge of the woods. A rifle report sounded in the distance, and she motioned him to come away from there. They went into the cottage, a house really, done in natural woods and with all the comforts. It lacked only a telephone, a convenience they had all agreed would be an intrusion, back when they had been a family. A large picture window in the living room gave a view onto an expanse of the lake, with a small island off to the right. Looking into other people's mouths had been pretty good to them after all.

"Now tell me what happened, Chris."

"I told you." He stood in the middle of the room as if there was nothing more to say. But then he added, turning his head and with a catch in his voice, "He went out this morning, and he never came back."

"Did he sleep in with you last night, Chris?" She tried to go to him, but he moved away.

"Yes." He seemed embarrassed. "I *told* you I didn't want to bring him."

"But, Chris, why not? You always wanted him with you." Then it occurred to her that he might have known it was hunting season, that he didn't want the dog with him because he knew something might happen. It made her feel guilty for having insisted. "Did you know it was deer season?"

He said he didn't, but not convincingly. He'd been secretive lately, poring over thick gun catalogues, reading all the hunting magazines he could get. She'd read about the gun craze of boys and how it would pass when the attraction of girls replaced it, but Mark had never been any help at all in such matters. He just said that some boys liked guns and some didn't, that he'd never understood the appeal himself, but then that maybe Chris was different, it would all work out okay.

She asked Chris to get Yukon's leash, and they got in the car and began to drive the roads. She told him to roll down the window and call, she'd do the same on her side. They did this awhile, yelling "Yuuu-kon," but after thirty minutes or so she saw the futility and thought that maybe Chris would be better off back home for now. He'd already tried for most of the day.

"Why would anyone want to shoot a *dog*?" she said, trying to put the right mixture of ire and sympathy into her voice, "And why would you think that someone did?"

Chris looked ahead as he answered. "If a dog tracks a deer during deer season, a hunter can shoot it."

"Who says so?"

"It's a law."

She looked at him. It had sounded as if he were saying that it was a law he agreed with, and she dared not question him on it. What would she find out, that her son was on the side of the hunter? Was the instinct so strong in him that even the loss of his pet could be tolerated if that's the way it was? But there had been a time when their positions were reversed. She had never been particularly squeamish before about the taking of animal life to sustain that of human. All meat had grim drama behind it: the beheaded chicken, the flopping tuna, the sledge blow or bullet to the head of a cow or hog. Never a disdainer of meat herself, she had always put the matter up to necessity. And when Chris was younger, he was always on the side of the quarry. Why, when he found out what veal was, he gave a little sermon that ruined dinner. And lamb! He'd taken to bleating as he pushed the shopping cart by the meat counter. She hadn't wanted him to be that way; he had to be tough for the ever-hardening world. But now that he had come around so completely, she was sad that he had. Oh, when had his love turned to its absence, and why did men track and kill when there was no longer any reason?

So she decided to talk it through, as if they were discussing the facts of hunting, which perhaps they were. Chris was a book of knowledge; the only thing was that, until then, she had thought that he was only a reader on the subject.

"Why would the law allow a hunter to do that?"

"A dog can run a deer to death, or attack it and kill it if it's hungry."

She could stand it no longer. "And what is the hunter going to do to the deer?"

"Shoot it."

That's all he said: *Shoot it.*

She started to argue against the modern killing-to-put-meat-on-the-table fallacy, but she knew now that she was on delicate ground. Her sensitive son, a reader, had had his head turned by the sound of the hunter's horn. He wasn't talking about necessity; he was taken with the *sport*. He'd suffered the loss of his dog, a Siberian husky of such beauty that even Ingrid, no lover of domestic animals, had become awed by its presence. But now she was implicated in that loss. It wasn't just that she insisted that Yukon be with Chris; somehow it was tied to Mark and her increasing responsibility to the boy. But she'd fix it: she'd find the dog, or the hunter who'd killed it.

That night after dinner Mark called and talked to Karen, then Chris. Ingrid could tell by what the children said that Mark was trying to assuage their grief. Then she talked to him, taking the telephone into the dining room. She didn't blame him, she said. She just wished he had thought about such things as safety before he encouraged Chris to go out there alone and "learn something about himself," as he'd put it. "It's because Chris is...alone that he's developed this attraction to guns," she said, knowing full well that the boy had had that before the break-up. When Mark offered to help find the dog, she asked him what he had in mind.

"Well, maybe we can hire a helicopter to fly over and spot him. If he's alive, he's got to be somewhere out there. He's not going to freeze, not with that coat of fur."

"I'll take care of it," she said. "If I need you, I'll let you know." And she hung up.

Karen was listless as she helped in the kitchen, and when Ingrid asked her about it, Karen turned away. She was crying.

"I know," said Ingrid, thinking how Karen used to pillow her head on the dog's side by the fireplace when he was allowed insides. "It's sad. But he might still be alive, and I'm going to find him if he is."

"Oh, Mom," Karen said, "it's not just Yukon," and she went upstairs.

Ingrid started to follow her, but she knew what Karen meant and she just couldn't discuss her father with her now. After a few minutes of idle work in the kitchen, she typed out a notice much like the one she'd called in to the newspaper that day: "LOST: SIBERIAN HUSKY. Answers to the name of Yukon," and the details of where he'd been seen. Then she began to embellish: "A family has been saddened by the loss of its beloved pet. Please, won't you help to make two children happy again?" And then, after debating it for several minutes in her mind, she decided to add: "Fifty dollars reward for any information leading to the recovery of our dog." She signed it "The Bergstrom

Family," then read it all over again and re-signed it "Karen, Chris, and Ingrid Bergstrom." Then she set the printer to REPEAT and let it run out 25 copies, while she found a picture of Yukon among the jumble of color photographs she had been meaning for months to put into the kids' albums.

She went to Chris' room, then Karen's, and told them to fend for themselves in the morning, not to worry if she wasn't there when they came from school. They both had activities anyway, they said, and wouldn't be there themselves until dinner time. She tried to assure each one that there was still hope, not to give up unless—she hated to say it but had to—unless Yukon's body was found. Before she left Karen for the night she asked her if she wanted to talk about what Karen had said earlier. Karen said she didn't . Then Ingrid asked her if she still had that large yellow T-shirt, the one with MINNEAPPLE printed on the front. Karen gave it to her, but she didn't ask why she wanted it, and Ingrid didn't say.

Stepping into the master bedroom, she felt, and immediately warded off, the gloom of her aloneness. For the first time in all the nights she had come alone to this room, as late as possible so that fatigue would put her under quickly, she was able to stop the feeling and turn it into something else, the single-mindedness of her mission. She would do what needed doing. She would go where she had to go, and she wouldn't give up or give in until she found the dog alive or dead. After she went to the large adjoining bathroom-dressing room and turned on the light, she was startled by the naked woman in the mirror. She had undressed without realizing that she had, and now she gazed at the face framed in short, brown hair, watched as the lips formed the sardonic grin that mocks the anguish of weeping. It was as if a sorrowful she had entered the room.

In bed, after she had cried out all her tears, she lay in tangible nightmare, as if she watched her sleeping figure dreaming, seeing into the other woman's head. And she was mortified as she witnessed that sullied weakling ravished by a brutal stranger.

***

She was out of the house by six-thirty, driving straight and fast to the lake.

Pickup trucks and campers were parked without design at the inn, and when she went in, its plastic tables already swarmed with men and a few hard women evidently fortifying themselves with food for the long day's stalking. Several children in down jackets played at an electronic bowling game, sliding the disk meanly. She went to the bar, where several men sipped steaming coffee and smoked cigarettes. One looked at her, and she looked back; then she asked the heavy, blue-jeaned woman behind the bar if she had heard from anybody about a Siberian husky. She showed the picture.

"Huh-uh," the woman said. Then she yelled to the crowd, "Hey, anybody see a husky dog?"

Ingrid turned, scanning the few faces that looked over blankly. Then she realized that these people were just going out. The ones from yesterday would not be here. She said that to the woman, who answered, "Not if they bagged one, they wouldn't but if they didn't they'll be here all week."

So Ingrid left a notice with the woman and gave one to the people at the nearest table and asked them if they would pass it along and call the number on the sheet if they heard anything at all. They nodded politely and looked at the paper as they passed it along without actually reading it. When she went back to the counter to ask the woman one more time to show the notice to everybody who came in, the woman told her that she'd lost her own dog three years ago on the opening day of deer season. "It never did come back."

"Did you ever hear anything about what happened to it?"

"Never did. But I always suspected." She gave Ingrid a look of sad sympathy. "Good luck."

She persevered by thinking of Yukon and Chris, imagining that she had only moments to spare before something awful happened, not to herself, but to the dog and the boy. As she drove to the cottage, the front windows down so she could call for the dog or talk more quickly to passing hunters, she considered too the pact she had made against the dreaming woman last night: she would have no pity for her, no matter how much she longed for it or even deserved it. For without pity, she would starve. And then she thought about what she might have been if her life had taken a different turn here and there—in short, if she had not married Mark.

Their courtship had been a time during which they showed only their best sides. She had primped and dressed well in advance and was always ready for him, as if that had been her normal self. He surely had done the same, showing up eager for the evening impeccably clothed and mannered. He had never seen the detritus she left behind, especially in the bathroom; they merely drove off in his shiny car and, disdaining the activities of other young college men in their junior year, he drove her, a young working woman, to theaters and concerts and restaurants. And she had not yet seen the clipped whiskers in the basin, the dark, curly hairs on the toilet bowl, the soiled jockey shorts. When they sealed their love in bed for the first time, she had done all she could to conceal the secret supplements to her outward beauty and had avoided looking directly at his nakedness. She simply felt that he was as physically perfect as a man could be. Then, after the wedding, he'd become so relaxed about personal things. She'd never known, for instance, that he wore a small partial plate until he removed it that first night, as nonchalantly as he had removed his clothing in front of her. And while he was tall and straight in clothes, without them he was thinner, his legs not so muscular or even straight as they'd seemed in good woolen trousers. These had not been disappointments to her, only revelations. In fact, it had been a relief to her to discover his even slight physical imperfections; she loved him more because of them and felt that her own flaws would be diminished in his eyes. But still she was careful to conceal as many as she could, especially in those regions men so often prize. But of course there was a limit, and she felt his displeasure as, through the years, the little revelations mounted. While she came to feel comforted at last, knowing that she had not married a god, she thought how easily the old attraction had died in him, and now realized it had because it must have been all, for him. And by then, as with Chris and the hunting of animals, his love had reversed itself.

A flash of bright orange interrupted her reverie. It was a hunter, walking the road, and she stopped and leaned out the window. "I'm looking for a dog," she said, showing the picture of Yukon. The man shook his head reasonably, gave a negative reaction by his look only, and walked on crunching in the snow. "If you see him or know of anybody who has, will you tell the people at the inn?" she called after him. "They have my phone number." The man exaggerated a nod, slowly, and kept going.

She turned the heater up full, yelling out the window, over and over, "Yukon! Come on, boy!" and drove to the cottage. She made herself hope that he simply found his way back to the cottage and would be there, lying outside waiting for someone to come and take him home. She saw in her mind the fine head lift trustingly as she approached; the eyes outlined in a black mask that trailed to the raised ears, edged in black, shaped like birch leaves; the full body of black-tipped white hair, tinged with the faintest tan. Above all, she felt at his throat the soft, white hair, thick with winter.

But he was not there, of course, and she went to the cottage and looked inside, thinking how foolish it was of her. So she went to the nude thicket across the road, where Chris had said he'd last seen him, and examined it like someone who knows what to look for. "Here, Yukon." She whispered it, making it sound like a wish.

When she returned to the car, she put the yellow T-shirt on over her tan down jacket and set her red ski cap. Then she started the car and drove the roads, calling from time to time out the windows. She encountered several hunters and was surprised to find so many of them rather mild-mannered, some cordial and sympathetic. One said, "I'm sorry," and hung his head. Another said, "I don't know what I'd do if I lost my dog." But she felt that they all knew something they wouldn't tell her.

As she came to unfamiliar turns, she took them, making a mental note about how to get back. Some of the roads were simply long driveways that led to cottages, and some of the cottages had smoke coming from the chimneys. Some roads led to others so that, on one, she became disoriented and had to stop at a cottage and ask a woman inside how to get back on the main road. She took the occasion to give the woman a notice and asked her to please call if she had any information.

The noise from the heater helped keep her mind from real thought. She made herself think only of what she had to do. When she became too cold, she rolled up the windows. But as soon as she was warm, she rolled them down again, yelling, "Yukon. Yukon. Here, fella." She looked from side to side, squinting through the birches and pines, as if at any moment she expected to see the dog come bounding from the woods. It kept her going all morning.

And then she came upon a place which caused her to slow, then stop. She was at the bottom of a slight rise. There before her the birches on either side of the road leaned slightly across, as if they yearned for one another, in vain. Perhaps in summer, when the branches were full, they touched, but now it seemed like desperation. Still, they formed something like an arch, pinnacles at the top rather than rounded, like a nave of an old cathedral. She turned off the heater. The sun was bright on the snow where she was; within the arch a network of shade, like black filigree, lined the road. The younger birches stood like skeletal poles; the bark of the older trees was the exact color of the husky. With the discovery she felt like a poet who had at last found the phrase she had searched for for years.

A truck came through the arch, and as soon as she saw the orange-clad men and the gun rack behind them a line from some long-forgotten story-poem came to her: *O, pity the sad-eyed doe.* In the time it took the struck to drive through the arch and come to rest beside her, she recalled the story of the mother deer that, trying to protect her twin fawns in winter, put them in separate cover, then ran herself to death between them.

"Stuck?"

"What?" She looked at the driver, an old man with a merry face. With the other two, a man and a boy, they might have been three generations of hunters, they looked so much alike, staring at her in kindly anticipation.

"Do you need any help?"

"No. I've just stopped here." She told them about Yukon, and she handed the drive a notice and showed the picture.

Something registered on his face, as the other two looked away, and she said, "What do you know about it?"

I didn't shoot your dog, miss."

She got out of the car and went to the window. "Have you seen him?"

"Yes, I saw him yesterday. He was chasing deer." He shook his head and sighed. "A hunter has the right to shoot a dog chasing a deer."

"What do you mean you didn't shoot him? Did somebody else?" She looked at the other two. "Did you?"

The one on the far side spoke up. "No, we didn't, but we should have. The men hunting nearby gave us hell for not killing that dog. You can't use a dog to hunt a deer.

"He wasn't hunting anything. You were!"

They gave her that look: you don't know; we can't tell you.

"Listen, miss," the driver said, "that's all we know. We didn't kill it, and we didn't see anybody who did."

She mentioned the law, and he said it was on the hunter's side. "Now, just let us pass."

"Wait. Where did you see him?"

He told her, pointing ahead, simulating the turns with his hand. "About half a mile, up the hill and around two turns, back in the woods to the right." Then he revved the engine and pulled away she she stepped back. After they were gone, she realized that she should have taken their names. And as she searched the rest of the day and into the evening where the man had said the dog had been, she didn't find so much as a print.

The next day she contacted the game warden. He was sympathetic, said he couldn't do much but he'd try to find out what he could. At least he didn't invoke any absurd law about killing dogs and, when she asked him about it, he said it might be written down somewhere but no real man would ever defend it. Then she called the animal shelter, and a man told her that they had a Siberian husky they'd found yesterday. He described where, and it seemed much too far, but she'd heard of cases where dogs had run miles to get home. So her hopes were high, when the man said the dog was bi-eyed.

"What does that mean?" she said.

"One eye's blue, the other's brown."

She spent the rest of the day out in the woods, hunting as much for the three men as for the dog. They knew more than they were saying, she'd bet. But she had no luck, and then she found herself going back to the arch of birches, sitting at the base of the rise, staring.

***

The next morning, after Chris and Karen had gone to school, a woman called, saying that her son had found a husky near their place and they were holding it. "It's friendly, and it answers to the name of Yukon, just like the ad said."

Ingrid yelled out mentally.

"But, now, it doesn't have a name tag or a red collar."

Ingrid's spirit deflated. "Is there another collar?"

"No. Nothing."

She wrote down the directions, telling herself that somebody could have taken the collar off; there couldn't be too many lost huskies. "Does it have brown eyes, both of them?"

"Why, I think so."

Ingrid asked her to check, and she did.

"I'll be there just as soon as I can," Ingrid said.

From the garage she took Yukon's old leather collar hanging on a nail. The leash was still in the car. On the way she imagined the drive back with the dog, licking at her from the back seat and just crazy to get home. The missing collar bothered her more now, but she thought about how if this was it, Chris and Karen would be spared another death, a real one, for she realized that if her divorce had been like a death sentence to her, what must it have been to them? Then, too, Mark would finally see that she could set right what he had started.

She found the house, several miles out of town, and parked the car. Barking sounded, and presently a large boy came into view. She gave a waist-high wave with her fingers, and he went around the house. She looked away, hoping, and then turned back.

The dog was thin and too small. She was so disappointed she turned to the car without a word, then remembered the woman and boy and yelled, "Thanks, anyway."

Instead of going back home—she had not eaten yet and wore only the tan coat, not even a hat—she drove to the lake area. She didn't want to waste time, and dejection urged her on. She went to the inn and, looking among the trucks and cars loaded already with their grim baggage, tried to recall the color and make of the truck with the three men in it. She could not, and so she went in and described them to the bar woman, but the woman just drew on a cigarette and shook her head tiredly. She was too busy to talk very much.

As Ingrid turned to go, a man said to the bar woman, "What's the matter, not getting enough?"

"Getting too much," the woman said.

Ingrid drove the roads, and after an hour of yelling out the window she found herself at the entrance to the arch of birches without consciously having driven there. Getting out of the car, she heard a distant rifle shot, but by now she was almost used to that sound out here. She walked the incline, slowly savoring the approach as if it held the secret to what she sought. Within the arch she felt release. Then the sound of the trees, like whispering, seemed to speak. The thought, absurd as it was, led her to others, until here all absurdities seemed possible. Here she could fancy that someday she would come upon the living dog; here she could think of her other self, not the nightmare woman but what she might have been. The thought was no comfort, but then it came to her that what she might have been in her human thinking was only another woman when, here, she might have been a bird or a deer, or even a lost dog. All things absurd were possible if what the trees seemed now to be saying was that, unaware that they made the arch what it was, they swayed, not in a show of acceptance, but in the agony that they must be forever in a place they yearned to flee, but never could.

A biting wind gusted, and she cupped her ears with her hands, then pulled the short collar of the coat around her neck and put her hands in her pockets. She was walking the roadside, when she saw tracks leading to the woods, and followed them in. In the ankle-deep snow the tracks looked at first like those of anything she might imagine, for whatever it was that had made them, it had trudged mightily until any discernible prints had become a trail of broken snow. She walked in the ditch of it—man or animal—looking beyond, through the trees, thinking that any moment she would come upon what had gone before her.

She had been stalking the trail for some time and was deep in, when she stopped. Suddenly, she was struck by the unassailable thought that she was following blindly a path that led nowhere or, worse, one that went the other way. What if it was the trail of a man, or an animal, hunting and she did catch up with it? A shiver shook her. But what if she walked in the trail of something being hunted? She turned her head, scanning the woods. A vast quiet was all around her. Then she turned full-circle to take it in, thinking with the dance-like movement that she might have been something graceful if her life had not led her here.

There was a movement through the pathless trees beyond and off to the side. It was not what she followed but something crossing that trail, just a streak. She stopped her breath and held a young birch, letting its cold bark touch her cheek, waiting. She heard something and closed her eyes—a wish—then opened them to see a large buck running, though not swiftly, through the curving path he must have seen through the trees. He was moving diagonally across her line of vision. Preparing herself for his passing, she gripped the birch and turned against the buck's direction.

And then he stopped. There were but several trees between her and the buck, and she could see all his splendor: the rack of horns, the white breast, the sleek hide. He turned his head in the direction from which he had run. Then he looked at her, briefly, and she felt shamed that he had caught her seeing him so privately, as his head went in a short down-circle and he snorted out a cloud of breath.

She began to walk in the unbroken snow toward him, saying what she might have to Yukon: "Oh, pretty you." She felt the presence of a powerful danger, but she was compelled to go to it. At any moment he could tear her apart with his—

But as she approached, his magnificence turned to something else. His antlers were broken; deep gouges pocked his scruffy hide. Waste seeped like liquid beneath his under-white tail, barely raised. Coming abreast of him, she saw an oozing hole in his side. Behind him lay a bloody spoor. He was breathing hard but not showing anything else, not pain or fear or even surprise that she was there. She moved nearer to the front of him. As she reached out with a finger to touch his muzzle, his head drooped; blood flowed from his mouth onto his white breast.

She did not hear the shot that sent the bullet through the animal to pierce her heart. The buck died on his feet, then settled into the snow as if he had simply tired. Her arm remained extended, as a searing radiance rose like smoke before her. She released the other woman then, saw her walk around the buck and into the blood-spotted trail, saw her see where the buck's path crossed that of whatever had led them into the woods, saw her stumble, then recover and begin to run, trying to grip the snow, like vanishing handholds, saw her grabbing at the birches, gaining speed as she heard what she could not distinguish as words, running wildly at the men—

But she had only crumpled. When the hunters arrived, they found her on her knees, her torso slanted across the buck, her arms stretched over it, like a final protection.

Achilles Speaks of His Deception in the Court of Lykomedes

by Michael Martone

I couldn't stand the blood. The forty daughters of the king lived so long together that the visitation of their monthly bleeding had synchronized before I got to Skyros. Preparing to hide me there, my mother, as she shaved my body, had rushed to tell me everything. How the broaches worked and how to comb and pin my hair, the way to look at a man and how to squat and pee. She had wheedled from Hephaestis, as she would later for my armor here, prosthetic hips and breasts made of gold and ivory, fragrant balsam and elastic willow, the minted nickel nipples. Whispering all the while, she wove the dyed fur of the cod piece into the scruff above my cock. The steps for the dances, the register of the dirge, goddesses I'd never heard of, all the ointments and unguents and where they go, the way I should let a man's hand slide over my rump. But she neglected to tell me how each month, beginning in ones or twos, then in greater numbers, the girls would

201

leave their father's court and secret themselves outside the walls of the acropolis in the tents pitched on unpure ground to bleed. I taught myself to wait and follow the last clutch of girls from the palace. I imitated them as they gathered up their kits. We took dried figs and raisins, olive oil for the lamps, wool to spin, a flute or lyre, and the wad of cotton rags.

Blood, I've seen. I learned the stitch that knit up your wounds, Danaans, from those girls in exile. The needle, lathered in blood from my sewing, draws its own blood with its work, red pips on the stems of black thread. My spear too does its mending, pulls ropes of gore through my enemies. But men you don't know what it's like to bleed the way the women do. To sit and seep like that. I watched them, a spot or two always in the folds of each crotch. The stains would slowly spread and soak through until one of them would stand and unwrap the girdle sopping now on the inside. She'd toss it on the pile to be burned, and her sisters would wash her wound and sponge her dry and hitch a new sheet around her waist and legs. The smell was something. It exhaled each time the dressings were changed. Then they would turn to help another. It didn't seem to stop. And the girls went on about their business, talking mostly like we are doing now.

I have never seen my own blood. Even as my mother's razor scraped the hair from my body, the blade whetted on my hide. Honed, the edge still dully slid over my thick skin, not a nick. I faked my menses, smearing jam on the cloth when no one was looking. At night in that stinking tent, I'd dream. Wrapped in sleep, I could not remember who I was. Reaching for myself, my hands burrowing in the rags between my legs, I'd feel the sticky puddle of what I took to be my bleeding. How could I be bleeding? In my mind, the jam had turned into the body's own syrup. I felt the stump of my cock nested in the fur sheath, everything smeared with blood. And I could also feel a cock, not mine, cut off stuffed up inside of me. I told you I was dreaming. I forgot what I'd become. I kept bleeding.

Men, we rape. That is what we do. Who hasn't drawn his cock bloody as a sword from some girl no older than the daughters of King Lykomedes? You strip the frothy coating off yourself and then pin her down to let your buddy have his turn. But for a moment, before you wring it clean, you hold it in your hand, this core of blood. It makes you think.

And there was the moon that night. Of course, there was the moon. I watched it slip out of the sea, red and full, into the black sky saturated with the smoke of smouldering rags. The moon tinged the water with its own diluted hemorrhage. My mother is a Nereid. I've seen her melt into a puddle. She dressed me up as a girl and never wanted me to suffer. I knew I was fooling no one. Though for a while, I wanted to be fooled. Now I know. Men, I am a man, like you.

Map of Rivers

by Kevin McIlvoy

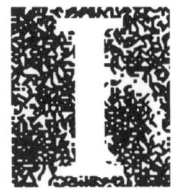

I still think everything my father did he did more for himself than for my younger brother, Ben. He could have visited Ben at the VA when he was medivaced there in early March. He could have seen for himself that Ben could not stay alive long.

He made himself believe Ben would leave the hospital and need a place to start recovering. Without so much as consulting my mom, he took out a loan in order to buy the Rado house two blocks away.

In a week, he had heaped up a pile of timbers, plywood, and other supplies; he set up a band saw in the backyard. He sketched some plans. Then he telephoned my older brother Anthony so he could take the two of us on the grand tour.

Mom and I were both angry with him, and angrier in each room he showed us. We saw the clothes closets, two spacious bathrooms. In the third bedroom she said, "Enough," and turned her back to him. But, as always, she followed after him again.

He pointed out how much nicer it was, the fixtures and appliances, the carpeting, the solid construction and generous insulation, than in our own home. Molly, afloat inside me, had dived into the deeper part of my pelvis, where she now swam more gracefully than she had in the months before. I was twenty. My husband James would be coming back from Vietnam in July. I should have been able to say to my father—but I didn't—that the money was wasted on Ben, that here was all their retirement money locked inside Mrs. Rado's walls.

Last, he took us to the master bedroom, where the south and east walls had floor-to-ceiling shuttered windows with iron framing and bright, new panes, each the size of your palm. He asked Anthony to open the shutters all the way, but it was late morning and the light didn't suit my father. "In the evening," he promised, "this'll be great."

He made us go into the walk-in closet to show that all four of us could fit. He showed how the closet light went on when the door opened, then shut off when it closed. In the dark, he said, "Nice, huh?" and, in the light, "What do you think?"

"Nice," Mom said. "A bargain."

"Let's go," said Anthony.

"Look," my father said. "Hey—"

Mom said, "We should. It would be better if we would just go."

Anthony took Mom's arm. "All right then." He led her out of the room

"Hey—come on, Anthony, don't."

Anthony's dark hair was ungroomed around his ears and neck. If he chose to look straight at you, he would shift his shoulders forward while drawing back his grimly handsome head and powerful neck. He came back from Vietnam two months before Ben was inducted, one month before my husband James went there. In James's family he and one of his two younger brothers were enlistees. Both his father and mine were World War II veterans. When you think about it, the odds were probably diminished for someone like Ben.

My father had rolled his navy blue work shirt sleeves just above his elbows. "Lots of work to do here, Little Peg."

"Sure is." I walked with him down the hallway to the dining room, then out through the kitchen to the backyard.

"About here," he said, losing his train of thought. "This. About here." He traced through the air with his hand and said, "I'm going to put a little patio down so he can get the sun." If you didn't look carefully, you'd have thought my father looked all right. But closer up, you could see the brick grit embedded in his face and arms and hands. Sometimes I would imagine my mother's body honed against that grit, which had become a part of him in his twenty years of work at the Rado & Sons brick factory.

"I was thinking," he said, "'how you could move in here with Ben when he gets here. You know—help out until James gets back, and the baby comes, and you two move somewhere else."

I didn't answer him at first. Because of my blessed maternal state, I had constipation and gas and bad nerves compounded by a cruelly indecisive bladder. I asked him for water. "Right," he said.

He called from the kitchen that the house didn't have glasses yet. He came out with water in a baked bean jar that had probably held nails. "It's clean," he said. "I rinsed it out."

I guess I was going to say no to him about moving into Ben's house. I think I might have if not for the worried way he looked into the water and then back up to me, holding the jar a second after my hand had closed around it. The dirty-rain taste of it was good.

207

At six-thirty the next morning, Mom and I brought my luggage, clothes, bedclothes and towels, and a box of borrowed silverware and cooking utensils to the Rado place. My father unfolded a cot in the living room. Before he went out in the backyard to work, I made him move the cot into the room that he said would be Ben's.

Mom neatened my bedmaking. She had always folded bathroom towels and ironed pants and made a bed in the same respectful way we were taught to fold the flag. One hand drew the sheet tight, the other expertly tucked it under a corner. "He's happy you'll do this," she said.

"Stay you mean?"

"Mm-hmm." Beneath her ears she blushed. At a certain part of her face her cheeks met the loose skin under her eyes and formed lines, definite as scars. "He's buying some furniture this afternoon. He's picking up a hospital bed somewhere in Chamberino, from a family, some people we know at church."

"In charge, isn't he?" I said.

She put her hand and arm inside the pillow to straighten the pillowcase. "Don't be snide, Peg."

"In the center ring, Peg and Mom—ferocious beyond–"

"Please dear."

"—beyond imagination."

Her teeth almost emerged through her thin white smile. A warning.

"You know what I mean." I offered my version of her smile. "Not really, huh?" I handed her my pillow, and went into the bathroom.

208

Afterward, I sat on the closed lid of the toilet and thought about Mom, and about how all the circus-goers admired the tigers more than the tiger tamers. Jumping through the hoops, posing on the platform, and bounding gracefully down on command. When the tamer's whip cracked, it wasn't his control but the rage the tiger held back that we watched. That's what I saw, anyway: the muscles moving in her face like crushing undercurrents.

When I met James, I was determined not to be like my mom. Then the first time James circled me and commanded, "Do this for me, Little Peg," "Wear this," "Don't talk like that out in company," "Make me this one promise," I heard him shouting, "Up, Up! and—how do I explain this?—I wanted to be good for him. When my skill was perfected, I wanted to be better. "*Good girl!*" I imagined everyone, my father and older brother and the whole penis gallery applauding. "*Good girl!*"

After James left for Vietnam and assumed I would stay with my parents, not rent an apartment; when he asked me not to take a full- or part-time job; and when he questioned whether I felt I really needed so many girlfriends; or if I really wanted to take courses at the university; when he asked all these things, I was the good housesoldier. *Make me just this one promise,* he said in letter after letter. What I did was what my mother would do. I followed all lawful orders. Patriotism.

I found Mom in kitchen, where she had removed the grate from the bottom of the refrigerator, and she was sweeping lint out with her fingers.

I stood over her. "Are you going to hang around until Dad gets back with his whatever-the-hell-it-is?" In so many words, I moved her out of the way, as Anthony had done the day before.

In some ways, I could not believe Mr. and Mrs. Rado and the Rado sons had ever lived in that house. In the mornings when I awoke I heard and smelled the empty house's perfectness: no odor of unclean cabinets or recooked cooking oils, no old carpet breathing years of spilled coffee and greasy ground-in bits of potato chip and popcorn; no burbling of drooling faucets or light fixtures humming like thumbnail locusts. Every board in the floor behaved and every door hinge and faucet handle noiselessly obliged me.

As the walk-in closet light came on all by itself, I smiled into the full-length mirror at my chunkiness, only some of which was pregnancy. I pulled off my silver-blue nightgown. I gave myself the quick once-over that James would give me if he were there. He never looked close. He preferred touching me, his uncomprehending hands trying to read me. After lovemaking, he was even less interested in looking. So though he wasn't there to speak for himself, I felt I could put words in his mouth. "Solid woman," I said. "Head to toe."

I'm not sure why I did not masturbate while he was in Vietnam, except that I somehow assumed it would have been a kind of dereliction of duty. I did permit myself body hair. I let my underarm hair grow, and the hair on my shins got shaggy. If he were there, James would ask, "Are you just going to let yourself go?"

I'm not an expert on this, but I think in 1970 housesoldiers did even stranger things. At least four days a week I devoted whole afternoons to writing him. I had imaginary conversations with him. I remember that when he eventually came back from Vietnam, I was disappointed he could not talk with me as intimately as my pretend-James did.

The sound of a snarling truck's engine outside made me look again at myself. I dressed there in the closet. When I shut the closet door behind me, I appreciated the automatic darkness.

My father unlocked the front door and quietly came into the house. He handed me a paper bag with a box of donut holes and a pint carton of chocolate milk inside it. "Well, Little Peg," he asked, "is it a good morning?"

True to our family custom, I answered, "Set sail!"

He blew the powdered sugar off a donut hole and ate it. "Mr. Aigley's coming over to help me set up the bed, get the place ready. Can you make him coffee?"

I said sure, that it would be good to see him. A half-truth. Andrew Aigley was my father-in-law and, while I didn't know him too well, I could have figured that if he were asked, he'd help out.

My father had also called my brother Anthony. He said he didn't think Anthony would come. "You never know," I offered. The men in my family had been one strong woven rope; now that a strand had been destroyed, the others had been unbraided.

The coffee made, we walked outside to the dismantled hospital bed piled in the truck. "The bed's a good one," he said, "I hope I can remember how it goes together. Needs a new mattress. But look, you've gotta see this." He drew a large black carboard cylinder from the open window of the trunk cab. He set his coffee on the trunk hood, pulled the cap off one end, and unsleeved the shiny, rolled-up vinyl. "Come on inside. I ordered this through the mail. I tell you, you can't believe it."

He carried the map inside to Ben's room. "You know how these places take forever. I ordered this thing for Ben in December."

"Okay," I said, "Show me."

He unrolled it on the bare floor, and we knelt down to look it over. About four by six feet, the Mercator world map was named The Map of Rivers in grand turquoise lettering at the bottom. All land was the lightest gray, with topographical variations rendered in only slightly darker shades so that the mountains, the land masses, the poles, all the geographic awesomeness of earth, even the oceans, was insignificant compared to the cerulean claws everywhere: the blue, slender branching arms and narrow, shell-blue curving wires. S upon S, the narrower threads branched out in pale, gnarled fingers or fanned into deltas, or sprayed into lines that the sharpest fingernail could not trace; they vanished and reappeared, always more important than the pale gray world beneath them. The Mississippi, the Murray, the Amazon, the Congo, the Nile, the Rhine, the Volga.

No nations, states or cities were named on the map; no monuments or ports or peaks were marked; the land was cleansed of highways and railways. The map's legend explained how the ten different shades of blue defined Stream Order, "the ranking of river systems in size and complexity." In silver lettering it said, "Streams of the first order (deepest blue) are spring-, rain-, or snow-fed brooklets without tributaries. Streams of the second order (lighter blue) are fed by those of the first order, and so on. A great river may have a stream order as high as ten."
The map had twelve eyelets at the top and twelve at the bottom and, as my father knocked tacks on the wall where the foot of Ben's bed would be, I joked that it always fell to women to hold up the world or hold it down while men hammered it in place.

He pretended to knock my forehead with the hammer. "You're overeducated, you know that?"

When Mr. Aigley came, we traded news about James. Whenever the Aigleys and I discussed my husband, I had the notion that we were sharing only a portion of what we knew. I felt it was fair enough for me to be stingy with them, but it angered me for the Aigleys to believe they should not let me know everything.

My father had been leaning against the truck in order to listen in on our conversation, and that angered me too. I know it all makes me sound immature.

We discussed again the gum disease that James had contracted in Ad Loc, which made it painful for him to eat. Since February, he had lost ten pounds. Mr. Aigley said, "So. Anyway, what can you do?" He turned to my father. "You know the drill, John." I guess that's true of VFW buddies like them: they know the drill.

"Yeah," said my father.

As far as I could tell, I didn't know any of it as men knew it. Who—a woman?—could know what they knew? A wife?

"I bet Mr. Aigley could use some java, Little Peg."

Mr. Aigley said, "Sure. You already got some on?" From the pocket of his work pants he fumbled out his leather gloves. "Black's fine. I could get it." He smoothed the gloves onto his fingers.

"No, no," I said, and fetched.

When I came back, he had closed his hands, and was holding his leather fists in front of him. "So, where do we start?"

"First, you gotta see something," my father said. He took his buddy inside to see the map.

* * *

By 10 A.M. they had neatly spread the skeleton of the bed over the front yard and then sensibly, systematically figured out how the contraption went back together. The gusty March morning sky brightened. I looked through the iron grates of the picture window, and I sized them up: Mr. Aigley, the flab of his arms and upper body quivering as he assembled the pieces he stood astride; my father, with his face asquint in concentration as he worked or, more often than not, as he stood apart from the whole mess and gave instructions. I took measure of the two men, because I liked little instances when I could promote myself to some imaginary military rank. Lance Corporal Peg O'Crehieh Aigley, SP3, IC, SU (In Charge of Sizing Up). There. That's how I was. Am.

I grinned openly at there bellies swaying in the sling of their shirts, and their fifty-year-old backs and awkward hands, and I decided I was (overweight—pregnant—nauseated) stronger than either of them.

And, later in the evening, when Mom and I visited Ben at the VA in El Paso, at first I coldly assessed the small part of my brother lying before me without his right leg, without his arms, without his slender, bony wrists, his almost unwrinkled hands. His narrow chest and his neck and face were drowned in bandages stiffening from drying blood. When I said his name, I was surprised to hear it come from me. *Ben.* Like a shutting door, the word sealed me off from everything but what I felt inside. I descended into myself as though I was made of cavern floors and could descend a level at a time to call a signal word out; then, a level deeper, a longer message; then, deeper yet, echoing sentences making nonsense out of the ones they over lapped. Outlined beneath the sheets, his body reminded me of a root pushing up through the earth or trying to claw deeper inside. His chest made a cooing sound, the murmuring of water flowing close under rocks.

My mother would have been helped by my tears if I could bring on tears, but here is what I did instead. I held her so she couldn't escape my arms. I said, "If he doesn't—can't—die before we get him to that house. Mother, listen. He's dead already if you look close enough." She wanted to get away, but I was too strong for her. If I was going to make her cry I wanted her right in my arms where I could feel what I had done. "I'll do it if I have too. If he can't die. If nobody else will."

On the drive home she was still crying. My baby tumbled, plunged deeper, and surfaced, and I could almost hear our shared blood splashing inside me. Instead of consoling my mother, whispering that everything would be all right, and walking her from the car to her home; instead of that, I sat and watched her fumble with her front door. I thought of the pretend trips Ben and I took as children, sitting in the front seat of my parents' Olds, reaching L.A. in five minutes, only turning left once to be in New York or, for that matter, Asia.

When I came to Ben's house, the perfectly clean windows seemed to me like shiny black marble panels placed over the fathomless darkness inside. I went into his room to sleep, but I chose Ben's bed rather than the cot so I could look at the map. The dams also were unnamed.

At first my father and Mr. Aigley had planned to do all the remodeling themselves. They did succeed in assembling the bed, constructing the front- and back-door ramps, lowering certain counters and shelves and tables. Then they unwisely tried to remake Ben's bathroom.

A plumber friend, Joe Prusczak, had to come out to repair the damage. The new toilet he brought was fabulous, the men agreed, a beauty of a can. The tank and toilet were all one sculptured unit. The lid and seat were padded. You think about a toilet, they said. What a thing, huh? You gotta see this.

"A beauty," I said. Despite myself, I was won over again by their adolescent enthusiasm. Still, Liberty Vitreous seemed like a bad name for a toilet, and I told them so.

We all laughed together then. Mr. Aigley read the bill (he had insisted on paying half), and said the price of freedom was three hundred and fourteen dollars and ninety-five cents these days, and we even thought that was funny.

Before the three men muscled and sealed and bolted the toilet in its place, they brought a chair into the bathroom so they could rehearse the transfer Ben would have to manage from wheelchair to toilet. To figure out placement of rails, they had Joe Pruszcak, a tiny man, move from chair to toilet and back again until they scratched brace markings on the wall. I watched from the door of the bathroom. Though Ben's build had once been twice Mr. Pruszcak's, there was logic now in adjusting things differently.

For determining the placement of the bath rails, Joe also pretended to be Ben. My father marked the walls with chalk and said, "Sit in there, Joe."

Joe sat in the tub. "Like this?"

"We've got to put the handles in there," said my father. "Where—" Looking down at the little man in the deep tub, he could only make enough breath for one word. "Where..."

Mr. Aigley leaned near his buddy. "Hey, John. We'll take a break."

Kneeling down, my father looked again into the tub. "What? Yeah. Okay, yeah." He handed the chalk to Joe, who made the marks where they needed to go. Helping him from the tub, my father almost lifted him completely up and out. When Ben and Anthony and I were very little, he would lift us out of the tub like that, and ask, "All right there?" He took his hands from Joe's waist.

Joe said, "I'm outta time guys. If I don't get home, I don't go home."

They knew what he meant: a wife's tyranny. Anyway, they avoided the whole shipwreck into intimacy that might have happened if my father had cried. After Joe left, they installed the handles, swept up after themselves, asked what I wanted on the pizza.

"I don't want pizza," I said.

"I'll bet the baby wants pizza," said Mr. Aigley.

"Oh God, I hate that."

My father asked, "What?"

"When people talk to my stomach."

"Our momma's crabby," my father said.

Mr. Aigley took our orders for soft drinks and said he'd be back in a jiffy.

When I was fifteen the Aigleys had lived near us. In one of the milestone scandals of the neighborhood, their home had been repossessed and they had completely packed up and moved out between midnight and 8 A.M. on a Sunday in December 1965. I don't think a house light went on anywhere in the neighborhood that night, but probably no bedroom window was left closed. We were so obvious, the Aigleys must have known we all were watching. My father had characterized them as a family that fouled its own nest.

Five years later, on the night I announced that Albert James Aigley had proposed and I had accepted, I imagined windows gliding open from one end of our neighborhood to another.

On our honeymoon, James had told me, "See how things turn out? After my dad had lost his job, and we went through that repo thing, we were white trash. That's how my parents thought of us after that. They fought a lot about my mom looking for work. We had fewer choices and we knew it. And once I accepted it, I could adjust myself.

We were fishing, our bobbers very far from us, too far to watch them on the glittering lake. I had asked him how he had adjusted, what he meant.

"We didn't talk about money. I didn't listen when kids told what they got—the bicycles and tennis rackets and things. That's part of what you do, you don't listen or look or imagine too much. I bet our bait's gone."

"I guess you got pretty mad sometimes," I said. We held on to our rods and reels.

"Nope. You stand far away from all the crap and you hit an Off switch. You know the things that make you mad are right in your face, but they can't reach you."

I listened carefully to him, my husband of two days. I looked out at the lake, out where my bobber might be, and I imagined just exactly where it was. I said to my handsome red and white bobber, *You have an Off switch. You don't listen or look or imagine too much.* I said it over and over. *You have an Off switch.* I did not yet understand how exactly that described the perfect soldier.

When he returned with the pizza, Mr. Aigley and my father talked about how they were going to hook up the television in Ben's room and what kind of remote control they would need to run the radio, room lights, television, and bed. This conversation went on forever. At first I heard both men; then I heard gibberish. At a certain point, their voices seemed clarified by distance, so that I could identify each word but no longer distinguish the men, even though I sat near them.

"It would be something if they could get one remote for all that, wouldn't it?"

That would be neat, but probably impossible, said the other.

"What?" I said.

"Yeah," said one. "but they order a satellite out in space to shift a quarter of an inch or spin slower and change orbit if they want."

Ben has no hands, I wanted to say.

"Problem is, the Pentagon doesn't buy its equipment at the Radio Shack."

"Hell if they don't! They just pay ten times what we do. Right?"

"Right."

"Peg?"

"Right," I said.

The men took slices of pizza with them to Ben's bedroom. I heard one quietly say, "She's awful upset."

A little before six the next morning, my brother Anthony stood at the back door, knocking lightly, probably unsure that he wanted me to answer.

When I let him into the kitchen he perfunctorily hugged me and said, " They've whipped the place into shape, huh?

"You can get what you want from the icebox," I told him. "I'll dress and be back."

I went to Ben's room. The baggy maternity jeans I pulled on were softened by fine dust. Hitting the knees and butt clean with my palms, I heard Anthony say, "You're mad at me for not coming around."

"Me? He might be hurt some about it. Not me." The dirty tube socks I pulled on were stiff, so I took them off. "He and Mr. Aigley have been removing stuff—their favorite thing to do. The doors, the bed, lights, radio. They're coming this morning to remote some of the windows, start building a deck."

"I'd like to, you know, be better to Dad." Anthony's voice was deep, fake.

I tucked my sweatshirt into my pants. That looked so bad I untucked it, held the waist of the pants out, and asked my bump, "Well, Baby, is it a good morning?" No answer yet.

Anthony said, "I've been talking with Mom, you know."

I nudged a brush into the front of my tangled hair. "You seen Ben?" I looked at The Map of Rivers. The Ganges, the Niger, the Thames, the Yukon.

"Mom says you hurt her feelings."

The Rio Grande, the Sao Francisco, the Khatanga. "Hell with the socks," I said and returned to the kitchen.

He asked for toast. I popped it in, asked him again, "You seen Ben?"

"Not yet." He asked for coffee. I put the coffee can, the filter and brewing equipment in front of him. "Put in five tablespoons," I said.

"Mom says Ben's about ready to come here."

"What?" I sat down at the table. "What did she say? What did she tell you?"

"Settle down, okay? She says Ben could, you know-"

"My God. Are you that cowardly?" When he pushed the brewer at me on the table, I said, "Look her straight in the face." I leaned across the table. "Okay, look me straight in the face."

Anthony set his elbows and arms up to prop his head, but then he lowered his hands on the tabletop and looked at them. "I bought a bunch of rose grafts. I've got a shovel. I told Dad I'd make a rose hedge out around Ben's deck. In the back."

"Anthony," I said, "he's–you go–you go see. He's like a shell something horrible has shed and left behind."

"It'll make Dad happy." He brushed the knuckle of his thumb against one heavy eyelids. His voice lower, he said, "Okay? You have a problem about it?"

I sized him up in a clownish, dramatic way—my head cantering up and down in order to show him I was sizing him up. I could have been helped by his tears if he could bring on tears. But he stood up. He looked down at me, and said, "You're a miserable bitch."

I'm not much for denying the truth. I let him go outside and get his shovel and rose grafts out. He had dug the first hole by the time I brought water to him. I uncoiled the lawn hose so I could soak each hole as he dug it.

Mr. Aigley and my father drove up an hour later with donut holes and milk. My father shook his prodigal son's hand and held on to it. He made Anthony eat. He showed him the map in Ben's room, then took him on the house tour again, asking his opinion of their work.

Standing in the backyard with the two men, Anthony was enthusiastic. "You're a miracle worker, Dad. You guys are something, you know it. Has Mom seen all this? Wait'll she sees."

After that, they knuckled down. They worked from ten to five, almost without a break. Mr. Aigley and my father conducted remote maneuvers in which they tested the probable sequence of commands. Timed lights operative? Inside and out? Garage, television/radio, air conditioner and heater remote functioning? Master bedroom remote operative?

When they tested the fire detectors, they let the warning alarm ring in every room and then in each room separately. Above the din, they shouted, "Functioning! Functioning!"

Anthony patted the mound around another green stick, and smiled at the two old soldiers. "Functioning?" he said.

"Yeah. They sure know the drill, don't they?"

He spoke to my face without looking into it. "They've been there. You haven't."

I thought of James, who was "there" now, while I was not. Because I didn't spit something back, I guess Anthony felt he had told me everything I didn't know and, now that I understood, I would shut up. "Water her," he said.

The three men eventually worked together to start making the little backyard deck. They stained the boards, rubbed them, restained and varnished. Maybe they shouldn't have varnished them yet, they said. They wanted Anthony's approval to strip off the varnish right way. He gave his approval, then got on his knees with them in the strong fumes of the acetone stripper, stain, and varnish. Before the boards were dry, the men began framing the deck.

At five, I drove to the DQ to get us all big malts for dinner. When I returned, Anthony and Mr. Aigley had their arms around my father, whose own stained arms helplessly enfolded my mom. Ben had died. All their arms would never be able to console her.

At home, Mom took some kind of prescription downer. She was pale but calm as she lay down, and when she started blubbering, "Ben Edwin!" she was already asleep. I left as soon as that ended. Mr. Aigley walked out the door with me, promising my father and brother he would telephone them in the morning. He offered me a ride.

"I have a car," I said.

He walked me to the curb, his eyes about to spill. "Nothing I can think to say. Wish there was."

"It's better to say nothing." For his sake, we hugged each other.

In Ben's bed at the Rado place that night, I took the remote control from the nightstand, but had to press four buttons before I got the shutters to open to let the moonlight into the room. It was a button with a tiny "L" sticker on it.

The next morning, just after dawn, I heard them banging around in the backyard. I dressed and tried to keep myself hidden from view as I watched through the kitchen window. Anthony was yanking rose grafts from their tamped mounds. My father was ripping apart the frame of Ben's deck, throwing boards toward a corner of the backyard. The noise seemed to awaken the baby.

"What the hell are they doing?" I asked her. I dressed quickly, telling her, "That's enough," then saying it to both of us, and then shouting as I buttoned my blouse, "That's enough!"

"Stop it!" I came out the back door. Neither man even unbent himself to look at me. I stood behind my father, and I said, "Stop." He pivoted to throw another board. "Listen to me," I asked, but he looked past me to make his aim true. I shouted beyond him and Anthony, "You make me sick! Stop. Some other family will want this. Some other soldier is going to need this and you know it."

Anthony said, "Little Peg. Come on."

"I'm—what is it with you pieces of shit and your stupid hands? Hammering away or tearing down—not happy it you're not hammering—and marching in your stupid parades—crying like goddamned babies at the cemeteries and heaping Honor on the graves." I kicked my father hard in one leg, which made him stop and which brought Anthony to his side.

"All the Bens—my Ben, my James—what do you purple hearts do about them?" I tried to slap my father but missed and hit him in the neck. He stepped forward as if to invite me to make the next slap count. The tears in his eyes streamed out.

"So stop," I said. "You make me puke—so just stop—because somebody's going to need all this—you know it—don't you?—some old vet will have to buy this place for his son." I made a fist and punched at the weeping, pitiful little man. I tried to push him down on the ground.

"Please," he begged, "for God's sake, don't."

Anthony grabbed my shoulders and held me back.

"Get away from me." I taunted my father, "You're too damn puny. I should pick on somebody my own size." Running back into the house, I was vaguely aware of them following.

An hour later, when I left the bathroom in which I had locked myself, they were gone. I perched on the edge of Ben's high hospital bed and looked at the map. The Song Hong, the Song Da, the Mae Nam Chi, the Mae Nam Mun, the Mekong. I was thankful Ben did not live to look at all the healing transpirations of this gray world, because he would have wanted to live then, and his dying would have taken longer. I rocked myself on the bed as I sang to my baby—some swingset song, the kind in which you're gulping air on the swing back and, on the swing up, singing yourself out past gravity. Out, far past.

The Walls of Dubrovnik

by Christopher Merrill

A good place to begin to understand the senselessness and horror of the continuing crisis in the Balkans is from the top of the walls encircling the ancient city of Dubrovnik. In an hour's walk from gate to tower, wall curtain to arsenal, you can see that more than half the buildings in the historic center of town were damaged in the series of attacks the Yugoslav National Army (JNA) and Serb irregular forces waged in October-December 1991 and again last May and June. *Urbacide* is the word coined by an architect from the destroyed city of Mostar to describe what has happened to the cultural legacy of this region; "urban cleansing" is what the Federal Army attempted in Dubrovnik—once "the pearl of the Dalmation coast," unemployed tourist guides will tell you.

Here is a city under siege: the tile roofs are covered with holes or sheets of nylon and tar paper; stairs and stone decorations are crumbling or have been blown away; piles of brick, stone, and broken glass line the narrow streets; and along the Stradun, the main thoroughfare, Croatian soldiers in U.S. Army issue combat fatigues wander around the monuments sheathed in protective planks of wood. The contemporary Ragusan poet Luko Paljetak has written that the Stradun is "not a street, but a world." Lately, this world has adopted a distinctly military air. Dubrovnik, which in 1979 was placed on the UNESCO Register of World Cultural Heritage and which is now on the Register of Endangered World Heritage, is waiting for the next battle.

Once the site of enormous tourist activity, this seafaring town of some 70,000 people, Croats for the most part, has only one hotel open for business; the others were either destroyed in the war or are now filled with displaced families from Dubrovnik and its surrounding villages or with refugees from Bosnia. In the Hotel Argentina, where the sign on the front door reads No Arms Please, you will find only journalists, soldiers, and UN personnel; old hands joke that a room with air conditioning means that the windows have been shot out. Gallows humor reigns: an EC monitor recalled a colleague who recorded the shelling of Dubrovnik from the terrace, refusing to seek the relative safety of the shelter. " 'Incoming, incoming, outgoing,' he would say, then call to the waiter, 'Another gin-and-tonic!' " said the monitor with a laugh.

There is little to laugh about in town. If the facades of most of the churches and buildings are still intact, shot up and pocked with shrapnel though they may be, the boarded-up doors and windows remind you that this is a city which has been hollowed out, physically as well as in spiritual terms. A woman told me that in addition to the 250 or so people killed in battle were those who in the aftermath of war died of shock. "One man returned to his farm," she said, "and drowned himself in his well. He couldn't take what it would mean to rebuild." Nor was he alone in his despair.

Dubrovnik Commune was one of the most prosperous regions in the former Yugoslavia, and its citizens say that they lost more than others in the Balkan war zone, perhaps because the invading forces both envied them and believed they had a right to their material possessions. How else explain the systematic looting of the occupied villages or the fact that more than 500 boats were sunk in Gruz harbor? I met a seaman who lost three of his four boats in a single day. To finance repairs on his damaged fishing boat and yachts he works on other sunken hulls. He cannot find credit or foreign capital, since investors are wary of the war as well as of the government's continuing inability to institute market reforms. Fortunately, he has enough work on the other boats to keep him going, as he said, "forever."

This he told me at the opening of an exhibition celebrating the role of Croats in Columbus' discovery of the New World. Which is to say: despite the damage, the people of Dubrovnik are trying to start over. Thus one night last week more than a hundred people gathered in an unheated building—through whose broken windows the cold sea breeze off the Adriatic blew—to look at a collection of maps, paintings, and shipping paraphernalia—a sextant, an hourglass, a small telescope—illustrating a local saying: "Stick a finger in the sea, and you are in touch with the whole world." While in another room *Batman Returns* was playing, I learned that Croats have been navigators for Columbus, and I suspected that in the end Dubrovnik would steer its way through this crisis, too. I could feel in this makeshift gallery and gritty determination to get on with life. Here was an artist who had lost his house and work in the most vicious bombardment of the war last December 6th; he commemorated the event this year with a party in what had once been his studio. It was raining that day, and so his guests drank brandy with their umbrellas open above their heads: the artist may have no roof, but he does have wit. And that is what may help him survive.

What is most appalling about this destruction is the simple fact that Dubrovnik had no strategic value in and of itself. If it was once a symbol of medieval power and poetry, now the city is nothing more than an artistic statement—and nothing less. It is difficult to imagine what the rump state of Yugoslavia would have done with Dubrovnik, which survived 93 days without water or electricity, had the JNA conquered the people who stayed behind to fight them off. The historian Slobodan Novak called his city "the Princess of the world; Venice is the older Queen." Then he told me that "this is not a town for soldiers. The walls are pure poetry; they have no military significance. But we need the soldiers now, and we'll need to remember in the future why they were here if we want this to be a city again for poets."

The poet and Nobel Laureate Octavio Paz recently wrote of "our own base era" that it "is in the habit of dishonoring the vanquished." Nowhere is that more apparent than outside the city walls of Dubrovnik, in the villages that, as an architect working to restore the region said, "belong to the same organism as the city." Now, however, whole villages have been razed. Marina Desin, Director of the Local History Museum of Konavle, took me through the ruins of Cilipi, where in the historic center of the town not a building had been spared. Her museum, which had once housed artifacts (evacuated, fortunately, before the onslaught) of the traditional culture of southeastern Croatia, was levelled.

"Every Sunday," she said on a warm, sunny afternoon, "we would have 2,000 visitors to see the people in traditional dress, tilling or pressing wine or olive oil, or dancing. We would serve wine for free, as much as you wanted. It was heavenly. And now look at what they did."

Every house and building in sight had been looted, then burned or dynamited. If the facade of the church was untouched, I was assured, repeatedly, that this was only for "propaganda purposes": the Serbian press used footage of this church to persuade its audience that the JNA was not targeting religious sites. The interior of the church told a much different story: it was gutted. Likewise, the priest's house, and the building across the square, and the gardens. "Catastrophic," was how an expert from the Council of Europe described the scene. Indeed.

We walked back toward the road, where two soldiers in two dump trucks filled with broken tiles and bricks were keeping watch. Around a corner we came upon an old man in a grey sport jacket and beret, balancing himself high up in a fig tree, pruning it with a hatchet. All his tools, he explained, had been stolen. The cafe he and his wife had run had been looted and burned; among the debris, which included smashed china and a ravaged espresso machine, were the scorched, skeletal frames of the chairs that used to line the bar and the charred spring from a mattress draped, like a rug over a wall. All that the invading forces had left him was a rack of empty wine bottles. Yet here he was in his tree, hacking away at the dead limbs.

"If that man comes to cut his fig," said Marina, "he will be back. That's what we need more than anything—people returning to the villages and starting to work on their places again. They can't stay in the hotels forever."

Herself in White

by John Milton

The mother is not in this story. She is dead. The father understands death and has adjusted to it. The daughter is different. She feels that she has lost her identity. Her anxiety contributes to headaches that do strange things to her. While walking to school, she stops by an old pine tree in the park, unbuttons her blouse, and embraces the tree, rubbing her small breasts against the bark until she cries out in pain. She does not know why she does things like that.

She loves her father, but whenever he talks about returning to the reservation she is fearful. Thoughts of the reservation breed hatred in her heart, but she cannot hate her father. He is a kind man; yet, she watches him closely when he is quietly resolute with his urge to leave the town. His deep brown eyes see to burn, and she peers closely as though she expects to see smoke. Then the fire goes out as abruptly as it has flared, and the entire face takes on the color of old embers. What makes her nervous, and adds to her headaches, is the thought that one day his latent desire will spring forth in full strength and he will take her from the white town and go to join the people. His people.

They are not her people, she keeps trying to tell him.

To her classmates in school she is an Indian. She is lovely, but she is brown. The only things she dislikes about school are the sections of American history that deal with the settlement of the nation and therefore lead to the discussions of Indian conflicts. It begins innocently. Early in the afternoon her teacher appoints a panel of students to report on the plight of the Indian. The panel struggles with the question of broken treaties. Yes, it was wrong of the government to make promises, to come to the tribes with honest-looking eyes and to guarantee grassland or woodland for eternity, and then make changes convenient to the white people who wished to settle on those lands. Even so, the panel says as though in one voice, it is not our fault. We did not do anything.

— What about the sins of the fathers visited upon their children?

— We can't help what they did.

— Wouldn't you have done the same thing?

— Of course not.

— Are you certain of that?

— Sure. Absolutely.

— And are you not guilty of racial prejudice today?

— What! How can you even ask?

Then it explodes: Well, let's ask Emmy.

She slides even lower in her chair, face turned to the side, eyes staring at the floor.

— Emmy?

She wants to be rude.

— Emmy, are you there?

— Yes.

— We don't want to embarrass you...

Then don't.

— but it would be very helpful if we could hear your point of view on this question.

She wants to get up and run from the room.

— Please?

— What was the question?

Her voice almost disappears among the chairs and the students but it carries down the wall and is delivered to the teacher on a small breeze from the open window.

— Do you feel that Indians are treated better now than 100 years ago?

The class looks at her, expectantly, perhaps waiting for an answer they can pounce on, devour, and spit out again, relieving themselves of a foreign object they cannot digest.

— I wasn't here then.

The class snickers.

— Come now, Emmy, that won't do. Please, we can use your help.

She hesitates. What can she know about such matters? She is white, like the rest of the class. They do not seem to realize, or remember, that her mother was white, white like a summer cloud, white like the snow in winter. Her mother is dead, of course, but that should not make any difference. She does not live on the reservation, knows nothing about Indian treaties, cannot be the speaker for the Tetons, the Oglalas, the Santees, the Little Yankton, or anyone else her father has talked about. She cannot remember the names of all the tribes.

— Emmy?

Yes, teacher, I want to be polite and gracious, like my mother taught me, but it's hard. Can't you see that?

— Emmy, we haven't much time left.

Time. Time. The white man and his damn time. It would do him good to sit on a butte or a mountain top and think. And have visions. And quit worrying about time, and clocks, and bells, and meetings, and appointments, and.... What is she saying? And did she say it aloud? Yes, she must have. Heat rises to her face as she realizes that she has betrayed herself. Her classmates cheer because they think they have been vindicated. Emmy One Horse is a real Indian. She can no longer deny it. Now she must answer the question. Clearly, she knows the answer.

— Speak! Speak!

The teacher stands beside her, places his hand gently on her shoulder.

She screams.

As the class looks on in amazement she pulls loose from the teacher's hand and runs from the room, down the hall, out onto the sidewalk, onto the grass, out to the street, the scream trailing behind her and pushing her onward until she runs so fast that she has no air for anything except running and it is not until she reaches the white house with brown trim and has collapsed on her bed that she is able to sob.

"How was school?" her father asks during supper.

"Okay."

"Gettin' along with the boys and girls?"

"Yes," she lies, as she always does when asked that question.

"Y'sure?" he persists.

"Yes." Her head aches as the lie compounds and swells until is bursts like a soap bubble and is no longer a lie but only a ritual, a ceremony to be celebrated five days a week as long as school is in session. But her head continues to ache.

"Good," her father grunts. "Simon, he was here, he don't believe you get along okay. He says we should come home."

At some point in her life, she knows, there will be no more school, no glances in the hallway, no more whispering when she appears to be listening. She can wait for that time. She can wait forever, if necessary. For now, "No," she says, "This is my home. I stay here."

Frank One Horse is uncertain about his home. Perhaps he has none. He is a quiet man with a well-fed and contented body, heavy although not flabby. He is given to periods of absent-mindedness that may be memories intruding from a somewhat confused past. When a friend drops in, either a town man or a reservation man, he often overcomes his normal reticence and talks with a measure of animation. He even laughs. But then the laughter turns to subdued anger as he tells of the whippings at the government school and the disease in the cold shacks on the reservation. He remembers. Above all, he resents the criticism from his relatives and friends who say he has turned white, moving to town and spending his time idly. What he does is draw Indian symbolsmeticulously, beautifully, on fine paper imported from Italy. Pretty nothings, they say. He is not practical. He does not work. He strings no beads for tourists, does not decorate moccasins, will not even keep the winter count on animal hide.

He respects those activities and their designs. He simply wants to go beyond them by incorporating essence, significance, into the designs. His relatives do not understand.

Perhaps his life now is an accident, a quirk of fate. He remembers, impassively, being already a grown man, languishing in poverty, scrounging for scraps of paper on which to draw. Then a woman from the white town drives her shiny car tentatively onto the reservation. The people are accustomed to this kind of visitor, the do-gooder, and expect nothing. They stand around and admire her car. She sees a few of Frank One Horse's drawings that hang in the dusty window of his boards-and-tar house. She hardly believes the tiny building to be a house, but she recognizes the quality of the pencil-and paper art work. She insists that Frank show the drawings in town. They will be appreciated there, she says. He stands straight and proud on the chipped linoleum just inside the door and stares at the white woman in her flowered summer dress. When the wind gusts, the dress swirls around her legs until she seems to be in motion, perhaps ready to fly. She speaks in clipped syllables, and it seems that Frank smiles in amusement, but she persists and soon is loading the artist and his drawings into her car and is speeding away from the distasteful reservation.

Frank has not yet said a word.

The woman is nice-looking as well as persuasive. She senses that Frank is looking at her, and now that she has removed him from the reservation she sees him less as an Indian and more as a handsome man, unmarried, who does what she tells him to do. She tells him to stay in town with her. He does. Eventually, after several exhibits of his drawings bring praise from the townspeople, and a number of sales, she tells him to marry her. He does. After a time, a child is born and named Emmaline after her mother's great-aunt. Frank respects ancestors but calls his daughter Emmy and the name sticks.

It is the mother who maintains the most influence on Emmy, convincing her during the first fifteen years that although her father is a full-blood Sioux—and that is all right, he is a good man—she, Emmy, is to consider herself a white girl.

"After all," the mother says, "you are more of me."

Emmy asks, "But what does Father say about that?"

"He does not say anything."

"Then, what does he think?"

The mother is thoughtful before she answers. "We do not ask him what he thinks."

By the time she enters junior high school, Emmy knows that she is white. Whatever Frank One Horse may think about his daughter's belief, he keeps it to himself.

And now the mother is dead. She is not here to reinforce her daughter's sense of whiteness. Emmy frequently stands before her mirror for a long time, after her father is in bed, determining that her skin is no darker than that of her friends who have been out in the sun and have become tan.

She waits now for her body to fill out. The popular girls at school are the ones whose bodies develop earliest. They wear tight sweaters to make their breasts look full and enticing, and in warm weather some of them have blouses cut low, so that when they bend over the fullness of breast is visible to the sharp-eyed boys who stand around, waiting.

Emmy waits in front of her mirror. She is slim, like her mother. Her ribs show when she stands fully erect, and there is little or no stomach to pull in. That much is good. But her breasts remain small and she looks at them in the dim light of one lamp, at night, and tries to push them up and pull them out until one night she has strange sensations throughout her body and she discovers that size has nothing to do with pleasure.

Her breasts are like half-oranges, one half on each side of her narrow chest, and she imagines that they are sweet like the citrus fruit, and no darker, except that the nipples are brown. In the shower room, after physical education class, she looks around carefully, not wanting to be obvious, and she observes that many of the girls have pink nipples, but the black-haired girls whose skin is off-white or even the same color as her own have brown ones. She wonders why these darker girls think they are different from her.

It is entirely unfair.

Bill, who is big and blond and wants to be a football player, sits by her in the lunchroom for several days, making small talk. She begins to think he likes her, and she responds in phrases of friendliness. One day he says in a husky whisper, "Hey, Emmy, let's go to the river after school and see what color you really are."

She turns her head in embarrassment. No, it is not that; it is anger. The brief friendship is over. All Bill wants from her is to see whether Indian girls are different from the other girls he has taken out. She knows that. She has heard all the jokes, has cried over them in her bedroom, and the sky has cried with her, pouring tears on a dark and gloomy afternoon while she lies on her bed and feels sorry for herself.

She thinks Bill and his friend Lester brag too much about their football prowess, and she is quite certain that she could outrun both of them. She is not afraid when Lester come to the table, exchanges glances with Bill, and joins the argument. "C'mon, Emmy," he says, "it's fun. You're a big girl now. Everybody else does it. And we got a nice quiet place, outdoors, grass, the river making nice sounds."

"No."

"When?"

"Never."

"How about tomorrow?" The scratchy whisper, much too loud, sends a shiver up her spine. Lester puts a hand on her shoulder, moves it along her back, and she tingles and jumps up and runs, runs to the white bedroom with the drawn curtains and the mirror, and she starts to cry and then looks in the mirror and wonders if the two boys like her that much and are not just curious.

She has forgotten that she is missing her afternoon classes.

She knows the river well.

The river curls in from the north and makes a ninety-degree turn at the southwest edge of town, then winds itself around the town and disappears into the east as it searches for the Big River. At the sand dunes, far out of town, it empties itself into the wide and rushing stream up which Lewis and Clark and fur traders have paddled furiously in their quest for whatever it was they wanted, far to the west in another land. Here the little river loses its identity now.

She loves the river although she despairs over the dirty color of the water, tainted by junked cars where it curls around the town, browned by mud washed downstream in the spring. It would be nicer in blue, perhaps a pale blue sometimes, suggesting a tint of white. The white could come from cloud reflections on the blue surface. She often sees the river that way, and she sits in the wild daisies and breathes the scent of pine, and watches the water flow slowly past below her.

She walks now beside the river. The sun shines on her and flitters on the water teasingly. She dodges around a cottonwood tree and into the coolness of shade. Behind her, grasses whisper.

Across the river a meadowlark warbles.

Amazingly, the bird calls her name. Delight rises in her and she answers: "Yes, I'm here. I'm here."

She peers across the river, waiting for the conversation she knows will come next. Suddenly her waist is grasped tightly and a different voice says, intimately but not at all like the voice of the meadowlark, "You came. Let's get to it." The hand on her waist moves up and begins to unbutton her blouse. Her squirming and screaming do not persuade it to stop. Her shouts dry to a hoarse whimper then to an icy white silence, and the hand continues to undress— the blouse, the tiny bra, pants and panties— and other voices now float through the haze, the red fog, and assault her body. "She's neat," the sound of one voice. "She's a real bitch," the sound of another voice. Then a question: "Well, is there anything different about her?" The reply, "No," cutting through a cloud of pain, is strangely satisfying. The grasses are harsh against her back and the sun hurts her eyes until she closes them and tries to withdraw from the river and the voices and the pressing hands. The sky now turns red beneath her eyelids and fills with black specks of birds darting and soaring as though looking for a place to set down. A great willful weight presses upon her, forcing the air out of her lungs, and she can make no sound, only feel that her legs hurt, ache, something terrible, and the ache moves up to her belly and she would like to cry out, to drown out the pain, but her mind will not recognize the source of the pain and she merely endures until the weight falls away and she gasps for breath as another weight falls upon her and she wants to die.

She has only one partially lucid moment, during which she hears the voices again: "Hey, Emmy, your body is okay. Really is." And, "Yeah, that was great. Have to do it again sometime." Finally, "You're in, kid." A perverse sense of pride overcomes her. She is someone special by being the same as the other girls. And then she is lost to the river and the grass and the trees and is running through an endless void until she is in her bed and has a sickening headache.

The next morning her father asks, "Anything wrong, Emmy?" She ponders the question, uncertain of the answer. She says, "I had a nightmare." She does not know if anything is wrong except that she aches in her entire body and the worst of all is the devastating headache. She goes back to bed after her father leaves the house. She is still there when he returns and he asks her to get up, have something to eat, and then they will talk. She cannot eat.

"You don't understand," she says to him in the twilight as they sit in the livingroom.

He sips his beer. When they have company he drinks whiskey and water, but when he talks to his daughter, alone, he wants to keep his head clear, he says. His broad face is dark and thoughtful. in the dim light. Between sips of beer he hunches forward in the chair, puts his elbows on his knees, and stares at the designs in the carpet as though he sees a story there, a story he must tell to his daughter.

"I understand," he says, his eyes following a scroll in the rug pattern, jumping to another scroll and following it, making a rough circle of the entire carpet and coming back to rest, staring now at his feet. "I understand."

"How can you?" she asks. "Your parents were both Indian."

"That don't matter," he says. He seems to be searching his mind for the permission he needs to tell her something. She has noticed this before, whenever he is to be critical of his people. It is like 'ancestors, forgive me, but I must tell the truth to my daughter,' and it is always followed by a sigh of resignation and a story that is not sympathetic to his people.

She waits for him to get his permission.

The room is almost dark know. Frank One Horse is not a poor man, but he remembers poverty and isolation and cruelty and depression, and he does not like to leave all the lights burning in his house. He has turned all of them off except one, and it struggles in vain against the growing darkness.

The darkness of the room is added now to the darkness of the man. Where the lamp touches him, a mahogany gleam reminds the girl of the sheen on a piece of sculpture. He is unmoving, like sculpture, carved from a block of wood, imperturbable on the surface.

She knows from their many talks in the evening that he is often shaken by his own kind of emotion from deep within, so that the stillness of the surface is misleading.

For this reason, she listens to him with respect.

"My trouble," he begins, "isn't with the white man. My trouble is with Inyans. I don't understand Inyans."

This much she has heard before, but he seems ready to expose a part of his past that she has not been exposed to. The potential of the moment unnerves her.

"I need a drink of water, or something," she says.

She goes to the kitchen, turns on the light, fills a glass with water, then empties it and gets a bottle of milk from the refrigerator. The cold milk opens her throat and relaxes her. She turns off the light and returns to the dark living room where she sits cross-legged on the floor near her father. "What don't you understand?" she asks.

He holds the empty beer glass in his large hands, turns it around and around. A lighted cigarette in the ashtray beside him burns slowly, forgotten. He clears his throat.

"You know," he says, "six, mebbe seven years ago—you were little—I was back on the reservation, visitin' my family. That's the last time. I don't go back again."

"I remember," she says.

"Mebbe so. Mebbe no."

She thinks she does, but says nothing.

"You know, my father is dead already then, but not my mother, or my two brothers. Your uncles."

"I know."

"Yeh, well, they don't like my town. This town. And they don't like me anymore. I'm rich, you know. The white man makes me rich."

She protests: "But we're not rich."

"It don't matter," he says. "They want money from me. They say old Inyan custom is sharing. What I have, they want it too."

"Mother said you gave them a lot of money."

"A good woman, your mother," he says. "Knowing all about these things."

The lamp flickers, and Emmy and her father look at it, waiting, but it does not flicker again.

"They don't like me," Frank One Horse says. "My brothers, I mean. I go to visit, and they take me to town and try to get me drunk. We drive back to the river, late, and dark. You see, it's late at night, and they're drunk. Edward and Henry. Both older than me. But they stay on the reservation. Edward is driving, you see, this night, and he goes from one side of the road to the other. He can't see where he's goin'. But I know he'll make it all right. It's his way."

Frank One Horse notices the burning cigarette stub in the ashtray. He snubs it out and lights another.

"Henry is in the back seat, with me. Ever'body is arguin' and cussin' and telling me I'm no good. I'm white. I'm an apple. I'm outside." He pauses, and he chuckles behind his cigarette, as though the memory is amusing even though the incident can't be tolerated. "Well, they get mean, with the bottle of whiskey gone. Henry throws the empty bottle out the window. And then Edward stops the car. I think mebbe he's too drunk to drive. He's gonna sleep it off in the car and then drive again. He reaches under the seat and comes up with a knife. Then I get worried. Edward, drunk, is mean with a knife. I open the door and get out, and Edward starts yelling and swearing. And Henry comes out of the car after me, and Edward after him, and we're all running through the dark."

The girl uncrosses her legs, recrosses them, and looks at her father in amazement. She has never heard this story. She wonders why. Was he ashamed, before?

She has been ashamed. He is joining her. Perhaps.

"You listening, Em?" he says.

"Yes," she says. "Yes."

"Do you understand?"

She is not ready for this. Her thoughts are confused and she cannot retain any part of the story except the dominant image: her father runs through the dark, pursued by his brothers. This is a disturbing kind of knowledge. She does not want it.

She dodges his question: "What happens? Do they catch you?"

"No. Nothing," he says, looking out into the night. He is reliving the incident in his mind, and it is a dark incident. "No. They stumble in the weeds, fall down, too drunk to catch anything."

"Then what?"

"I walk back to town. Catch a bus. Come home. And I never see my brothers again."

"That's awfully sad," she says, softly, as though in the presence of tragedy.

"Yeah."

She wonders, then, why he sometimes talks of going back. Everything is a puzzle.

Timidly, holding back part of her breath, she asks, "Then you don't really want to go back? Not really?"

He cannot seem to answer her, and she cannot repeat the question. She is afraid that she might have missed something in the story, in the tone, and that in spite of his brothers Frank One Horse might still one day wish to return to the reservation, having left only because of her mother.

They are a tableau in the midwestern darkness, figures caught not in flight but in perplexing indecision. The weak light of the one lamp mysteriously adds darkness to his face. Her black hair catches an errant ray from the streetlight outside, but the black of her hair is merely illuminated, not brightened. Neither figure moves when a passing car backfires noisily into the night.

When it appears that the room and its figures are lifeless, the father mumbles, "I dunno. Edward is dead. Your mother is dead."

The girl begins to understand death, but the understanding brings back her headache. The attack upon her sensibility in the schoolroom is a kind of death. The attack upon her person by the river is a kind of death. The attack upon her father, by his brothers, is another death. Death is all around.

The mother is not in this story. She is dead.

For the first time the girl feels sorry for her father. He has been hurt on the reservation and does not want to go back. She has been hurt in the town but does not want to leave. Her resolution is more final, more determined, than her father's, and it is this also that increases her headache. The difference does not seem to mean anything and yet it will always be there because she must be white. She cannot speak further of this to her father. She can only hug him, hard, and stumble upstairs in the dark to her bedroom, holding her painful head between brown hands.

She lies on the bed now, eyes closed, seeing herself in white beside her mother, the mother who is dead but who will enter the story whenever the daughter rewrites it.

Unsent Letter 2

by Carol Muske

You say you don't know who you are. I take the plate of the homeless man and fill it with macaroni and salad. Does he know who he is?
The next man comes up and I say "Would you like
a roll?" and he says "In the sand?" and laughs.

The next one is a woman, pregnant,
young. She asks in a small voice
if she can have some extra food.
We give her noodles, meat, greens.
She looks at her plate and begins

to cry. *I'm so tired*, she says
and stares into space, then at me.
I want to take her in my arms, but
I keep serving food, my hands in
the clear plastic gloves ice-cold

from the ocean wind. After a while
the pregnant girl has finished eating
with the others on the grass and wandered
away. I don't know who you are either.
We turned to each other,

once in blinding sunlight,
once in darkness. Going nowhere, in unnatural
transit—as if we'd been abandoned
by our lives, cut free of every expectation of identity.

St. Augustine said to the crowd around the magus
that we do not understand miracles because we
do not understand the nature of time.

The magus collapsed duration: in his palm
the bean-pod unfurled into a shoot, flowered. I felt
your touch, not in time: in charmed space
where that seed accelerates, cycle by cycle.
And if we sped up transition—she'd have
another human being in her arms, an infant,
—just like that—but she is homeless,
nothing to hold her outside her self.

He has left her, as we are all left, so we do not want
to hurry it, the miracle. It's better that it be served
in gradual sequence, do you see?—child, seducer,
  mother,
father, child, seducer...do you see? Faces: a food-line, a
  you,

one frozen location of mercy: a final divided portion
to set on each plate.

Romeo and Julio

by Jay Neugeboren

Julio lay on his side, as if, Tony thought, he had been folded into position like a paper swan. An aide gave Julio an injection, then wrapped him in a straitjacket. Patients swarmed around, chattering like birds, shuffling in carpet slippers, bare feet, broken shoes. They asked Tony for money, for golf lessons, for candy bars, for skate keys.

Tony imagined that Julio's skin was made of glass, that he could see through to the skeleton below. Julio was a large prehistoric bird—more deadly and beautiful than an eagle, his bones held together by gleaming black railroad spikes. Julio was flying home, his wings spread to the width of the highway, his eyes bright as emeralds.

Tony went over his lines, so that, afterwards, when he brought Lynne home to Brookline from the dress rehearsal of Romeo and Juliet, he would be ready. *O, Wilt thou leave me so unsatisfied?* he would ask. He saw Lynne lean against her door, smile, take her cue. *What satisfaction canst thou have tonight?* she would reply.

He wondered: if he were to tell her he had spent the afternoon visiting his brother Julio in a mental hospital, would that make her like him more? He did not want to be liked *because* he had a brother who was mentally ill. Still, it pleased him to imagine Lynne asking questions, gazing at him with admiration while he talked about how close he and Julio were.

You really love him, don't you? she would say, and he would shrug, modestly. *Sure—Romeo and Julio, that's us*, he would reply, and then apologize quickly for the bad joke, so that sensing his embarrassment, she might like him even more.

He has met Lynne at the Cambridge Public Theatre, where, three months before, they were chosen, along with ten other high school seniors, to serve as apprentices. After rehearsals they would go with the other apprentices to a nearby luncheonette, and often they would stay and talk long after the others had gone. He loved being with her—loved her directness, her sometimes strange sense of humor. She seemed always to say just what she was thinking, without worrying how it would play to others. And he loved, too, the way her hazel eyes flickered, as if filled with fine gold shavings.

Tony dressed, looked past closet mirror, to the window. Below, in the courtyard of their apartment building, Julio had become a small mud-colored lizard. Julio scurried under hedges, leapt to the wall, began climbing. Julio appeared at the window, crawled onto the sill, dropped to the floor, skittered behind the bed.

After the rehearsal, they rode the train back to Lynne's home. The train rose from a tunnel into the night-lights of the city, then crossed over Longfellow Bridge. Tony saw Julio slipping down from one of the bridge's old stone towers, riding the roof of the train like a cowboy, hanging by his ankles, peering upside down into the subway car, grinning brightly.

The instant they were inside Lynne's apartment building, Tony's chest constricted, as if, he felt, the muscles around his heart were drying out, so that the blood had to force its way through. When, on the second floor landing, Lynne turned away to put her key in the lock, Tony touched her arm. She faced him at once, smiling so warmly that he sensed she did want him to kiss her, and yet, his heart pounding, he told himself to wait, to follow through with his original plan.

"O, Wilt thou leave me so unsatsified?" he asked.

"Why not?"

"Why not?"

She laughed and he found himself too surprised to know what to do next.

"The questions from the play, " he said. "I was saving it. I was hoping you'd remember—that maybe you would recite Juliet's reply back to me. . . " He felt dizzy. "I'm sorry," he added.

"Oh Tony—don't be sorry—"

Her eyes seemed nearly transparent, as if made of the thinnest gold leaf. He shrugged. "I just. . ."

"You just what?"

I was just thinking about my brother, he wanted to say. I just love looking at you. I just can't believe a girl as pretty as you would like me as much as I like you. I just don't know what I'm doing and I don't want to put on an act and make a stupid joke from my brother's name and yet. . .

"Nothing," he said.

She smiled and brushed her hair back. He wished he were her hand. He wished she could know, without words, how much he loved being near her. But he was frightened that if he began telling her about Julio he wouldn't know where to stop and the moment he'd been hoping for would pass and never come again.

He felt faint. He imagined a twister of frigid air swirling up the staircase, tunneling around him, wrapping him in white. He blinked, looked down, saw nothing but her mouth, her lips.

"Would you like to come in for a few minutes?" she asked. "I have to get up early tomorrow to help my mother bake. Before ten o'clock mass. Then we're going to my aunt's house."

"I'll be visiting my brother Julio tomorrow," Tony stated. "He lives in a mental hospital. He's been there for almost three years. He's my only brother and he's a year younger than I am. We were always very affectionate with one another."

Lynne cocked her head to one side, and he saw a look of such intense compassion on her face that it made him stiffen.

"That must be hard for you," she said.

What Tony wanted more than anything in the world was simply to hold her and to have her hold him, yet when her fingers touched his cheek, gently, he was too ashamed of himself, and too furious with her, to risk being repulsed again. What right did she have to know about Julio's life, and why—what he would never be able to take back, he knew, and what she would surely despise him for—had he been so weak as to mention it?

"I'll see you on Monday," he said, stepping back. He moved toward the staircase.

"Call me in the morning," she said. "All right? I'll be home until at least nine-thirty. Please?"

Tony slept. When he woke, near dawn, thirty years had passed. He reached over to stroke Julio's hair, the way he often did, but Julio was not there. Tony sat up. He saw himself taking Lynne by the the hand, leading her to this point in his life. They were driving north of Boston, past low rolling hills and endless green fields of gravestones. Tony's wife was beside him, his two children in the back seat. Tony was a well-known film director, his wife a beautiful movie star who had given up her career to raise a family with him, but who, every few years, appeared in a film he made.

They drove on, Lynne invisible, yet strapped to the rear of the car, forced to watch and listen. Why was he so angry with her? he wondered. Even if she found out the way his imagination worked sometimes—how it could contain the craziest and most violent and most beautiful scenes at the same time—why would this scare her away? Did love and friendship *have* to be opposites, the way sanity and insanity were?

When they drove past an enormous complex of tall prison-like buildings, he explained to his children, as he did each time, that this was where their Uncle Julio had lived once upon a time. They cruised along curving tree-lined roads, stopped in front of an elegant colonial home. The front door opened and Julio appeared, smiling radiantly. He walked down the steps. Tony emerged from the car and he and his brother embraced. Julio asked him why it had taken him so long to get there.

"Long?" Tony said. "But it's only been thirty years—"

Tony put on a bathrobe, left his room. The apartment was wonderfully still. In a few hours his parents would be eating breakfast, going through the *Sunday Globe*, talking about their visit, later in the day, to Julio. It was just past five-thirty. Tony opened the refrigerator. He could eat breakfast, dress, go out and get the paper, tale a walk, come home, shower, shave. Time would pass more easily if he kept busy. He didn't want to telephone Lynne's home before nine.

A Measure of the Sin

by Kristy Nielsen

1. A Bucketful of Sin

I walk through the town with one of the women, her baby on my hip, weighted with rain that just keeps falling. We pass men with bandaged heads, men with hats under their arms singing prayers, women clicking like squirrels crouched under low trees. They quiet once we pass. Only the wind swirls behind us.

The baby clings to me so that I almost don't have to hold him. The woman is weak and chilled, but the rain doesn't bother me. I press on and let people inside houses and stores stare at my wet, hardened nipples. We don't know why we came out or how we got so far from the house. The water keeps pouring over us. The baby is pale and cold.

We pass out of town, but the woman doesn't think she can make it. She coughs blood. I swing the baby to my front and she climbs onto my back. With lowered head, I watch trees pass as we reach the country and move out toward the house, to safety. Rain flattens flowers by the side of the road and even field cows move under trees.

When we reach the house, the man says the water washed us clean. He tugs in the buckets of rain he's collected, a measure of the sin.

2. There Is No Bear

A bear prowls the house. I've seen him climbing out of the front closet and smelled him in my room. At night, I hear him walking the third floor. The women say, "There is no bear," and run themselves a hot bath. The man tells me we are too far south for bears, watches a mouse run across the kitchen. I still hear the bear snorting in the next room.

Finally one night I awaken to find the bear on top of me. I fight, of course, but he is so heavy. I claw at his hair and call to the man for help. The man says, "There is no bear. Go back to sleep."

There is a bear: I feel his weight on top of me, smell his bear breath, hear his bear grunts. The women upstairs are tittering. In one of their dreams, I am smothered by the bear's great weight and lie frozen on my back forever.

3. At Least One Bitch

The man strips down the house, except for one long upstairs room overflowing with stuffed chairs, rugs, flowered paper, and five wooden bureaus, light ones and dark-colored ones with curving mirrors above drawers that overflow with silk and soft cotton. Two long-haired women with newborns take short steps, mewing softly, and one bitch licks her puppies clean.

I, the childless one, am awkward in the cramped room. I must help him downstairs to move everything into the opened-up house. He herds two cows into the living room, their tongues working in confusion, shoos chickens onto rafters. With the wall board down, he uses crossbeams as shelves—tomatoes, a potato placed alone, then a bucket of beans. Through the open wall I see him walk by urgently, carrying an armful of lettuce pressed to his chest.

From my own tiny garden, I bring unripened vegetables. I place tomatoes on the window sill, side by side in the sun. He stops me. "These are no good." Then more gently, "See," stabbing one with his pocketknife. I see that it is filled with worms.

At night we breathe quietly among animals and food. I watch moonlight move slowly across shapes in the darkness, make each in turn a solitary portrait.

4. Somewhere to Begin

I sit heavy with the bear's child when the man tells me I must carry a twenty pound bag of potatoes through the woods to the stream and wash each carefully. The two women come with me to learn the way. They think it is a dangerous mission; they run zig-zag through the woods and stop behind trees to peer ahead. I walk straight through with the bag over my shoulder, the bear's child clawing inside.

At the water, I squat and roll each potato between my hands in the stream's current. The two women splash and giggle downstream. Occasionally they stop to pose before mirror-like patches of water.

I look up when I hear my name. A brown woman in a red shift stands with her feet planted square in the stream bed, staring at my potato. She squats in front of me, her breasts swaying with the movement. She carries nothing. "How do you survive alone?" I ask. She tells me, "That is the second most important question."

5. The Hummingbird Between My Legs

I carry my pelvis gently, like a wounded hand, and search for a quiet place to sit. The tension between my legs is a clenched fist, a hummingbird. I could think up metaphors all day, but for the work that must be done: we plant the new garden where it can't be seen from the road. The man and I silently break up dirt with a shovel, and I avert my eyes. He smells me in the dirt I've walked over, looks at me with cow eyes.

With each seed I punch into the ground, I look for signs; I sniff the air. The tension between my legs is a moss-covered rock, a bowl of fruit, a secret letter. When the seeds are finally planted, I lie back on newly plowed soil in midday sun, spread my legs to let the hummingbird beat against my dress and fly away.

6. Everything's Going to Be All Right

The women on the third floor squawk with fear: one of the babies is lost in the house. I hear the man's heavy bootsteps as he moves through the house opening closets, calls to the baby in a funny, high voice.

I think of pet snakes or mice that get loose in a house and live and breed behind walls, slithering along trails of wires and pipes, staring out knotholes at breakfast, lunch, and dinner. I drop to hands and knees and crawl at baby level to the cellar. I move slowly along the dank wall, wind around the monstrous furnace and look up only as I climb into the old potato bin. The child sits naked and quiet, breathing through his mouth.

I cannot bring myself to say, "Shh, everything's going to be all right." I can only stare back, rise to my feet and return to the chair in my little room where I can look out the window.

7. Any Woman

Outside the kitchen, I sit on the stairs and press myself to the side rail. I lift flakes of white paint with my fingernail to reveal blue underneath. The bear storms through the house again, but he does not want me this time. When I hear noise, I do not startle. I do not reveal my presence. I do not betray a single emotion.

The rumbling starts low. I wait for it to build, flicking paint chips silently. The noise is rhythmic and soothing. When the train comes finally through the valley, its roar deliciously overwhelms the sounds of everyday life. I look up. While the train lasts, I am in any soundless picture of a woman on the back stoop. I am any muted woman waiting for bread to rise so she can punch it down again.

8. The Only Weapons I Have

When my time comes, I run barefoot down the dirt path toward water. Animals watch silently, and the canoe only whispers as I push it from the shore. I wind down the canal throughout evening. The water's surface reflects orange in the swirling pools of waste behind abandoned factories at the edge of the city.

Evening darkens the sky. Snakes dangle from branches, from metal rods hanging off viaducts; some look like coils in the water. I let the water propel me as long as it will. When my canoe stops in the city, I start swimming and pull the canoe by a rope in my mouth.

I must glide through the water, unnoticed as a rotted branch; the snakes must not get angry. My body brushes a water snake, and I resist the kick. Ahead, a purple and green snake coils up and down in the water. I know I have to skim the surface of the water, my body flat, but I want to curl up, cover my belly with knees, fingers, elbows, the only weapons I have.

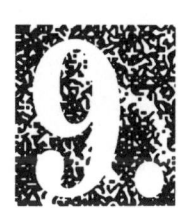

9. Such Blueness

This barn in a flat grazing pasture has been a hiding place for someone else. In corn cribs, I see rusted cans, stacks of chipped plates, flatware, broken glass, moth-eaten linen, a saucepan. Along one wall, someone carefully lined up house plants where they could receive sun from the slats in the loft. Furniture is stacked everywhere, chairs four high and rotted through with mice and spiders, wooden dressing tables, chests of drawers and end tables all twisted and buckled.

On a stool in a corner I sit partially hidden from the others. Here I find pieces of paper protected in a cookie tin. A woman has erased recipes to write messages: "I wouldn't want you to see me this way, with my head bandaged, stark against the blue sky."

From where I sit, from where she must have sat, I see a tiny piece of the afternoon sky through a gap in the barn boards. My sliver of sky is blue also.

On Encountering Passionate Lovers of Poe in the Former Soviet Union

by Karen Lee Osborne

Like the French, the Georgians love him.
When a dark-haired
Georgian mother recites
"Annabel Lee"
I nod and smile.
They love Allen Ginsberg too
and what he does in the dark
doesn't bother them much
though they can't do it
freely here.
They know there's room,
there's space in the heart
for many things.

I refuse
to choose
between heaven and hell,
angels or demons,
excess or restraint. It's

a dangerous ruse. Let each
one love whom she may.
Let's each try to be of use.
I'll take Tsvetayeva **and**
Akhmatova, Sturua **and**
Kalandadze. I'll admit no
scarcity, not paranoia of praise
among such plenty.

Georgians use the word
guest-loving. Always they have
many guests, always they make room,
despite the undeserving.
In a land
taken many times, where
a Soviet tower long stood
on *M'tatsmindu*, Holy Mountain,
language claims
more than they know.
Lay me down, when I die,
in such a place, between
two mountains facing each
other, each one speaking
its ancient, irrefutable tongue.

The Miracle

by Harry Mark Petrakis

He was weary of tears and laughter. He felt perhaps he had been a priest too long. His despair had grown until it seemed, suddenly, bewilderingly, he was an entity, separate and alone. His days had become a burden.

The weddings and baptisms which once provided him with pleasure had become a diversion, one of the myriad knots upon the rope of his faith. A rope he was unable to unravel because for too long he had told himself that in God rested the final and reconciling truth of the mystery that was human life.

In the middle of the night the ring of the doorbell roused him from restless sleep. His housekeeper, old Mrs. Calchas, answered. Word was carried by a son or a daughter of a friend that an old man or an old woman was dying and the priest was needed for the last communion. He dressed wearily and took his bag and his book, a conductor on the train of death who no longer esteemed himself as a puncher of tickets.

He spent much time pondering what might have gone wrong. He thought it must be that he had been a priest too long. Words of solace and consolation spoken too often became tea bags returned to the pot too many times. Yet he still believed that love, all forms of love, represented the only real union with other human beings. Only in this way, in loving and being loved, could the enigmas be transcended and suffering be made bearable.

When he entered the priesthood forty years before, he drew upon the springs of love he had known. The warmth of his mother who embodied for him the home from which he came, bountiful nature and the earth. The stature of his father as the one who taught him, who showed him the road to the world. Even the fragmented recollection of the sensual love of a girl he had known as a boy helped to strengthen the bonds of his resolve. He would never have accepted his ordination if he did not feel that loving God and God's love for all mankind could not be separated. If he could not explain all the manifestations of this love, he could at least render its testaments in compassionate clarity.

But with increasing anguish his image seemed to have become disembodied from the source. He felt himself suddenly of little value to those who suffered. Because he knew this meant he was failing God in some improvident way, a wounding shame was added to his weariness.

Sometimes in the evening he stopped by the coffeehouse of Little Macedonia. There the shadows were cool and restful and the sharp aroma of brandies and virulent cigars exorcised melancholy for a little while. He sat with his old friend of many years, Barbaroulis, and they talked of life and death.

Barbaroulis was a grizzled and growling veteran of three wars and a thousand tumbled women. An unrepentant rake who counted his years of war and lechery well spent. An old man in the twilight of his life with all the fabled serenity of a saint.

"Hurry, old noose-collar," Barbaroulis said. "I am half a bottle of mastiha ahead."

"I long ago gave up hope of matching you in that category," the priest said.

Barbaroulis filled both their glasses with a flourish. "Tell me of birth and marriage and death," he said.

"I have baptized one, married two, and buried three this last week," the priest said.

Barbaroulis laughed mockingly. "What a delightful profession," he said. "A bookkeeper in the employ of God."

"And whose employ are you in?" the priest asked.

"I thought you knew," the old man said. "Can you not smell sulfur and brimstone in my presence?"

"An excuse for not bathing more often," the priest said.

"You are insolent," the old man growled. He called out in his harsh loud voice and a waiter exploded out of the shadows with another bottle of mastiha. Barbaroulis drew the cork and smelled the fragrance with a moan of pleasure. "The smell of mastiha and the smell of a lovely woman have much in common," he said. "And a full bottle is like lovely woman before love."

"Your head and a sponge have much in common, too," the priest said. "Wine and women are ornaments and not pillars of life."

"Drink up, noose-collar," Barbaroulis said. "Save your sermons for Sunday."

The priest raised the glass to his lips and slowly sipped the strong tart liquid. It soothed his tongue and for a brief illusive moment eased his spirit. "The doctor has warned you about drinking," he said to Barbaroulis. "Yet you seem to be swilling more than ever before."

"When life must be reduced to an apothecary's measure," Barbaroulis snorted,"it is time to get out. I am not interested in remaining alive with somber kidneys and a placid liver. Let the graduate undertakers who get me marvel at my liver scarred like the surface of a withered peach and at my heart seared by a thousand loves like a hunk of meat in incredible heat."

"You are mad, old roué," the priest said. "But sometimes I see strange order in your madness."

"Even a madman would renounce this world," Barbaroulis said with contempt. "Why should anyone hesitate giving up the culture of the bomb and the electric chair? We are a boil on the rump of the universe and all our vaunted songs are mute farts in the darkness of eternity."

"You assemble the boil and the fart," the priest said, "from the condition of your liver and your heart."

"When will you admit, noose-collar," Barbaroulis laughed, "that the limousine of faith has a broken axle?"

"When you admit," the priest said, "that the hungry may eat fish without understanding the meaning in its eye." He finished his drink and rose regretfully to go.

"Leaving already?" Barbaroulis said. "You come and go like a robin after crumbs."

"There is a world outside these shadows," the priest said.

"Renounce it!" Barbaroulis said. "Forsake it! Join me here and we will both float to death on exultant kidneys."

"You are a saint," the priest said. "Saint Barbaroulis of the Holy Order of Mastiha. Your penance is to drink alone."

"What is your penance?"

The priest stood for a moment in the shadows and yearned to stay awhile longer. The taste of mastiha was warm on his tongue and his weariness was eased in the fragrant dark. "Birth and marriage and death," he said and waved the old man goodbye.

On Sunday mornings he rose before dawn and washed and dressed. He sat for a little while in his room and reviewed his sermon for the day. Then he walked the deserted streets to the church.

There was a serenity about the city at daybreak on Sunday, a quiet and restful calm before the turmoil of the new week. Only a prowling tomcat, fierce as Barbaroulis, paused to mark the sound of his steps in the silence. At the edge of the dark sky the first light glittered and suspended the earth between darkness and day.

The church was damp from the night and thick with shadows. In a few moments old Janco shuffled about lighting the big candles. The flames flickered light across the icons of the white bearded saints.

He prepared for the service. He broke the bread and poured the wine for the communion. Afterward he dressed slowly in his vestments and bound the layers and cords of cloth together. He passed behind the iconostasis and through a gap in the partition saw that the first parishioners were already in church awaiting the beginning of the service. First the very old and infirm regarding the ornaments of God somberly and without joy. They would follow every word and gesture of the liturgy grimly. Their restless and uneasy fingers reflected the questions burning in their minds. Would the balance sheet of their lives permit them entry into the city of God? Was it ever too late to take solace in piety and assurance in sobriety?

After them the middle-aged entered. Men and women who had lived more than half their lives and whose grown children had little need for them anymore. Strange aches and pains assailed them and they were unable to dispel the dark awareness of time as enemy instead of friend.

Then the young married couples with babies squirming in their arms, babies whose shrill voices cried out like flutes on scattered islands. In the intervals when they were not soothing the infants, the young parents would proffer their devotions a little impatiently while making plans for the things to be done after church.

Finally the very young boys and girls, distraught and inattentive, secured to the benches by the eyelocks of stern parents. They had the arrogance of youth, the courage of innocence, and the security of good health.

When the service was over they all mingled together for a moment and then formed into lines to pass before him for bread. Old Janco began snuffing out the candles in the warm and drowsy church. The shadows returned garnished by incense. The church emptied slowly and the last voices echoed a mumble like the swell of a receding wave. In the end only he remained and with him the men and women standing in the rear of the darkened church waiting to see him alone.

"Father, my daughter is unmarried and pregnant. A boy in our neighborhood is guilty. I swear I will kill him if he does not marry her."

"Father, my husband drinks. For ten years he has promised to give it up. Sometimes there isn't money enough to buy food for the children's supper."

"Father, all day I look after my mother in her wheelchair. I cannot sleep at night because I dream of wishing her dead."

"Father, my child is losing his sight. The doctors say there is nothing that can be done."

"Father, ask God to have mercy on me. I have sinned with my brother's wife."

"Father, pray for me."

Until the last poor tormented soul was gone, and he stood alone in the dark and empty church. In the sky outside a bird passed trailing its winged and throaty cry. He knelt and prayed. He asked to be forgiven his sins of weariness and despair and to be strengthened against faltering and withdrawal. For a terrible instant he yearned for the restful sleep of death.

There was a night that summer when the doorbell rang long after midnight. He woke from a strange and disordered sleep to the somber voice of Mrs. Calchas. Barbaroulis was dying.

He dressed with trembling hands and went into the night. His friend lived in a rooming house a few blocks away and the landlady, a grim-faced Medusa, let the priest in. She told him the doctor had come and gone. There was nothing more to be done.

Barbaroulis lay in an old iron-postered bed, a decayed giant on a quilt-and-cotton throne. When he turned his head at the sound of the door, the priest saw that dying had refashioned the flesh of his face, making the cheeks dark and tight and the eyes webbed and burning.

"I was expecting Death, the carrion crow," Barbaroulis said. "You enter much too softly."

"Did you wake me for nothing?" the priest said. "Is your ticket perhaps for some later train?"

Barbaroulis grinned, a twisting of flesh around his mouth, and the husks of teeth glittered in the dim light. "I sent for you to get it," he said.

"Get what?"

"The bottle of mastiha," Barbaroulis said. "My mouth is parched for some mastiha."

"The custom is for communion," the priest said.

"Save it," Barbaroulis said. "There is a flask of mastiha in the corner behind the books. I have hidden it from that dragon who waits like a banshee for my wake."

The priest brought him the flask. The great nostrils of Barbaroulis twitched as he smelled the sharp aroma. He made a mighty effort to raise his head and the priest helped him. The touch of the old man's expiring flesh swept the priest with a mutilating grief. A little liquid dribbled down the old man's chin. Breathing harshly, he rested his head bach against the pillow. "A shame to waste any," he said.

"Tomorrow I will bring a full bottle," the priest said, "and serve to you out of the communion chalice. We might get away with it."

"Drink it yourself in my memory," Barbaroulis said. "I will not be here."

"Where is your courage?" the priest asked gruffly to cover emotion. "I have seen men sicker by far rise to dance in a week."

"No more dancing for Barbaroulis," the old man said slowly and the mocking rise and fall of his voice echoed from the hidden corners of the room. "the ball is over, the bottle empty, the strumpets asleep. Pack me a small bag for a short trip. Only the lightest of apparel."

"A suit of asbestos," the priest said.

"I have no regrets," Barbaroulis twisted his mouth in weird grin. "I have burned the earth as I found it. And if word could be carried far and fast enough a thousand women would mourn for me and rip their petticoats in despair."

"Are you confessing?" the priest asked.

"Just remembering," Barbaroulis said and managed a sly wink. "When I see your God," he said, "shall I give him a message from you?"

"You won't have time," the priest said. "The layover between trains will be brief."

The old man's dark parched lips stirred against each other in silent laughter. "Old noose-collar," he said, "a comfort to the end."

"Saint Barbaroulis," the priest said. "The Holy Order Mastiha."

"What a time we could have had," Barbaroulis said. "The two of us wenching and fighting and drinking. What a roisterer I could have made of you."

"What about you in church?" the priest said. "You might have become a trustee and passed the collection plate on Sunday. Who would have dared drop a slug before your fierce and vigilant eyes? Gregory of Nazianzus would have been a minor saint beside you."

Barbaroulis laughed again with a grating sound as if bone were being rubbed against bone. Then the laughter faltered and a long shudder swept his body. His fingers, stiff as claws, curled in frenzy upon the sheet.

The priest watched the terrible struggle and there was nothing he could do but grip the old man's hand tightly in his own.

Barbaroulis made a sign with his raging eyes and the priest moved closer quickly. A single moment had transformed the old man's face into a dark teeming battleground of death. His lips stirred for a moment without sound and then he spoke in a low hoarse whisper and each word came bitten slowly from between his teeth.

"I have known a thousand men and women well," he drew a long fierce rasp of breath. "I have loved only one." His voice trailed away and the priest moved closer to his lips that trembled to finish. "A priest who reflects the face of his God."

Then his mouth opened wider and his teeth gleamed. For a moment he seemed to be screaming in silence and then a short violent rush of air burst from his body.

The priest sat there for a long time. In death the old man seemed to have suddenly become half man, half statue, something between flesh and stone. Finally the priest rose and closed the dead man's eyes and bent and kissed his cheek.

He left the room. The street was black but the roofs of houses were white in the glow of the waning moon. A wind stirred the leaves of a solitary tree and then subsided.

His friend had been a man of strife and a man of contention. But into the darkness the old man had borne the priest's grief and his sorrow. In his final moment, Barbaroulis had fed his loneliness and appeased his despair. And as he walked, he cried, and the great bursting tears of Lazarus ran like wild rivers down his cheeks.

Revolutions

by James Plath

for Brian

Tears are always the epicenter
beneath the fissures of our vision.
Even a child, my son
suspects the center of things
must always change, as water seething
shapes itself to the volatile moon,
as a Popsicle
melting warms to the stick.
When stiff arms fold, his back toward me,
it is almost as if the whole earth
has turned, leaving me
to my own
rebellion, speaking
not to the boy he is, but to the boy
I used to be. Shouting and pointing
to rooms unclean or bicycles
left to rust in the rain, to freeze,
to grind arthritic circles. . .
none of it matters at times like these.
In revolutions, words are lost
and whole worlds melt
into borderless shapes, a darkness
which, though temporary,
no one can ever hurry
or change.

Divine Attention

by Paulette Roeske

The Board of Education had its reasons
for sending me across the racial border
into the ramshackle high school
where I would grapple with street gangs
on the turf of remedial English.
On day one in the dust-covered classroom,
shot-out windows admitting jigsaw pieces
of true sky, I learned the meaning of anarchy.
At the first bell, Rat shook up
a bottle of Pepsi and sprayed Weasel,
then someone snatched a tampon from DeeDee's purse
for a game of catch. In the front row,
with divine attention, Carmen painted
her nails chartreuse. I pounded the textbook
on the desk, a trick I stole from Krushchev.
I thanked them for their attention.

Day after day I followed the carefully
prepared script the Board believed would open
closed doors. Diagrammed sentences
marched across the blackboard like stick figures
in a learn-to-draw-me book. While I droned
about the parts of speech, on the bulletin board
they posted the school news—what babies
were born, who held up which gas station or
corner store, which gang crossed what line,
who bled from what wound, who was arrested,
who arraigned, who sent up the river,
who checked in at the morgue.

2. The day a brick crashed through
the last whole window,
I told the class we were lucky
no one was killed and to leave
the glass on the floor.
William, myopic, overweight, a bully,
picked up the biggest shard
and entered the center aisle, testing
the point on his palm. The world
was Fat William, slow-stepping
down the collision course, and me,
adrift beside the small island
of my desk. When he reached the front,
he raised his arms inch
by inch above his head, forty-five
pairs of eyes climbing after him.
Stretched like a victim on the rack,
he paused. Lost in the wavering
pools of his magnified eyes,
I didn't will his hand
away from the soft edges
I call me, nor did I invite it.
As for him, he must have guessed how little
the difference between cutting
me and cutting himself.
With an angry sleight of hand
he brought down the glass
at my feet.

3. When I wore the black mini-skirt
and black and white striped blouse,
puffed sleeves buttoned to my forearms
like gauntlets, red bow draped at my neck,
DeeDee said she liked my dress.
From her purse she fished
a well-thumbed copy of *Glamour* stamped

DO NOT REMOVE. Women—thin, white,
too happy—rose from the clutter
of candy wrappers, crushed cigarette packs,
action comics, cosmetics swept straight
from the shelf into DeeDee's purse.
The women summed up her dog-eared
ambition. She tortured her hair
blonde and powdered her face as if
to erase herself. Again she said, "I like
your dress." In the next row, Carmen
added another point to the black star
she was painting on her thumbnail.
Without glancing up, she said, "So? She got
a job. She working." DeeDee said she wanted
my dress. I imagined myself naked
in front of the class as in those dreams
teachers sometimes have. I imagined her
as me, the red bow in a stranglehold
around her neck.

4. "Hey, white girl, the name's Rat.
I'm a poet. I'm crazy," he said,
leaping onto my desk, executing
a soft-shoe that broke pencils
and footprinted the detailed
records required by the State.
"That's Mrs. to you," I said. "You're
no more crazy than I am. And
get off my desk." Barely clearing
Carmen's bowed head, he jumped
from one nailed down desk
to the next until he reached
the door at the back of the room.
On the school's one reluctant
mimeograph machine, I cranked out
copies of poems signed *One Crazy Rat.*

Purple smudges bruised every page.
Personally he handed them out
to the thirty students left,
saying, "I'm a poet. I'm famous.
And her? She's Mrs. White Girl." He
didn't come back after that day.
Maybe he turned sixteen, maybe
he turned his back at the wrong
time, or maybe he figured that day
was as good as life got and
how much wiser to bow out
with both barrels smoking. Daily
I checked the bulletin board for news.

5. During the strike the teachers
called me a scab and worse, but Weasel
ditched class to guard my car.
I could see him from the window,
lounging on the hood of my Chevy,
rolling joints. By then I had thrown
away the script and spent the days
reinventing my favorite books—talking
up Kurtz's crimes in the Congo,
ascribing him tortures borrowed

from the Bible, Dante, and de Sade.

Iago was misunderstood, cried the twelve

who remained, and the minotaur

merely confused by his odd

combination of hands and hooves.

They warmed to the world where everything

is permitted, and believing at last

they could imitate art in their lives.

6. After school in the girls' john,
empty except for the ineradicable
odors of urine, smoke, and lilac cologne,
where lipsticked walls cursed
honkies, pigs, spicks, the fucked-over world,
where cracked plaster leaked roaches
and forgotten books spilled their undecipherable formulas
beside the overflowing toilets,
I abandoned the false metaphor
calling life a blank slate.
For a year I had watched them turn
desecrated page after desecrated page
even though they already knew no idea
was ever whole or pure
and salvation was a profane word.

Epitaph for Contemporaries

by Maura Stanton

The year of our Lord 1946—?

Millions of us, blind and slippery,
    Emerged with our bloody scalps.
Somebody grabbed our ankles
    And held us upside down
Until we gasped and squalled.
    Tucked into bassinets
Or old laundry baskets,
    Silky haired or bald,
We were given earth names
    From Morocco or Ireland
And kissed for good luck.
    Prince of years, 1946,
Post-war, baby-boom—
    Our parents smiled at our faces
Not knowing what they rocked.
    They dressed me in white organdy,
Lined with red rickrack,
    Brushed out my curls.
In my patent leather shoes
    I danced myself dizzy
Trying to reach someplace
    Beyond the ordinary.
My twin wore blue overalls,
    Banged on his xylophone,

A dazed look on his face,
    And slowly we forgot
What we knew before language,
    Our babble and shriek
Trained into syntax and error.
    We sat at school desks
Where some of us learned to read
    And some of us learned to weep,
Growing into ourselves,
    And thought we'd forgotten
That other planet, our home.
    But deep inside our brains
Instructions were planted
    Like a computer virus
And here at the millennium
    We squint and can see
Beyond our Good Intentions.
    Smoke rises from grasslands
Replacing the rainy jungle,
    And the bees, without winter,
Multiply and swarm north
    To scorched Alpine valleys.
We look away from each other
    And this one still goes to market
And this one stays home
    And this one eats more roast beef
And this one eats none
    And this one cries wee wee wee wee
Frightened of home.
    Brother humans, Sister humans,
Soon all of us will be
    Crushed into caskets or urns
Or dumped into mass graves
    To resemble each other exactly
Without sex or color or speech.
    When our Masters come to view

All we've conquered and poisoned
   They will not distinguish us
From the fruits of our grim labor
   As they stride over the globe
Triumphant, unfurling their wings.

Night Shift, After Drinking Dinner, Container Corporation of America, 1972

by Kevin Stein

Through the cheap iron gate and its mythic
irony (for who would storm and sack
a box-making plant?); down the cigarette-
stained

hall and past the super's all-glass office,
I lurched and reeled and had, as the boys
who play the ponies say, to piss like a racehorse.

It wasn't the urinous light, puddled
and wavering as if a mirage in some
bad Abbott and Costello Sunday movie;
not the yawing and clanging, the squeal
of machines in heat, for reproducing,
after all, is their anointed duty;

not the scent of sulphur and hot glue,
those belching and farting fork lifts,
not even "death valley" steaming cardboard.
It was a raspy *Jesus Christ* I heard
above the six pack hiss (Pabst Blue Ribbon,
a buck sixty-none, cold), a voice which beckoned

me to Shipping where acid-tripping Bill
had metal-strapped his hand to a pallet.
Efficient, even when stoned, he'd stencilled:

SHIP TO: PITTSBURGH, PA / HEINZ 57
200 COUNT / SCORED / DOUBLE-NOTCHED.
That, my introduction to LSD and political subversion,

so little of either in my GM town:
alternators, headlamps, the domino theory,
"An Okie from Muskogee" our jukebox anthem.

What I knew of war I got from Cronkite's
daily tally, each lurid tone of death
on camera, that Vietnamese girl napalmed

and naked. This was what I watched—
mind you, watched, and took to saying "peace"
instead of goodbye, easy enough if your draft

number's 185. So it was when oh so wild Bill
lifted the stub to his lips and sucked it
as he would a paper cut, Mr. Natural's

going to keep me out of 'Nam, he said,
which meant: would keep him whole,
notwithstanding the lopped-off index finger;

which meant: no trigger, no Uncle Sam
poking his chest. He laughed
the bellyful laugh of shock,

the giddy electric giggle of lysergic acid.
We pried his finger from the skid,
buried it in a cup of ice, our ship

of state scuttled in rose waters.
There was beauty in the mind's eye,
which could afford to be inconsolably

clumsy with facts. "Keep on Truckin',"
said the little blotter acid man—
his boots huge, arm raised, finger pointed

to some constellation of loss
and promised rebirth. There was
irony, too, in a rush to hide the cup,

red-faced paramedics screaming,
"Where is it, man?"—how cleaving
may cleave a part unto the whole.

An Essay on Liberation

by David St. John

He stood naked at one of the two windows
She kept open in all weathers in her
Corner room at the back of the old building
As the sun rose he watched a man
Dragging a handcart along the narrow alley
  below
& across the court a young boy was turning
His face from side to side in a freckled mirror
From the temples in the old section of the city
He could hear the first sequence
Of morning prayers & to the west he could see
The dulled bronze domes of The Church of the Orthodox
Where at any moment the bells would begin to chime
& in the streets crisscrossing the city
From the old section to the sea
The tanks & personnel trucks began moving quietly
Into position in their orderly & routine way
& as the bells began sounding from their tower
They were answered by the echoing concussion of
  mortars
As the daily shelling of the hills began
& she was slicing small pieces of bread the size of coins
To fry in goat butter & chives she was naked
Kneeling on one of the worn rugs thrown at angles
  across

The scarred floor she glanced up at him & smiled
Nodding for no reason in particular & in spite of
The fact the one phrase he'd taught her perfectly
Began with the word for *free* though it ended
With *nothing*

Oh Rage and Fury

by Jonathan Strong
for Mike and Alisa

Fucking goddamn psychiatrists! Blinking, twinkling, coaxingly smiling across the darkened room—that was Dr. Schoen anyway. Or how about Dr. MacNamara, the second-opinion showman I saw last week, lazing back open-armed: "I'm the one who can solve the mystery. That Schoen just didn't get it. You deserve to be *loved*, you need to be seeing someone like *me*! Unfortunately I don't have any free time at present..." A couple of years ago, there was Dr. Bartholow, on the edge of his chair, face wrinkled in concern, all for me. Or in ancient days, Dr. Krespel, the adversary, our long-term entrenchment: "You have to want to change." "I want to want to change, but I don't *want* to change." Oh, there've been others. Fuck them all.

Instead, now, there's Donny. Talk about transference. Virtually instantaneous. Lanky ballplayer type, brimmed Padres cap, brown deep-set eyes. Or in his noontime incarnation, a waiter at Minnie's: white sleeves rolled up to his tight little biceps, black vest, the Old West saloon look.

Well, which would you pick? Dr. Lewis Schoen? And why shouldn't a fantasy be just as salutary? Lord knows, they bear the same likeness: a one-way relationship. All in the head—"It's all in your head." Isn't everything?

So let's stick to Donny Rosen from San Diego; let's just say he admires me, thinks I've got it together. He volunteers to help next Sunday. We're giving out water to the marchers at the Walk For Life. Turns to me, whispers: "I think I'm falling in love with you." That'd be enough to get me going again. So what if my boyfriend of three years has decided to settle in with my previous boyfriend of seven years? So what if they got the apartment? My new little low-rent bunker on the wrong side of town has its attractions—for Donny, at least. We can play music as loud as we like, lie in bed as long as we please.

As for my last boyfriend, the one with the three-year warranty, I'm writing an opera libretto about him: *Gentleman Johnny or The Punished Dissolute*. It's an attempt to purge him from my soul. Everyone needs a creative hobby these days; mine is putting new words to old operas. At least I don't have to worry about collaborating with anyone. My ex-ex, Leon, the one with the seven-year itch, got his opera, too: *Infidelio, or Conjugal Fuck-up*. Infidelio is, naturally, a trousers role, perfect for, oh, Hildegard Behrens in biker drag. But Gentleman Johnny, now there's a part! Soloflex taut, tofu lean, lots of elusive eye movement. Somehow never quite there, always calculating the next *scena*, escape hatches his specialty. Exasperating Elvira, too-easy Zerlina, agonizing Anna: the Disappointer Sisters. But which one did Johnny really want? And what was he looking for? Why *wasn't* one of us enough for him? Well, he gets *his* in my opera: a basso-profundo six-foot-tall vibrating butt plug drags him off to his ultimate sexual encounter.

It's all part of an effort to make the music of the masters palatable for the so-called Nineties. I've built up quite a repertoire already: there's *Car Men* (which climaxes beneath the grandstand at a demolition derby), there's *Un Ballo Emasculato* (with the infamous semi-botched castration scene), and my maiden effort, chronicling the culinary price wars of colonial Philadelphia, *The Pie Rates of Penn's Aunts*. I started out goofing around, but now it's an obsession. It's all in my head. Donny, you deserve better.

So then, a real-life scenario—well, say, Donny's too late to catch his bus cross town. My king-size bed is easily big enough for him to feel uninfringed upon in. And I never infringe in these little duets. It's always earnest sweet Donny who makes the move: "You know, Richard, I've been feeling sort of confused lately." "How so?" "I don't know...Are you really sleepy? Do you mind talking?" "Of course not, Don." "Well, it just means a lot to me to be getting to know someone like you." "Ditto." "And I never really felt this comfortable, you know, I mean *at home* with anyone before." "Mmm." "I mean, it's really nice to be here." "I'm glad..." "Richard?" "Mmm?" "I think I'm falling in love with you." There's that line again. It keeps cropping up.

Johnny had a line like that. Same words, in fact, but the stress fell on the second beat—I *think* I'm falling—like a question. It would require a different melody for Donny's line: I think I'm falling in *love* with you. It's all in the stress.

Now as for what ended in the Conjugal Fuck-up, it was altogether different. Life with Leon: no fantasy, no seduction, just settling in. After my war with Dr.

Fucking Krespel, it came as a welcome alliance. Why not? Let's risk it! What else does life have to offer that we should keep waiting for it, Leon? This! It's enough. It's here. It changes everything.

For seven years. Then Leon goes and dredges up Marcell, that imbecile, and eventually, after a bout with Dr. Batholow, I get entangled with Gentleman Johnny. Even the high-priced Dr. Lewis Schoen couldn't redeem that one. So now I'm consulting some Dr. MacNamara for his fucking elixir of love bullshit?

Donny doesn't have to consult, Donny knows: he hangs on after exams, waits tables all summer so he can afford an apartment with his buddies and stay as far away as he can get from Dr. and Mrs. Rosen of San Diego. And when he gets lonesome? And when he needs the feeling of home? "Donny, you can stay over whenever you want. I like having you here." "But, Richard, you won't mind if I toss around in my sleep a lot?" Toss away, Donny.

Oh Jesus—toss him away, a mere figment, a quick glance, a fleeting vision. *"Vision fugitive..."* What's that from? Memory failing. Or don't I care as much anymore? I used to practically memorize all my records. Massenet—but which? By now I've branched beyond the even remotely familiar. In this CD age, the used-record shops are coughing up the oddest things: *Las Golondrinas* by Usandizaga (the first and only U in my alphabetical shelving system), *Giulietta e Romeo* by Riccardo Zandonai (Hey, Riccardo, you got it backwards!).

This little bunker of mine was formerly a two-car garage. It's all cement, even the roof. Nothing to leak, to catch on fire. Record collection—safe! The old driveway has just been pulled up, so my plate-glass sliders look out on weed-sprouting stubble. By the end of summer I can pretend it's a meadow. Donny and I will wake up in each other's arms when the first sunlight hits the goldenrod. "That was great last night, listening to *Tristan*." "Thought you'd like it." "My dad's been trying to get me to listen to his opera records for years. Before the divorce, he and Mom used to fly to New York each spring for the Met. I never wanted to go along. I always disappointed my dad. You sort of remind me of my dad, Richard, some ways." Instantaneous transference. "You'd rather fly to New York each spring for the *Mets*, eh, Don?" "Only if they're playing the Padres." "Hey, I see where the Padres are coming east next week. Want to buzz down to New York with me?" "Richard Johnson is following sports now?" "Since we got to know each other—but I only check San Diego, helps me know what kind of mood I'll find you in. "But I'm always happy when I'm with you." "Mmm." "Richard?" "Mmm?" "I wish you'd say something more than mmm. I'm never really sure how you feel about me." "You mean you can't tell, Donny?" "Not really..." "You can't tell, my Guy of the Golden West?" "No..." "My Rosen Caballero?" "Come on, Dick." "But *of course* I love you!" Christ, it's all in the stress. "Leaving out 'of course' maybe, Richard?" "Don?" "I'm serious." "I guess I really am falling in love with you." "But are you over Johnny? Really?" "I don't know." "Are you even over Leon? I mean, you only moved out of the apartment from hell a month ago. Ten years..." "This is home now." "With me?"

But you (my latest and only you) aren't here. Your noontime shift just started. You're hung over. You were out last night drinking with your buddies. You can't stand opera. And there I was, last night, that goddamn glowing digital fucking clock on the VCR blinking away at me. I got up, walked across the darkened room and unplugged it like a high-tech Marschallin. Aha, the germ of a Donny libretto! What is it she sings?

>   Sometimes I get up...
>   middle of the night...
>   and make the ticking tocking
>   clockwork stop.
>   And yet why should I find
>   the passing time so fearful?

So is it back to Schoen? What an unoperatic way of coping! Basta! Let me see. How do they usually do it in an opera?

Voyage

by Lucien Stryk

1.
That was the year midsummer's
heat wave knocked us all
for loops: cats, squirrels

up, down, round the oak and
sycamore, mobbed the birdbath,
scratched in frenzy at the camel-

back packed earth. Birds veered
cockeyed, whomped the kitchen
window. Grass snakes frizzled

on the concrete path. That
was the year mosquitoes
failed to guzzle, as I drifted

by the parched Kishwaukee river,
caught up with my wife
and daughter for a turn around

the park.
          Faltered as I
stepped down from the bridge.

2. That was the year the paramedics
strapped me in the helicopter,
pointed me to stars, in fits

and starts between the cockleburs
of galaxies, my eyes blurred up
with ghosts of mayhem, fireflies,

outcasts sifting garbage on hot
city streets. That was the year
on hold. Riddled with lifelines

in an alien bed, I thumbed the Sunday
bookpage, stared at the faces of those
Auschwitz children waiting a turn
upon the Zyklon carrousel—near
the last photograph of Primo Levi,
their fire-eyed witness, before

he took his life,
                    slamming
the door on half a century's pain.

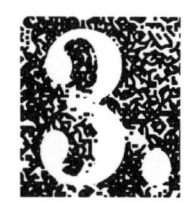

3. And this year, botched up
once again, oxygen mask in
place, heart monitor intact,

cut off from warzone static,
buzz and scuttle of the
misery out there. My wife,

my dearest friend, stroked
the blue flower round
the IV in my arm, coaxed

darkness from my eyes.
With tapestries of words
sent acrobatic sparrows

rising like last autumn's
leaves from fresh-turned soil,
wove flocks of scarlet tanagers

above gold-sovereign dandelions,
unthreaded winter hair of
willows greening into spring.

And this year, back full
circle in the summer heat,
I know for all it lacks

this world is still the only
place, and walking in a flame
of sunset I have things to do.

Compost

by Martha M. Vertreace

She hears old stories: twisted homes,
   unlived, untouched
for years as plaster whitens spectral vows
   heard
in cold bedrooms. Could this happen to her, who lives
within his diamond ring of promises, the veiled story
maidens tell of a comet's tail which twists
black holes of perfect omens? Home,

a spiral galaxy; he, the center of her home,
the young blue star whose morning rays touch
the garden she weeds where spring vines twist
elms; willows whose sough she hears
at night, breathing as she breathes. Her story:
tomorrow she walks on white satin, her life

in her father's hands one last time, one life
traded for another, one home
for another. The village whispers stories
which sting her face, a nettle's touch:
stories she would rather not hear—
how a woman, with a sewing basket, threads twisted
around wooden spools, on a frayed scatter rug twisted
her ankle as she carried a white shirt; barely alive
after she tripped in a rain of pins. No one heard
the needle plunge near her left breast, its home
until her body hated the hollow eye which touched
her. One hundred fifty such stories

in female medical records, this story
with its own twist:
"In your heart, a needle," the doctor touching
the red mark said. "How could you not know?"—"Live
for now," the widows smirk, at home
with bald fate when no one heard

footsteps scuff her stone path. The house hears
her sobbing for her ghostly groom, his story
bursts, a supernova. Blind, she makes her home
in the garden, under black buckthorn; her twisted
mind nests on straw mulch, alive
with phlox and lilac, no human touch,
the final twist, for thirty-five years. She hears
new stories: "touched in the head," they say,
"alive, but at home among the dead."

amalek

by S. L. Wisenberg

and you want to know why buchenwald and i ask, why amalek? and you say who? and i say amalek. for you should never forget amalek, the bible tells us, amalek is evil, the tribe that tried to kill us all, amalek, pure as evil can get. we have forgotten amalek but the pain is passed down and through. we have forgotten the scars, the specifics of amalek, but still we look over our shoulders for an oncoming, onrushing shadow—an arm, upraised.

yesterday i learned of the custom, i read of this custom in a book, standing in the jewish section of a bookstore run by a chain, not at home, not at the table, not at the desk, not at the synagogue, i learned from a book in the middle of manhattan that when testing a new pen, the jew write the word amalek and crosses it out. it says in the bible to remember this amalek and cross him out. amalek is the enemy. and i come from a people for whom the word is sacred. for whom the pen is not mightier but for years that is all we had. on yom kippur we write our sins on paper and let them float in water.

we are all making marks against amalek, against our own annihilation. we write amalek in our own terms. we cross it out in our own hand. ashkenazi jews give babies the names of our dead. each name is a statement against amalek.

there are people who say: you are inventing this amalek. it is an ancient enemy, this amalek, this antique devil at the door, clownishly clattering his rusty sword. there are people who say this amalek is merely death, that he carries a scythe, not a scabbard. your deaths are the same as those in the bubonic plague, in the war of roses, in vietnam, cambodia. in salvador. sabra, chatilla. the balkans. you are not chosen, in death or in life. gypsies died in the ovens. and—the list too long to bear. throw down your arms against amalek, forget this amalek and dance to a tune that all nations can hear.

but without amalek, there is no history. we are accustomed to being chosen. we are accustomed to our holidays, our apples and honey, our haroset like mortar, our parsley like life dipped in salt water tears. and after the death of masses we cling to individual voice and spirit, we believe again in capitalism, we publish books of holocaust children's drawings amazing to us because they are so much like other children's drawings.

but no person is wide enough to hold the sorrow of a generation. we become a collective again in order to mourn.

somewhere in the synagogue is a prayerbook dedicated to the memory of my grandfather. i remember the cinnamon smell of the silver havdalah box, used in the weekly farewell ceremony to the sabbath. i yearn for the ghetto, life without telephones, the shtetl, my version of pastoral. and for the city of vilna, once-golden hub, a western jerusalem—now vilnius, its jews ghosts. we are learning to live without vilna. we are learning to live with amalek, to raise our faces against amalek, to look him in the eye in the darkness of his vision and to raise whatever we can raise and strike this amalek with our ink, with the factory-made ink we buy by the box in stores, strike out this amalek, cross him out without becoming amalek ourselves—because he is the storm he is the void he is everything that will swallow us up, jonah in the whale, jonah alone in the whale, fearing above all that on land he is forgotten. we fear no one will mourn us so we mourn ourselves first and remember this amalek and make a strike through his name that will lead us to our own.

The Same Old Hatreds Only More Deadly Now!

by Maia Wojciechowska

When I was child living in Poland it was taken for granted that Germans and Russians had to be hated and the Hugarians disdained, that the Gypsies were all thieves and worse, that the French lost their collective soul during their Revolution (and their brains during the Age of Enlightenment) and that the Jews were smarter than we were. All of those prejudices and stereotypes were reinforced many times over by facts, observations, experiences and general acceptance. If you did not hold all those traditional beliefs you were considered somewhat dense, or compared to the village idiots, who didn't deal in reality.

But the Poles were not as good at hating as they were good at dying. Hating was like bridge, or tennis, a game rather than a serious business. It only came in handy and was useful during wartime. It made the cause just. It never got associated with our beliefs, in God, Christ who said to love your enemy, his mother who hated no one, or the church who, before giving out the bread of life made you say: "Peace be with you."

Poles were the last true Catholics left in the world, I used to think, during the long decades of communism in my native land. During that long night of oppression they turned to their Church and found solace and the kind of arms that each Christian has to bear in a world gone bad. We did not kill, during that long night, maybe we became more civilized, more Christlike in our knowledge that our true enemy was no longer the same as before. Maybe (I say maybe because I was not there, just wish it to be so), we finally had learned that the enemy lives in every sin committed against our Father. Maybe, I thought, Poles had finally learned that they had to give up what they were so good at: dying. Maybe, I prayed, they figured out that dying is but the other side of the coin that says: "Thou shall not kill."

* * *

We live in an age that makes all the sins ugly. And the uglier sin looks the harder someone tries to package it to look pretty. Hunger is ugly but it looks almost necessary when you wed it to politics and begin to talk about "politics of hunger" rather than people starving to death. But then we look again, at hunger, through that eye we cannot escape, the eye of the t.v. camera, and we are reminded that sin is ugly and it must be stopped.

There is something very confusing in the eyes of those who starve, are starving, those who kill and are killed, those who cry and don't cry, in that country that is so close to my native land. What is happening in

Yugoslavia makes little sense in the nuclear age. We don't want to see that confusion, or get infected by that confusion that is in those eyes, whether they are looking at us from behind wires, or across desks, or over the barrel of a gun.

We go easier to *Samalia*. In *Samalia* it could be two, four centuries ago. Time had stopped there, or maybe even moved backwards. But Europe always kept track of the ticking clock. Going back in time is not European. After all everything progresses, nothing regresses. Except, what? Hatreds? Resentments? Unfinished feuds? Holy wars?

* * *

"That's the trouble with evolution, it catches you with your pants down." The old man used to philosophize and I used to learn a lot from him, but it was a diagonal sort of learning, not vertical.

We used to be on opposite poles, "sitting with our backsides to each other," he'd often say. He did not believe in God, I saw God in everything. We had our profound differences about evolution as well.

"I believe in God's evolution," I once said and continued in spite of his arms waving the Presence away. "Once He created us He gambled on the unknown."

"What unknown? He's supposed to know everything, your God!"

"I figure He didn't count on how attached He could become, how obsessed He'd become. With us. That's the whole story of the Old Testament, as I see it. His grand, solitary passion for his people."

"So what's the evolution you're talking about?"

"For God to the Creator and then, when He did not know how else to show us his love, from Father, to Son, to Saviour on the cross, to the Holy Spirit inside us all! What an exquisite, mad, great, divine, evolution of love!"

He did not laugh, he only shook he head. And looked at me with sadness.

"So how do you account for the folly of men with that scenario inside your head?"

"I can't." I said. At fifteen I could not. At sixty-five I gave up trying to understand, why people would betray God while fighting over Him.

* * *

I suspect that in Yugoslavia they did not spend fifty years, as they had in Poland, practicing how to fight the enemy without killing. I suspect that in Yugoslavia on Sunday morning they played ball, went swimming, slept late. In Poland there was a fight that went on Sunday mornings. The State promised young people all sorts of goodies, held for them all sorts of sports activities, enticed them with rewards one could only dream of. And yet the young resisted those temptations in favor of standing in crowded churches, hearing the words about the Kingdom that was not of this world. And that Kingdom reigned during that long night.

I can only guess that in Yugoslavia, where they endured that same long night, fewer looked to that Kingdom. They might have blamed those who were traditionally to blame, those that it was traditional to hate. But maybe they did not fight as hard, without killing, all through that long dreadful night that stretched across fifty years, as the Poles fought. Maybe they did not, as the Poles had, learn that the most worthwhile of all the wars is the one that does not spill blood, but which restores what had been ours since the beginning of time.

I'd rather think that this might have happened. For I can't figure out any other, plausible, explanation. The Yugoslavs did not evolve during those fifty years. Maybe because it was all so dreadful they simply decided to go back. To a time when enemies were easier to identify than they are today. Maybe what's happening there is for a purpose not a cause, but a purpose. Maybe it's for us, who have tried to get rid of sin, a chance to look at it and identify it for what it is.

The Earnest Man

by Paul Zimmer

Now the earnest man who cleans
Our offices has lost his newborn
First grandson. I watch him come
To work in desolation, composing
Himself before he enters. Days ago
He'd told me of his joy in holding
This tenuous creature in his arms,
Spoke of it as a gem so translucent
He could see through its skin to
The pumping of its diminutive heart,
To the slow, steady stream in
Its arteries, and this had seemed
Like a love he could count on.

Recurring Dreams: The Neglected

by Al Zolynas

The feeling always of an exquisitely painful
shock of recognition—followed by great
   relief;
the glowing aquarium

into which I've dropped no food
in what seems like a millennium, still holds
its two fish, nonetheless, floating, serenely alert,

their regal, soulful eyes regarding me;
the chickencoop in the backyard three
new generations of chickens among

the tangled weeds, also unfed, but
miraculously unharmed, scratching in the dirt,
preening bright feathers; the mysterious garden, lush

with vegetables and fruit, ladybirds and aphids.
How could I have forgotten to water
it for so long? How could I have forgotten

its very existence? Though I know I'm supposed to,
I haven't fed any of these wild beings
of the dream world, these fish

and fowl, these flourishing vegetables. And yet
something has sustained them—more
than sustained them—allowed them to thrive,

secretly and continuously, away
from the day's fading and disappointments, beyond
any arrogant husbandry.

Contributors

JONIS AGEE has published a book of poetry, two collections of short stories (*Pretend We've Never Met* and *Bend This Heart*) and a novel, *Sweet Eyes*. Her new novel, being published by Ticknor & Fields in September 1993, is called *Strange Angels*. She loves country music, Dwight Yoakum, the shopping channel and the sandhills of western Nebraska. She prays that in some age we'll learn not to kill each other.

TONY ARDIZZONE is the author of two novels, *In the Name of the Father* and *Heart of the Order*, as well as two collections of short stories, *The Evening News*, which received the Flannery O'Connor Award for Short Fiction, and *Larabi's Ox: Stories of Morocco*, winner of the Milkweed National Fiction Prize. He is also the recipient of other awards, including two National Endowment for the Arts grants. He currently teaches literature and creative writing at Indiana University.

THOMAS FOX AVERILL is Writer-in-residence and Professor of English at Washburn University of Topeka, where he teaches courses in Creative Writing and in Kansas Literature, Folklore and Film. The author of numerous articles, poems and short stories, he has also published two collections of short stories—*Passes at the Moon* and *Seeing Mona Naked*—and is a monthly commentator for KANU, National Public Radio from the University of Kansas.

MARVIN BELL's eleven books of poetry included his *New and Selected Poems, Iris of Creation* and *The Book of the Dead Man*, which is forthcoming early in 1994. He is a longtime faculty member of the Writers' Workshop at the University of Iowa and lives both in Iowa City and Port Townsend, Washington.

CHRISTOPHER BUCKLEY's fifth book of poems, *Blue Autumn*, was published by Copper Beech Press in 1990; in the fall of 1993, Copper Beech will bring out his sixth book, *Dark Matter*. He is the editor of On the *Poetry of Philip Levine: Stranger to Nothing*, and was poetry editor for the Pushcart Prize, 1992-3. Buckley spent six weeks in Yugoslavia on a Fulbright award in creative writing and is the recipient of numerous other awards.

JANET BURROWAY is the author of plays, poetry, children's books, and seven novels, including *The Buzzards, Raw Silk, Opening Nights*, and most recently *Cutting Stone*. Her text, *Writing Fiction*, is used in more than three hundred colleges and universities in the U.S. She is McKenzie Professor of Literature and Writing at the Florida State University in Tallahassee.

ANDREI CODRESCU, poet and National Public Radio announcer, is editor of *Exquisite Corpse*. His latest book is *Road Scholar*, Hyperion Press, 1993

PHILIP DACEY's fifth book of poetry, *Night Shift at the Crucifix Factory*, was published in 1991 by the University of Iowa Press. Co-editor of *Strong Measures: Contemporary American Poetry in Traditional Forms* he recently resigned from full-time teaching to devote more time to writing. He and his two musician sons have formed a poetry-music trio, Strong Measures, which has begun performing in the upper Midwest.

ROBERT DANA is the author of five collections of poetry, one of which, *Starting Out for the Difficult World*, was a Pulitzer nominee. He was awarded the Delmore Schwartz Award in 1989, and he has taught creative writing at Cornell College in Iowa for more than thirty years. Another Chicago Press published Dana's *What I Think I Know: New and Selected Poems* in May.

CONNIE DEANOVICH is the author of *Ballerina Criminology*, a chapbook of poetry, and has had her poems published in a variety of journals and had her work included in the anthology, *Under 35: The New Generation of American Poets*. In addition, she is a recipient of the General Electric Award for Younger Writers and the Fund for Poetry Individual Artist's Grant. Deanovich is also editor of *B City Review*.

HELEN DEGEN-COHEN has published in a number of journals, including *Partisan Review* and *Another Chicago Magazine*, and has had her work anthologized in, among others, *The House of Via Gambito: Writings by American Women Abroad*. She is the recipient of a National Endowment for the Arts grant in creative writing and has won awards for her fiction, poetry and non-fiction. She is currently a member of the Illinois Arts Council's Artists-in Education roster.

EMILIO DeGRAZIA is both a fiction writer and a poet. He is the author of *Enemy Country*, a collection of short stories about the Vietnam experience, and *Billy Brazil*, a novel about mental illness. A second novel, *The Savior of America*, will be published in 1994 by Guernica Editions of Montreal. DeGrazia lives in Winona, Minnesota.

STEPHEN DIXON has published five novels and nine story collections. His newest collection, *Moon*, will be published in the fall of 1993. In 1991, his novel *Frog* was a finalist in fiction for the The National Book Award and a finalist for the P.E.N./Faulkner Fiction Prize in 1992. He teaches writing seminars at Johns Hopkins University.

JIM ELLEDGE's two collections of poetry are *Nothing Nice* and *Various Envies*, and he has published five scholarly books. *His Sweet Nothings: An Anthology of Rock and Roll in American Poetry* is due from Indiana University Press in 1994. He teaches at Illinois State University and serves as editor of The Illinois Review.

S.P. ELLEDGE has been published widely in literary magazines, including *Paris Review*, *Beloit Fiction Journal* and *Farmer's Market*. A native of Iowa and current resident of Boston, Elledge has taught at Wellesley College and the University of Massachusetts. He is currently finishing work on his first novel.

LUCIA CORDELL GETSI's latest book of poems, *Intensive Care*, won the 1990 Capricorn Prize. Other books include *Teeth Mother Letters*, *No One Taught This Filly to Dance*, *Bottleships: for Daughters*, and *Georg Trakl: Poems*, a translation. She is the recipient of a 1992 NEA fellowship and several Illinois Arts Council fellowships. She is professor of Comparative Literature and co-director of Creative Writing at Illinois State University and edits The Spoon River Poetry Review.

ALVIN GREENBERG's most recent collection of poetry is *Why We Live With Animals*, from Coffee House Press. He teaches at Macalaster College in St. Paul, Minnesota.

DAN GUILLORY teaches literature and writing at Millikin University. For the past fifteen years, he has been a poetry reviewer for Library Journal. In addition to publishing in many literary journals, he has published two books, *Living With Lincoln* and *Alligator Inventions*, both from Stormline Press. He has served as an Illinois Poet in the Schools and is a recipient of an Illinois Arts Council's Artist's Fellowship.

RICHARD JACKSON's most recent book of poetry, *Alive All Day*, was nominated for a Pulitzer Prize. He has been a Fulbright exchange poet in Yugoslavia and has lectured and given readings in Yugoslavia and Central Europe. He has won the Agee prize and an NEH fellowship for his criticism, poetry awards from Crazyhorse and the NEA and a Pushcart Prize. He is also editor of *Poetry Miscellany* and teaches at the University of Tennessee-Chattanooga.

DAVID JAUSS is the author of the story collection, *Crimes of Passion*. His fiction has appeared in *O. Henry, Best American Short Stories* and *Pushcart Prize* collections. He is also a poet and teaches at the University of Arkansas-Little Rock.

W.P. KINSELLA is the author of three novels, *Shoeless Joe*, for which he won the Houghton Mifflin Literary Fellowship Award, *The Iowa Baseball Confederacy*, and *Box Socials*, along with eleven short story collections. He lives in the Pacific Northwest, where he and his wife, Ann, are card-carrying scouts for the Atlanta Braves.

TED KOOSER is an insurance executive in Omaha, Nebraska. His books of poetry are published by University of Pittsburgh Press.

PAUL LAKE has published two collections of poetry—*Another Kind of Travel* and *Walking Backward*, and a novel, *Among the Immortals.*. Recipient of the Mirrieless Fellowship at Stanford while working on his M.A. in Creative Writing, he has had his poems and essays appear in a number of journals. He teaches at Arkansas Tech University.

JEAN C. LEE is an editor of *Farmer's Market* and director of the Publications Unit at Illinois State University, which manages production for several literary journals and presses. Lee has previously published poetry, art essays, and a history book, *Prairies, Prayers and Promises*.

JOSEPH MAIOLO is a professor of English at the University of Minnesota-Duluth. He has won a number of awards for his fiction, including two NEA fellowships, the Loft-McKnight Award of Distinction in Fiction and three PEN Syndicated Fiction Awards. His work has appeared in several literary magazines, and he has published a novella, *Elverno: A Tale from a Boyhood*.

MICHAEL MARTONE is the author of *Fort Wayne Is Seventh on Hitler's List*, *Safety Patrol*, and *Alive and Dead in Indiana*, all collections of stories. He has edited two collection of essays: *A Place of Sense: Essays in Search of the Midwest* and *Townships*. He lives in Syracuse, New York. He lives in Syracuse, New York.

KEVIN McILVOY is the author of two novels, *The Fifth Station* and *Little Peg*, and is editor of *Puerto del Sol*, a literary magazine. He teaches at New Mexico State University and is past president of the Council of Literary Magazines and Presses.

CHRISTOPHER MERRILL spent two months traveling in what used to be Yugoslavia. He hopes to publish a book about his experiences.

JOHN MILTON has written and edited fifteen books, including fiction, poetry, biography, history, and literary criticism. Since 1963, he has been a professor of English at The University of South Dakota and in that same year founded *The South Dakota Review*. In addition to awards for writing and editing, he has also been honored for his photography.

CAROL MUSKE's newest book of poetry, *Red Trousseau*, was published in the Spring of 1993 by Viking Press.

JAY NUEGEBOREN is the author of ten books, including *The Stolen Jew*, which won the American Jewish Committee's prize for Best Novel of 1981. His stories and essays have appeared widely and have been reprinted in several dozen anthologies. He is Writer in Residence at the University of Massachussetts in Amherst.

KRISTY NIELSEN's poetry and prose poems are forthcoming in numerous journals, including *The Illinois Review, Mid-American Review, Prose Poem*, and *Poet & Critic*. She has received the Intro Award in poetry and Amelia's prose poetry award.

KAREN LEE OSBORNE is the author of the novels *Carlyle Simpson* and *Hawkwings*. She is the edtior of the forthcoming *The Country of Herself: Short Fiction by Chicago Women* and co-editor, with William J. Spurlin, of the forthcoming *Reclaiming the Heartland: A Midwestern Gay and Lesbian Reader*. Her third novel will be published in 1994 by Third Side Press.

HARRY MARK PETRAKIS is the writer of fifteen books which include eight novels, four collections of short stories, two works of autobiography and one work of biography. He was twice nominated for the National Book Award in Fiction and holds honorary degrees from a number of universities.

JAMES PLATH is the editor of *Clockwatch Review* and director of the Hemingway Days Workshop and Conference in Key West. Poems of his most recently appeared in *Apalachee Quarterly* and *Men of Our Time: Male Poetry in Contemporary America*.

PAULETTE ROESKE's first collection of poems, *Breathing Under Water,* was published in 1988 and a chapbook, *The Body Can Ascend No Higher*, won the 1992 Illinois Writers, Inc. chapbook competition. A number of her short stories have also appeared in print, and she has just completed a novella, *The Ecstacy of Magda Brummel*. She is the recipient of three Illinois Arts Council literary awards and an Illinois Arts Council fellowship.

DAVID ST. JOHN is the author of four collections of poetry: *Hush, The Shore, No Heaven,* and *Terraces of Rain: An Italian Sketchbook*. In 1994 Harper Collins will publish *Study for the World's Body: New and Selected Poems*. He teaches at the University of Southern California and is Poetry Editor of *The Antioch Review*.

MAURA STANTON is a poet and fiction writer who teaches at Indiana University. Her books of poems are *Tales of the Supernatural, Cries of Swimmers,* and *Snow on Snow*. Her most recent collection of fiction is *The Country I Come From*.

KEVIN STEIN's collection of poems, *A Circus of Want*, won the 1992 Devins Award and was published by University of Missouri Press. A recipient of fellowships granted by the National Endowment for the Arts and the Illinois Arts Council, he's also published the critical study, James Wright: *The Poetry of a Grown Man*.

JONATHAN STRONG was brought up in Illinois and now teaches at Tufts University and lives in Somerville, Massachusetts. Zoland Books has published his novel *Secret Words* and his two novellas *Companion Pieces* and will bring out *An Untold Tale* late in 1993. His earlier books are *Elsewhere, Ourselves*, and *Tike*.

LUCIEN STRYK is the author of numerous books of poetry and volumes of translations. One of the country's leading practitioners of Zen poetry, he is Professor Emeritus at Northern Illinois University.

MARTHA VERTREACE is poet-in-residence and associate professor of English at Kennedy-King College in Chicago. Her work frequently appears in literary magazines and has earned her three Illinois Arts Council Literary Awards. A fiction writer and essayist as well as a poet, her first collection of poetry, *Under A Cat's Eye Moon*, was published in 1991.

S.L. WISENBERG runs Red Fish Studio Writing Workshop in Chicago. She has lectured at Elgin Community College and has been published in *The New Yorker, Tikkun, The Kenyon Review, The North American Review* and other publications. She is working on a novel about memory.

MAIA WOJCIECHOWSKA is known chiefly as a children's writer and Newbery Award winner. She has also published a novel, *People In His Life*.

PAUL ZIMMER lives in Iowa City, Iowa. His poetry is widely anthologized.

AL ZOLYNAS teaches writing at United States International University in San Diego. His work is widely published and has been included in a number of anthologies, including *Maverick Poets, Editor's Choice III* and *A New Geography of Poets*. He has published one collection of poetry, *The New Physics* and is co-editor of *Men of Our Time: An Anthology of Male Poetry in Contemporary America*.